PILGRIMAGE IN EARLY CHRISTIAN JORDAN

PILGRIMAGE
IN EARLY CHRISTIAN JORDAN

A LITERARY AND ARCHAEOLOGICAL GUIDE

Burton MacDonald

Oxbow Books  Oxford & Oakville

Published by Oxbow Books, Oxford, UK

This book is available direct from

Oxbow Books, Oxford, UK
(Phone 01865-241249; Fax 01865-794449)

and

The David Brown Book Company
PO Box 511, Oakville, CT 06779, USA
(Phone 860-945-9329; Fax 860-945-9468)

or from our website

www.oxbowbooks.com

The Scripture quotations contained herein are from the New Revised Standard Version Bible, copyright © 1989 by the Division of Christian Education of the National Council of the Churches of Christ in the U.S.A., and are used here by permission. All rights reserved.

The photos by David Bjorgen, Jerzy Strzelecki, M. Disdero and David Shankbone are licensed under the Creative Commons Attribution ShareAlike 3.0 License.

Aerial photographs:
Aerial Photographic Archive of Archaeology in the Middle East (APAAME), archive available from: www.classics.uwa.edu.au/Aerial_archaeology

Cataloging data available from the Library of Congress.
A CIP record for this book is available from the British Library.

Text type 11 pt Adobe Garamond Pro
Display type 18/12/10.5 pt Hypatia Sans Pro

Printed in China on acid-free paper.

CONTENTS

LIST OF FIGURES

ACKNOWLEDGMENTS

A great deal of the archaeological information in this work is taken from articles published in both the *Annual of the Department of Antiquities of Jordan* and *Studies in the History and Archaeology of Jordan*, both publications of Jordan's Department of Antiquities. I wish to express my gratitude to the excavators who have done the field work and published the results of their work. I am particularly grateful to Basim Mahamyd, Mohammed Al-Balawneh, and Rustom Mkhjian, members of the Department of Antiquities, who help me in the field.

Translations from many of the pilgrims' texts are taken from Wilkinson 1981 and 2002. I am indebted to Wilkinson (2002) for this material.

I appreciate the help provided by librarians and staff at: the American Center of Oriental Research, Amman; Dumbarton Oaks, Washington, D.C.; Pontifical Biblical Institute, Rome; St. Francis Xavier University, Antigonish, Nova Scotia; Washington Theological Union, Washington, D.C.

Trianos Gagos, the University of Michigan, Ann Arbor, helped with some of the Greek inscriptions. His help is especially appreciated with those inscriptions from Tall Mar Elyas.

Sherry M. Hardin, North Carolina State University, Raleigh, took some of the ground photos in 2007. In addition, she accompanied me in the field in June–July 2008 and took more photos. She drew the figures for the publication and contributed to its final design. Her contribution to the work has been invaluable.

David L. Kennedy, University of Western Australia, Perth, granted permission to use his aerial photos of some of the sites. He is given credit in the text for these photos.

Rosemarie Sampson read drafts of the work. I appreciate her editorial comments which helped me focus the subjects more clearly.

My in-class students at St. Francis Xavier University were especially helpful in the preparation of this work. They asked the questions that helped me understand what future readers would want to have clarified. Moreover, they made invaluable suggestions relative to the improvement of the work.

1 INTRODUCTION TO THE SITES

IN the minds of many Christians, the area west of the Jordan River – present-day Israel and the West Bank – is the Holy Land. Very few view the land to the east of the river as an important center of Christianity in its formative years. However, as this book will show, there is much to the east of the river that is of interest to both pilgrims and tourists.

The major pilgrimage sites and related areas treated in this work indicate the high level of pilgrimage activity in Jordan during the early Christian period, between the fourth and seventh centuries of the Common Era. In fact, there is inscriptional evidence at both the Church of the Virgin Mary in Madaba and the Church of Saint Stephen at Umm ar-Rasas for the continuation of Christian practice in the region up until at least the late eighth century, or into the Abbasid period.

Our focus is not on every early Christian pilgrimage site but only those that have a biblical basis and have been excavated. It is at such sites that the visitor can see, on the ground, at least the footprints of the churches, chapels, tombs, and, in some cases, the remnants of hostels that played a part in pilgrimages east of the Jordan River.

The site of **Gadara/Umm Qays**, located in the northwestern corner of Jordan and overlooking the Sea of Galilee, may have been a pilgrimage site for two different reasons. The four tombs and five reliquaries found in association with the two churches on the Church Terrace could have been the object of pilgrimage for those who wished to visit, pay homage, or pray for assistance, such as a cure or miracle, to the martyrs or holy persons buried there. In fact, the tomb in the square church on the Church Terrace may have been the grave of a venerated martyr.

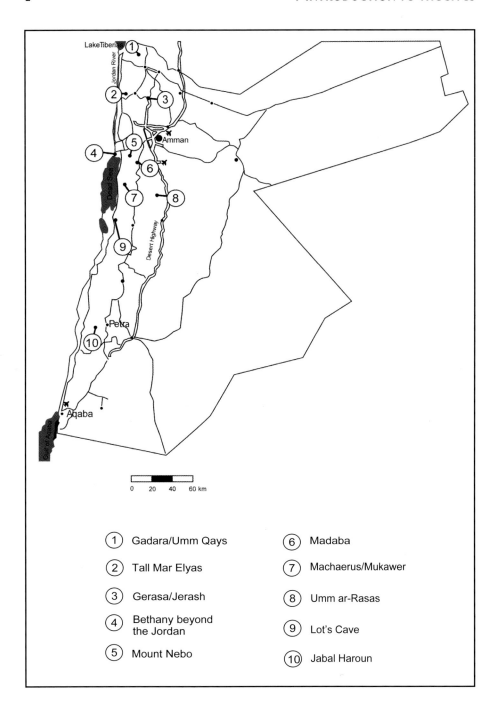

(1) Gadara/Umm Qays   (6) Madaba

(2) Tall Mar Elyas   (7) Machaerus/Mukawer

(3) Gerasa/Jerash   (8) Umm ar-Rasas

(4) Bethany beyond   (9) Lot's Cave
    the Jordan

(5) Mount Nebo   (10) Jabal Haroun

FIG. 1.1   Map of Jordan with early Christian pilgrimage sites indicated.

Also at Gadara, the complex consisting of the Roman Mausoleum, Christian Crypt, and Five-Aisled Basilica may have commemorated the New Testament story of Jesus' "Casting out Demons" (Matthew 8.23, 28–34; 9.1). In addition, the crypt could have contained the remains of holy persons. If so, Christians would have come to the place to pay homage or seek assistance from these holy persons.

According to Mark 5.1 and Luke 8.26, "the country of the Gerasenes" is the region where the story of the "Casting out Demons" took place. This would locate the exorcism in the region of Gerasa/Jerash. However, there is no ancient textual evidence that the site, based on the story, became a place of pilgrimage. Nevertheless, during the early Christian period, Gerasa was an important ecclesiastical center; some of the Roman structures in the center of the site became churches. In addition, many churches were built on the site's periphery.

The miraculous fountain, which is the one that now probably lies between the Cathedral Church and the Church of Saint Theodore, is thought to have become the center of the greatest complex of Christian buildings at Gerasa. While it does not seem to have had anything to do with the exorcism narrated in Mark and Luke, it could have attracted pilgrims and the curious because of reports of the annual miracle of the fountain spouting wine instead of water.[1]

Through the centuries, the site of **Tall Mar Elyas** has attracted pilgrims from different religions, since it is connected to the prophet Elijah who is reverenced by Jews and Muslims as well as Christians. In addition, the persons who were buried in the tombs in proximity to both the site's small and main churches may have been individuals who were considered holy. If so, their places of burial would have attracted pilgrims to the site.

The practice of pilgrimage to Tall Mar Elyas continues to the present day. There are indications of candles still being burnt in the apse of the small church, and the large number of pieces of cloth tied to trees throughout the site is also a witness to the devotion of those who come to the site to pray, to seek assistance, or to pay homage to Elijah and possibly the individuals buried in the tombs.

Bethany Beyond the Jordan is perhaps the country's most pre-eminent Christian site. Its connections are with the New Testament as well as with the Old Testament/Hebrew Scriptures.

---

1 There are certainly biblical parallels between the story of the miraculous fountain at Gerasa and that of Jesus turning water into wine at the wedding feast at Cana (John 2.1–12).

Like Tall Mar Elyas, this site is connected with the Prophet Elijah. His parting of the waters of the Jordan River with his mantle, the separation from his disciple Elisha by a chariot and horses of fire, and Elijah's ascension into heaven in a whirlwind (2 Kings 2.6–11) are all thought to have happened here. People expected Elijah to return to earth; in the minds of the New Testament writers, this was fulfilled in the person of John the Baptist (Matthew 17.12) who is also commemorated here.

The Gospel according to John places John the Baptist's ministry at Bethany Beyond the Jordan (1.28), but it was also the place where he lived and gathered disciples around him. Jesus came from Galilee to be baptized by John at Bethany Beyond the Jordan, and it is also here that John declared that Jesus was "the Lamb of God who takes away the sin of the world" (John 1.29; see also 1.36). The first disciples of Jesus, who were former followers of John, joined Jesus while he was at the site. After John's death, Jesus retired to Bethany Beyond the Jordan at least on one occasion to escape persecution from the religious authorities in Jerusalem (John 10.40).

There is a large body of extra-biblical, early Christian literary evidence that points to Bethany Beyond the Jordan as a site of pilgrimage. This textual material provides information about the structures built at the site to commemorate Elijah, John the Baptist, and Jesus.

Bethany Beyond the Jordan has been recently excavated. The excavations show structures along the Wadi al-Karrar indicating pilgrimage activity. At the eastern end of the wadi, there are structures that relate to both Elijah and John; at its western end, close to a former course of the Jordan River, there are structures than commemorate the place where John baptized Jesus. In the cliffs of the wadi are the remnants of cells in which monks from the early Christian centuries lived.

Bethany Beyond the Jordan is once again becoming an important site for Christian pilgrimage. It is being developed to accommodate the many pilgrims from various religious faiths, but especially Christians, to honor the three biblical individuals who made it a center of religious importance.

The **Memorial of Moses on Mount Nebo** has been a center of pilgrimage since at least the fourth century AD. Egeria, one of the earliest Christian pilgrims to the Land of the Bible, visited the area and wrote about the monks who lived both on the mountain itself and at Wadi 'Ayoun Mousa, just below and to the north of its summit. It is this latter place that is often associated with the burial of Moses, although "no one knows his burial place to this day" (Deuteronomy 34.6). Egeria was followed by a number of other Christian pilgrims to the area who witnessed to the continuation of religious life there well into the Middle Ages.

Archaeologists from the Studium Biblicum Franciscanum (SBF) began their excavations at the peak of Mount Nebo (Ras al-Siyagha) in 1933. Their work resulted in the discovery of a basilica and a large monastery that had grown up around it in the early Christian period. The archaeological evidence shows that the monastic presence at Mount Nebo extends from the second half of the fourth century to the ninth–tenth centuries AD.

The SBF began the restoration of the basilica at Mount Nebo in 1963. Work at the site, now known as the Memorial of Moses, has continued, and the Memorial of Moses is presently a place of pilgrimage. People from all over the world come to commemorate Moses. Pilgrims, whether they are Christian, Jewish, or Muslim, as well as other visitors to the site will discover there a place of prayer and peace.

The plains of Moab, located in a desert environment to the northeast of the Dead Sea in the southern extremity of the Jordan Valley, are linked to Moses' memorial. It was from these plains that he climbed to the top of Ras al-Siyagha to view the land that God had promised his ancestors, and it was from the plains of Moab that the Israelites set out to cross the Jordan River and began to take possession of the Promised Land.

Ancient Livias (Tall ar-Ramah) in the plains of Moab was on an important route from Jericho to Esbus (Hesban) in the early Christian period. Because of this, it is mentioned as a place through which pilgrims passed from Jerusalem and Jericho on their way to Mount Nebo. It was at the sixth Roman milestones that pilgrims would turn off to make their way to Moses' memorial. Here again, Egeria is one of the early Christian pilgrims who provides information about the route from the Jordan River to Mount Nebo.

Madaba is known as the "city of churches and mosaics." Together with the surrounding region, it can be associated with Moses, since it was at nearby Mount Nebo that Moses first viewed the Promised Land. But the town is also associated with Jesus by means of the Madaba Mosaic Map, one of the best-known Christian features of the city, located in the Greek Orthodox Church of Saint George. As Christians participated (and can still participate) in the liturgy within the church, the map, which is oriented towards the east, is between them and the altar area and draws their attention to the central facts of Christian religion. The map's focus is the city of Jerusalem, and the central location within Jerusalem is the

Holy Sepulchre, the place where Jesus was crucified, buried, and rose from the dead. This places Jesus at the center of the map and the liturgy and connects him to Madaba.

The present practice of introducing pilgrims and tourists to both the significance of the Church of Saint George and its world-renowned mosaic map in a nearby building to the south of the church has made the church itself more of a place of prayer and devotion. Now it can be visited and its mosaic viewed without disturbance from the explanations of tour guides.

A number of impressive early Christian churches form part of the Madaba Archaeological Park. The remnants of these churches and their mosaics can be visited. As pilgrims and tourists make their way through the archaeological remains, they ought to be aware of the Roman street and other features from previous periods. In this way, they may relate to how the early Christians of the city used the previous architectural features for their religious purposes.

The Madaba Archaeological and Folklore Museum houses the Aitha Chapel / Twal Chapel, a good example of a private or family place of worship from the early Christian period.

There are other churches within Madaba. A number of them are closed to visitors, but the Church of the Apostles located on the south side of the city is well worth a visit. It provides a good idea of how large some of these early Christian churches were. It has been well preserved with a modern "covering" that helps protect it from deterioration.

Umm ar-Rasas, a UNESCO World Heritage Cultural Site, is located ca. 30 km to the southeast of Madaba. Although a large number of its sixth–eighth century churches have been excavated, mostly in the area to the north of the Roman–Umayyad period fort, there is still a great deal of it that has yet to be uncovered.

The Jordan Tourism Board is presently emphasizing the churches of the "Saint Stephen Complex" by building a Visitors' Center at the entrance to the archaeological park. The "Saint Stephen Complex" has a "covering," and raised walkways allow the visitor to view the several churches and chapels comprising the complex while avoiding further destruction to the antiquities. The Church of Saint Stephen is the central church. It is dedicated to one of the first deacons of the Christian church in Jerusalem and its first Christian martyr. It is now a place of pilgrimage for Christians, as it would have been in antiquity.

To the south of the "Saint Stephen Complex," a number of other churches have been excavated. These ecclesiastical structures indicate the importance of the area for early Christians. Along with the Saint Stephen Complex, they are proof that Christianity continued to thrive in the area well into the Abbasid period (late eighth century AD).

Around 1.5 km from Umm ar-Rasas is a tower/pillar that was probably the place where a stylite resided. Nearby is the Tower Church with its reliquary containing the cremated bones of an adult. Pilgrims would have come to the tower to consult the stylite and/or to pay homage to the holy person buried in the church.

Although Josephus places Herod's beheading of John the Baptist at the palace-fortress of **Machaerus**, there is no evidence that the site and its neighboring village of **Mukawer** ever became a place of pilgrimage for the Christians of the area. The Studium Biblicum Franciscanum found no evidence of a church or chapel dedicated to John the Baptist at the palace-fortress of Machaerus, and the presence of two churches and a chapel in the village of Mukawer does not in itself indicate pilgrimage activity. However, the palace-fortress and the village have been included in this work because of their close association with John, who was imprisoned and beheaded there.

Lot's Cave/Dayr 'Ayn 'Abata, along the southeast side of the Dead Sea, was a place of pilgrimage in the early Christian period. There is, in fact, an early Christian account that indicates it as a place of pilgrimage at least during the period of Lent. In addition, the Madaba Mosaic Map places a church dedicated to Saint Lot at the spot. Further evidence for the site as a place of pilgrimage comes from the excavation of the monastic complex with its likely hostel for pilgrims.

Although the Bible associates Lot and his daughters with incest, the man was honored as a saint in the early Christian period. Inscriptions at Lot's Cave/Dayr 'Ayn 'Abata indicate his saintly character. Furthermore, an inscription in the Church of Saints Lot and Procopius at Khirbat al-Mukhayyat near both Mount Nebo and Madaba indicates the high regard in which Lot was held in the early Christian centuries.

Of all the early Christian pilgrimage sites presented in this work, the hardest to access is that of the **Memorial of Aaron on Jabal Haroun** to the southwest of Petra. Nevertheless, in the late fifth to eighth centuries of the Christian era, a church was built on the peak of the mountain and a monastery on the plateau to its west. Both were associated with Aaron, the brother of Moses and Miriam.

Although the peak of Jabal Haroun is now the location of a Muslim shrine (*weli*) dedicated to Aaron, it was at one time the site of a Christian church, built in the sixth century. This church would probably have been contemporaneous with the monastery. Both would have drawn pilgrims to the area. The site continues to be a place of pilgrimage for the local people and the Bdul Bedouin of the region. They hold an annual festival there in the autumn.

It is evident from the above that the area to the east of the Jordan River was a place of pilgrimage during the early Christian period from the fourth to the eighth centuries. The earliest evidence from literary sources comes from the late fourth century and the writings of Egeria. This witness to pilgrimage activity is supported by archaeological excavations at both Gadara / Umm Qays in the north of the country and Mount Nebo in the center of the country. Both places indicate church structures dating to the fourth century that were associated with pilgrimage activities. The building of churches east of the Jordan River intensified during the fifth to the seventh centuries. Some of these churches, especially at the sites presented in this work, were pilgrimage centers.

For the most part it is quite easy to visit these sites, some of which are still pilgrimage sites today. Using Amman as the principal set-off point, the sites may be visited in a logical fashion.

Visits to the three sites of Gadara / Umm Qays, Tall Mar Elyas, and Gerasa / Jerash can be done in a day from Amman. One may wish to start with either Gadara / Umm Qays or Gerasa / Jerash. At each site, a visit to the secular as well as the ecclesiastical features of the site is advised. In this way, the churches at each site can be set within their proper historical context. After a visit to one or the other, one can visit Tall Mar Elyas and then proceed either north or south to visit the site not already seen. Visits to both Gadara / Umm Qays and Gerasa / Jerash will take the longest, since there is much to see and walking is required to visit their various features.

Using Amman again as a base, one can visit Madaba, Mount Nebo, Khirbat al-Mukhayyat, and Machaerus / Mukawer also in a day. Once in Madaba, you can begin with a visit to the Church of Saint George and its Madaba Mosaic Map. Proceed southeastward to the Madaba Archaeological Park and visit the church and chapels within it. You may then wish to visit the Madaba Archaeological and Folklore Museum. Finally, you may want to visit the Church of the Apostles which is located on the southern edge of the city and immediately north of the King's

Highway. From Madaba you can proceed westward to Mount Nebo. After a visit to the site you can stop at Khirbat al-Mukhayyat and visit the Church of Saints Lot and Procopius on your way back to Madaba. Then, you may go south along the King's Highway to Libb. At Libb turn to the west and visit the palace-fort at the top of Machaerus. On your return, you may wish to visit the churches and chapel within the village of Mukawer.

Still using Amman as a base, one can visit Bethany Beyond the Jordan and Lot's Cave / Dayr 'Ayn 'Abata in a day. Since the weather is very hot during the summer months at both sites, it is advisable to visit them early in the day. At the same time, one will pass through the plains of Moab and pass by Tall ar-Ramah as one proceeds to the Baptism Site.

One of the hotels along the northeast side of the Dead Sea may also be used as the base for visits to the sites and regions indicated above. That way, you can also experience a swim in the sea and a visit to some of its nearby hot springs.

Umm ar-Rasas and the tower and Tower Church to its north will take a half-day. After a stop at the Visitors' Center, one goes on a guided tour to the "Saint Stephen Church Complex." From here, one may be able to visit some of the other churches that have been excavated at Umm ar-Rasas. Finally, a visit to the stylite tower and Tower Church is worthwhile.

People who wish to visit the Memorial of Aaron on Jabal Haroun will usually stay in Wadi Musa or its vicinity the night before. An early morning start is advised, since the walk is both long and strenuous. One may wish to visit the monastery complex to the west of the peak first. Following this, a visit to the Muslim shrine is recommended. If you have a guide, which is advised, he/she will generally know a Bedouin in the area who has a key that will permit you to enter the shrine and its crypt.

In conclusion, and from a purely secular point-of-view, due to the selection of Petra as one of the "new seven wonders of the world," there is more of an interest in Jordan nowadays as a place of tourism. But as the present work points out, there is much more than Petra in Jordan for those who have an interest in pilgrimage in early Christian Jordan.

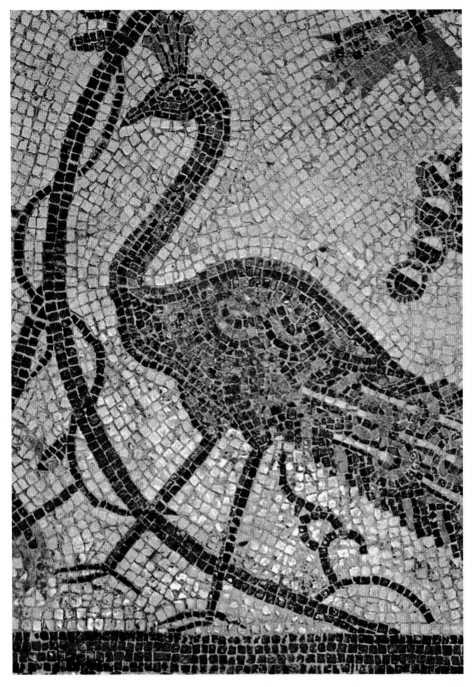

FIG. 2.1 Detail of a peacock from a mosaic at the Memorial of Moses on Mount Nebo (photo by Jerzy Strzelecki, 2001).

2 EARLY CHRISTIAN PILGRIMAGE IN JORDAN

AN interest in places of pilgrimage is very much a part of the life of many people in the modern world. In the west, these sites are of interest to Jews, Christians, and Muslims, while in the east, pilgrimage sites are also of interest to many religious groups, including Hindus and Buddhists. In addition, many people who do not align themselves with any particular religious tradition have a tourist's interest in pilgrimage sites. There is constant mention of these sites in our mass media. As a result, many people wish to go on pilgrimage or visit the sites about which they have both heard and read.

The practice of going on pilgrimage is ancient. While the focus of this book is on prominent and excavated early Christian pilgrimage sites within the country of Jordan, this chapter also provides some background on the practice of pilgrimage in the ancient world in general, early Jewish pilgrimages, the Jewish practice of pilgrimage as reflected in the New Testament, and early Christian pilgrimages and pilgrims in general.

The place of Jordan's early Christian pilgrimage sites relative to other sacred places in the Holy Land also must be put in context. Although the country is not at the center of the Land of the Bible, it still has importance as a place of pilgrimage for Jews, Christians, and Muslims. As a consequence, it is necessary to begin with a consideration of the terms that are used in the title of this publication.

PILGRIMAGE

There are various understandings of the word "pilgrimage," which is derived from the classical Latin word *peregrinatio,* "to travel or sojourn in

FIG. 2.2   Pilgrims' and tourists' path to Machaerus/Mukawer (photo by Sherry Hardin).

foreign parts." What is generally meant by the practice in today's world derives from its usage in ecclesiastical Latin, where it came to be closely associated with religious pilgrimage. Among those who study the early Christian or Byzantine era today, the term is used rather loosely. It can refer both to long-distance journeys to visit a holy shrine or a living holy man and to short-distance trips to a local or regional church for the sake of prayer or in search for healing. What is stressed is not so much the journey itself but the veneration of relics upon arrival at the tomb of a holy man or woman (Talbot 2002: 73)

Whatever the description, the motivation for pilgrimage is primarily religious: to visit a site of special religious or numinous significance. Thus, a pilgrimage may be described as "sacred mobility / religiously motivated travel / sacred journey / devotional travel" or a journey undertaken by a person or a group in quest of a place or state that is believed to embody a sacred ideal. It involves "going to pray at" a place. Associated with such a journey is the ritual activity, such as prayers and/or the veneration of relics, at the religious site (fig. 2.3). Thus, prayer and penance are often a distinctive activity of the pilgrim. In addition, pilgrimage is sometimes the means by which people come into intimate contact with a shared cultural or religious tradition; an example is the annual journey to Mecca on the part of Muslims.

For many pilgrims, the assumption is that the physical world and the spiritual world come together at certain special places, *loca sancta*. They believe, that at these places, the powers of heaven are more easily tapped, either for earthly benefit or for aid in salvation. Christian pilgrims to the Holy Land also hope to pray in places made holy by Christ and his followers. The process of using one's imagination to recall biblical events is an aspect of why Christians respect the holy places. A visit to a holy place nourishes faith by stimulating the minds of pilgrims to imagine biblical events taking place, which provides an opportunity for deep prayer and contemplation.

FIG. 2.3 Modern-day pilgrims and tourists in the Church of Saint George, Madaba (photo by Sherry Hardin).

A journey to a place where there is a relic, the tangible remains of a departed saint, is often very much a part of what is involved in a pilgrimage (fig. 2.4). The relic is seen as a means for the pilgrim to connect with the saint and, through him, also with Christ in heaven. Thus, the pilgrim's visit to the place where the relic is kept can, it is believed, lead to the saint's intercession with Christ for the hope of miraculous cures and good fortune (Harpur 2002: 68–69).

There are many forms of pilgrimages undertaken in our modern world. These include:

⊙ devotional pilgrimages, which have as their goal the encounter with and honoring of the shrine's divinity, personage, or symbol;

FIG. 2.4 Reliquary in modern Greek Orthodox Church at Bethany Beyond the Jordan (photo by Sherry Hardin).

- instrumental pilgrimages, which are undertaken to accomplish finite, worldly goals, for example, cure for an illness.

Examples of these first two types would be Fatima in Portugal and Lourdes in France, shrines to Mary, the Mother of Jesus, where pilgrims go out of devotion to Mary and/or to seek a cure.

- normative pilgrimages, which occur as part of a ritual cycle, relating either to the life cycle or annual calendrical celebrations. An example from the Old Testament/Hebrew Scriptures is the Israelite practice of going to Jerusalem for the Jewish festival of Passover;
- obligatory pilgrimages, such as the Muslim *hajj*;
- simple wandering. This form of pilgrimage has no structure, but the pilgrims will be guided to places that satisfy their inner craving;
- initiatory pilgrimages, that is, those undertaken with the purpose of being initiated into some society and/or rite; included here would be all pilgrimages that have as their purpose the transformation of self (Morinis 1992: 4).

It is not easy to distinguish between pilgrimage and tourism. In fact, the Vatican City State in Italy has a "Pilgrim and Tourist Office" that operates in St. Peter's Square. The route (*Camino*) to the tomb of the apostle Saint James the Great in Santiago de Compostela in northwest Spain is promoted as much for touristic as religious purposes.

Tourism is generally undertaken for either mere recreational purposes or to visit beautiful buildings, landscapes, or works of art to evoke an aesthetic response of wonder. Tourists will often visit a place out of curiosity. They will frequently have a guide book to help them understand what they are looking at. While pilgrims will usually put up with hardships in their travels and visits to sacred sites and offer these up as worthwhile sacrifices, tourists will generally demand "a bang for their buck." If this is not forthcoming, the tourist will usually complain. However, pilgrims are not immune to complaining!

There are many examples of the practice of people making pilgrimages to certain places. The pilgrimage that perhaps attracts the most attention in the Western world today is the Muslim *Hajj*, the annual pilgrimage to Mecca during the 12th lunar month of the year, in which millions of the faithful participate. But Jews, both secular and religious, make pilgrimages to Jerusalem and other holy places of the Land of the Bible. And Christians too have their pilgrimage sites, for example, to the Holy Land, to St. Peter's in Rome, and to places associated with appearances of Mary, such as Fatima in Portugal and Lourdes in France.

For the Muslim, pilgrimage is a sacred duty. In the words of the *Koran/Al-Qur'ān*, "Perform the pilgrimage and holy visit in the service of God" (2.196; see also 3.97) (Ali 2001: 35). Moreover, what the Muslim pilgrim is required to do once reaching Mecca is spelled out (*Koran/Al-Qur'ān* 2. 196-203) (Ali 2001: 35–36). Unlike Islam, however, Christianity lays no obligation on the faithful to make pilgrimages. As a consequence, there are also no specific guidelines for the Christian who visits a holy site.

THE PRACTICE OF PILGRIMAGE IN THE ANCIENT WORLD

There is evidence for pilgrimages as early as the third millennium BC. For example, in the land of Sumer (modern-day southern Iraq), Gudea of Lagash (last half of the 22nd century BC) recounts a journey he made from his home town to the sanctuary of the goddess Nanshe some distance away at Isin. In Egypt, according to the Greek historian Herodotus, pilgrims attended the festival of Osiris at Abydos in Upper Egypt and visited healing sanctuaries on the west bank of the Nile River as early as the second millennium (Elsner and Rutherford 2005: 10).

A common motivation for pilgrimage in classical antiquity was the consulting of oracles, for example, a consultation at the major shrine of Delphi in Greece. Another reason for pilgrimage in the ancient Greek world was for healing, such as a journey to a shrine of the god Asklepios. At least two hundred sacred shrines were dedicated to this healing god. His chief pilgrimage centers, Epidauros, in modern-day Greece, and Pergamum, in modern-day Turkey, were not unlike a sanatorium or spa, where the infirm went to bathe, drink mineral water, and place themselves under the care of a physician.

In summary, pilgrims were a familiar sight in antiquity. At shrines and cult centers throughout the Mediterranean world they could be seen bringing their offerings, joining in sacrifices, fulfilling vows made in times of distress, seeking relief from pain or healing, giving thanks for benefits, and participating in processions and banquets (Wilken 1992: 103).

EARLY JEWISH PILGRIMAGE

Before Solomon (ca. 970/960–930/920 BC)[1] built the temple in Jerusalem, Israelites made an annual pilgrimage to the central shrine of the tribal confederacy. The practice of a man named Elkanah is a good example:

---

1 The dates in this publication generally follow those in Freedman 1992.

> There was a certain man of Ramathaim, a Zuphite, from the hill
> country of Ephraim, whose name was Elkanah.... Now this man used
> to go up year by year from his town to worship and to sacrifice to
> the LORD of hosts at Shiloh, where the two sons of Eli, Hophni and
> Phinehas, were priests of the LORD (1 Sam 1.1, 3).

Following the construction of the temple (built between the fourth and
eleventh years of Solomon's reign [1 Kings 6.37–38]), it and the city of
Jerusalem, in which it was located, became the focus of Israelite pilgrimage or festival: "Three times in the year you shall hold a festival for
me" (Exodus 23.14); "You shall observe the festival of unleavened bread"
(Exodus 23.15); "You shall observe the festival of harvest, of the first fruits
of your labor, of what you sow in your field (Exodus 23.16); "You shall
observe the festival of ingathering at the end of year, when you gather in
from the field the fruit of your labor" (Exodus 23.16); and "Three times in
the year all your males shall appear before the LORD God" (Exodus 23.17).
This latter command is reiterated in Exodus 34.23, and in Deuteronomy
16.16 it is stated: "Three times a year all your males shall appear before the
LORD your God at the place that he will choose: at the festival of unleavened bread, at the festival of weeks, and at the festival of booths."[2]

These times of pilgrimage brought Jews to Jerusalem not only from
the land of Israel but from the diaspora as well. We have evidence for this
in the New Testament:

> When the day of Pentecost had come.... Now there were devout
> Jews from every nation under heaven living in Jerusalem.... And how
> is it that we hear each of us, in our own languages? Parthians, Medes,
> Elamites, and residents of Mesopotamia, Judea and Cappadocia,
> Pontus and Asia.... (Acts of the Apostles 2.1, 5, 8, 9).

For the Jews, pilgrimage centered on Jerusalem, the city that stood "in
the center of the nations" (Ezekiel 5.5). Even after the Romans destroyed
the holy city and its temple in AD 70, Jews came to Jerusalem on the
ninth day of the eleventh month of their calendar to mourn its loss.

In addition, religious Jews made trips to other sites that were associated with biblical persons and events. Jewish religious leaders encouraged
the faithful not to abandon their practice of visiting Palestine and its
many holy places, even after the fall of Jerusalem. Wilken states:

---

2 These Jewish festivals/pilgrimages are now known as Passover, Pentecost, and Booths/
Tabernacles.

> For Philo the land of Israel was more than a spiritual idea. It was a place to which Jews from all over the world looked for inspiration and comfort. The act of pilgrimage, for example, was not only a spiritual discipline or a religious duty; it was a social rite that united the people and created in them a sense of unity… (1992: 36).

The Jewish Practice of Pilgrimage Reflected in the New Testament

The Israelite practice of observing the three festivals, especially the Passover, in Jerusalem is very much a part of the New Testament (see, for example, Matthew 26.2; Mark 14.1; Luke 2.1, 22.1; John 5.1). The writers of the accounts of the Gospel have Jesus in Jerusalem for these festivals; this is especially the case in the Gospel according to John: "After this there was a festival of the Jews, and Jesus went up to Jerusalem" (5.1); "Now the Jewish festival of Booths was near" (7.2); "But after his brothers had gone to the festival, then he also went, not publicly but as it were in secret" (7.10); "Six days before the Passover Jesus came to Bethany" (12.1) … "The next day the great crowd that had come to the festival heard that Jesus was coming to Jerusalem" (12.12).

Jesus' death took place during the festival of Passover (Matthew 26–27; Mark 14–15; Luke 22–23; John 13.1) and, afterward, the Descent of the Holy Spirit upon the Apostles took place on the Jewish celebration of Pentecost: "When the day of Pentecost had come, they were all together in one place" (Acts 2.1).

The New Testament also demonstrates that during the time of its writing, the Christians accepted Jewish holy places. When Peter mentioned King David, he said, "His tomb is with us till this day" (Acts 2.29).

EARLY CHRISTIAN PILGRIMAGES AND PILGRIMS

In the early centuries of Christianity there existed no wholesale encouragement for going on pilgrimage. Even in the New Testament we have a good example of this. In a passage from John, Jesus is in conversation with the Samaritan woman whom he had met at a well on his journey through her region on his way to Jerusalem.

> Jesus said to her, "Woman, believe me, the hour is coming when you will worship the Father neither on this mountain nor in Jerusalem. You worship what you do not know, for salvation is from the Jews. But the hour is coming, and is now here, when the true worshipers

will worship the Father in spirit and truth, for the Father seeks such
as these to worship him. God is spirit, and those who worship him
must worship in spirit and truth" (4.21–24).

It is evident that going to holy places is not an obligatory activity on the
part of the followers of Jesus. Moreover, outside the New Testament, not
all early Christians accepted the necessity of visits to holy places. There
were those who rejected the whole notion of pilgrimage. In AD 351, Saint
Basil of Caesarea came to the east to follow a route taken thirty years later
by Egeria. He visited Palestine, Alexandria and the rest of Egypt, Coele-
Syria, and Mesopotamia, hardly mentioning the holy places. His interest
was in the monks and ascetics of the region, the secret of whose lives he
wanted to learn (Wilkinson 1999: 6).

In about AD 380, Gregory, Bishop of Nyssa (Cappadocia in modern-
day Turkey), wrote a letter condemning the whole notion of pilgrimage.
He was far too concerned with the spiritual beliefs of the Christians in his
diocese to waste any time over the historical places of Jesus.

The opposite reaction came from Jerome (see below), a biblical com-
mentator who actually lived in Bethlehem. He was very hard on ignorant
guides to the Holy Land and took the trouble to work out the correct
places for biblical events (Wilkinson 1999: 6).

For the three hundred years after the time of Christ, the Christian
historian and bishop Eusebius (see below) names only four Christians
who visited the homeland of Jesus because of its historic associations.
The first was Melito of Sardis who, motivated by the study of the Old
Testament/Hebrew Scriptures, came to the Holy Land and wrote about
Jerusalem in about AD 180. He records how, in order to establish accurate-
ly the books of the Old Testament, he had traveled to "the place where
these things were preached and done." Alexander came next; in about AD
200, he traveled from Cappadocia to the Holy City "for prayer and inves-
tigation of the sites." He later became bishop of Jerusalem. Sextus Julius
Africanus, who lived in Emmaus, came in about AD 220. Finally, Origen
(AD 184/185–253/254), a principal theologian of the Greek Church and a
biblical scholar, came to the Holy Land from Egypt in about AD 235. He
traveled around Palestine seeking out the location of events recorded in
the Scriptures. For all of these early Christian pilgrims it was a combina-
tion of biblical tourism and Christian devotion that brought them to the
Holy Land. Thus, "pilgrimage" before AD 325 for the most part was likely
a local phenomenon.

Constantine's Conversion and the Beginnings of Pilgrimages to Palestine

The idea of the Christian holy places began in the fourth century with the innovations of the emperor Constantine (reigned 306–337). His involvement led to the establishment of hundreds of holy sites and churches in Palestine throughout the Byzantine period, and Christian pilgrimage began in the wake of his innovations.

It appears that the primary reason for Constantine's new belief in the power of the Christian God was that this God provided him with military victories, in particular a victory over his Western rival Maxentius in the battle for the Milvian Bridge, outside Rome, on the 24th of October, 312. According to Eusebius, Constantine saw a vision of a sign of the cross inscribed with the words "By this conquer" (εν τούτω νίκα) drawn in the sky in light, whereupon "the Christ of God" appeared with the same sign. After his victory, Constantine had the Christian symbol incorporated into his standard, the *labarum*, with the *chi-rho* abbreviation used by scribes to mean 'good.' For the emperor, and perhaps others before him, the *chi-rho* also stood for *Christos*, since the letters *chi* and *rho* were the first two letters of the name. The *labarum* became a symbol of the alliance between God and Constantine; it affected a kind of magical power over the battlefield.

Whatever Constantine's commitment was to the Christian God, it resulted in a radically changed world. When Constantine and Licinius, his co-emperor, met in Milan in AD 313, they agreed on certain legal provisions in favor of the Christians. The result is often referred to as the Edict of Milan or the Edict of Tolerance, and it prescribed that everyone should be given the freedom to follow their personal religion, that ordinances hostile to Christians were lifted, that general and unrestricted freedom of religious practice was guaranteed, that confiscated Church property was to be restored, and that Christians were given the right of forming a legal corporate body (Ziegler 2003: 625).

When Constantine defeated his rival Licinius in 324, he took over the rule of the East, which included Palestine. He rebuilt the city of Byzantium, changed its name to Constantinople, and decided to make it the new Rome. He immediately set about a program of Christianization. The resolutions of 313 had already halted the persecution of Christians, begun by Diocletian in 303, throughout the Empire. However, positive steps in favor of Christians had not been taken by Licinius in the East. With Constantine, there was a purge of prominent pagans.

When the Roman Empire turned to Christianity, pilgrimage to the Holy Land was encouraged. Conversely, the fact of pilgrimage was decisive in the development of a Christian Palestine. But pilgrimages only began on a large scale with the Christianization of the country. For example, Eusebius writes that as early as 315, Christians from all corners of the world were coming on pilgrimage to Jerusalem and praying on the Mount of Olives. The news of the discovery of the Holy Sepulchre, the place of the burial and resurrection of Jesus, and the Christian reclamation of Jerusalem must have substantially increased the number of pilgrims visiting the Holy Land.

Constantine is the first person known to have built churches in Palestine at places Christians regarded as holy. These churches were begun shortly after he became emperor of the East as well as the West. The four places that were developed by imperial order are: Mamre/ Terebinthus (Ramat el-Khalil), the tombs of the Jewish patriarchs and matriarchs at Hebron (Abraham and Sarah; Isaac and Rebekah; Leah [Gen 49.31]; Jacob [Gen 50.13]); Bethlehem, the site of Jesus' nativity (Matthew 2; Luke 2); Golgotha in Jerusalem, the place of Jesus' death and burial (Matthew 27.32–66; Mark 15.16–46; Luke 23.26–55; John 19.17-- 42); and *Eleona*, a church on the Mount of Olives commemorating the Ascension of Jesus (Luke 24.51; Acts 1.9). Following the Synod of Tyre in AD 335, Constantine urged the participants to go to Jerusalem, at state expense, to celebrate the inauguration of the newly built church of the Holy Sepulchre.[3]

As the news of Constantine's works in the holy places began to spread, the flow of pilgrims increased. The first of them whose writings have survived came from Bordeaux in AD 333 with the express purpose of seeing the Holy City and, no doubt, of describing it for the benefit of his neighbors in Gaul. This Pilgrim of Bordeaux describes in his writings a stage in pilgrimage when there were as yet hardly any Christian buildings; he mentions only two: Constantine's basilicas at the Holy Sepulchre and on the Mount of Olives.

---

3 There is archaeological evidence to support the fact that some churches were also built east of the Jordan in the fourth century, for example, at Gadara (Umm Qays; Chapter 3) and Mount Nebo (Chapter 6). However, it was during the fifth and sixth centuries that this building activity reached its height. The increase in building activity in the sixth century is attributed to the flourishing economy and the stable political activity of the Byzantine Empire or Eastern Roman Empire, with its capital at Constantinople, during the long reign of Justinian I (reigned 527– 565). It was Justinian who gave both spiritual and financial support to the building of churches in Palestine. A political change in the form of the Muslim conquests led to the decline in the building of churches from the mid-seventh century.

The Bible and the Christian Pilgrim

Whatever the varied experiences of the journey that brought the early Christian pilgrims to the Holy Land, it was always the Bible that inspired their enterprise and, indeed, shaped their whole conception of the Holy Land.

The Pilgrim of Bordeaux labeled each of the sites he visited in the Holy Land with its precise scriptural associations. His descriptions always include the biblical event, usually a matter of Old Testament history, that was commemorated there.

The Bible was Egeria's guide-book. It also was a dominant influence on the language and presentation of her narrative. All that she saw was in response to her demand to be shown the settings of the events of the Bible. In her words: "So we were shown everything which the Books of Moses tell us took place in that valley beneath holy Sinai, the mount of God… it may help you, loving sisters, the better to picture what happened in these places when you read the holy books of Moses" (*Travels* 5.8, Wilkinson 1971: 97–98). Egeria explicitly states the relationship between familiarity with the text of the Bible and the desire to visit the holy places of Palestine.

Jerome used the Bible as a motivation to encourage visitors to the holy places. He urged Marcella to come to the Holy Land and re-live before her eyes the Gospel narratives (Hunt 1982: 87).

And what did the early Christians do when they reached a holy place? An answer may be found in the accounts of Egeria (see below), one of the first Christian pilgrims to the places of the Bible. She writes:

> … This is Horeb to which the holy Prophet Elijah fled from the presence of King Ahab, and it was there that God spoke to him with the words, "What doest thou here, Elijah?," as it is written in the Books of the Kingdoms…. Thus the holy men were kind enough to show us everything, and there too we made the Offering and prayed very earnestly, and the passage was read from the Book of Kingdoms. Indeed, whenever we arrived anywhere, I myself always wanted the Bible passage to be read to us (*Travels* 4.2–3; Wilkinson 1999: 111).

> And it was always our practice, when we managed to reach one of the places we were able to see, to have first a prayer, then a reading from the book, then to say an appropriate psalm and another prayer. By God's grace we always followed this practice whenever we were able to reach a place we wanted to see (*Travels* 10.7; Wilkinson 1999: 120).

FIG. 2.5   Ancient roman road at Gadara/Umm Qays (photo by Sherry Hardin).

Egeria's practice of commemorating the person or event by reading passages from the Bible, from the Lives of the Saints, and by saying prayers is still followed by many pilgrims today.

Road System and Hostels

Although some pilgrims came to the Holy Land from the west by means of ship, most came on mules or donkeys or by foot. For these, the Roman road system of the time made pilgrimages from both west and east feasible, since it provided a means of communication throughout the entire Roman Empire (fig. 2.5). In the Roman Orient it included roads from the Mediterranean into Syria, Mesopotamia, and Asia Minor and then southward to Egypt. In addition, there were roads that crossed the Jordan River and continued into the *Provincia Arabia* and then, as desert tracks, into the Arabian Peninsula (Roll 1999: 111).

Local bishops considered it their responsibility to provide hospitality for pilgrims on their way to pilgrimage sites as well as to those at the holy places. However, the responsibility went far beyond the person of the bishop himself. There also was the frequent establishment of hostels (*xenodochia*) supervised by monks or the clergy (Hunt 1982: 63).

Hospitality was one of the virtues cherished by the monks and was often recommended by monastic leaders in the rules dictated to their disciples. Feeding the poor was considered but one aspect of the virtue of openhandedness. Thus it may be assumed that even small monasteries and hermitages made some arrangement for overnight guests (Hirschfeld 1992: 196). The standard policy was for a maximum stay of two days (unless the visitor earned his keep by working) (Dietz 2005: 97).

The monasteries were in the forefront of meeting the demands created by the concentration of pilgrims. Since they were deliberately sited in the proximity of the leading holy places, it could hardly be otherwise (Hunt 1982: 181). Moreover, desert monasticism was largely dependent on the stream of pilgrims to the holy places, not only for the income they brought with them, but also – and primarily – for their manpower (Hirschfeld 1992: 2).

The hostel could be situated outside the walls of the monastery so as not to disturb the life of the permanent residents. It could consist of a series of bedrooms and dormitories and there would have been spaces for cooking and an area where the animals that frequently brought the pilgrims to the site could be tethered and fed. Lodgings in the hospice were offered free of charge. In some cases, the needy even received a parting gift of money or food (Hirschfeld 1992: 199).

The excavators of the pilgrimage sites at Bethany Beyond the Jordan, Lot's Cave, and Jabal Haroun indicate that they have uncovered evidence of pilgrim hostels; they will be treated when considering these particular sites.

EARLY CHRISTIAN JORDAN

Today, 95 percent of Jordan's population is Muslim. However, many people are unaware that the country was at one time predominantly Christian. Due to its past, there are hundreds of Christian sites throughout the country. Some of these sites were and still are places of pilgrimage, such as Bethany Beyond the Jordan and the Memorial of Moses at Mount Nebo. Traditionally, emphasis has been put on the Christian sites to the west of the Jordan River, while little attention has been devoted to those on the river's east side.

Archaeological Sources

For archaeologists and historians with an interest in the Near or Middle East, the early Christian era is generally referred to as the Byzantine period, which is dated to AD 324–640. AD 324 is the year when the Eastern Roman Empire became distinct from the western one and Constantine the Great became its leader. Beginning with this date, and for three centuries thereafter, Christianity was the main religion of the Near East. AD 640 is the date when the area became part of the Islamic or Muslim Empire. From then on, as far as Jordan is concerned, this area was under Muslim rule, and Christianity began to decrease in importance. It is most probable that at this time the Bedouin tribes of the area converted from Christianity to Islam. However, as we will see throughout this work,

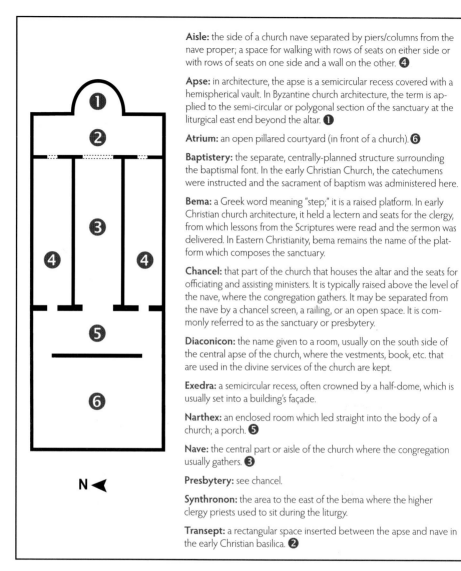

Aisle: the side of a church nave separated by piers/columns from the nave proper; a space for walking with rows of seats on either side or with rows of seats on one side and a wall on the other. ❹

Apse: in architecture, the apse is a semicircular recess covered with a hemispherical vault. In Byzantine church architecture, the term is applied to the semi-circular or polygonal section of the sanctuary at the liturgical east end beyond the altar. ❶

Atrium: an open pillared courtyard (in front of a church). ❻

Baptistery: the separate, centrally-planned structure surrounding the baptismal font. In the early Christian Church, the catechumens were instructed and the sacrament of baptism was administered here.

Bema: a Greek word meaning "step;" it is a raised platform. In early Christian church architecture, it held a lectern and seats for the clergy, from which lessons from the Scriptures were read and the sermon was delivered. In Eastern Christianity, bema remains the name of the platform which composes the sanctuary.

Chancel: that part of the church that houses the altar and the seats for officiating and assisting ministers. It is typically raised above the level of the nave, where the congregation gathers. It may be separated from the nave by a chancel screen, a railing, or an open space. It is commonly referred to as the sanctuary or presbytery.

Diaconicon: the name given to a room, usually on the south side of the central apse of the church, where the vestments, book, etc. that are used in the divine services of the church are kept.

Exedra: a semicircular recess, often crowned by a half-dome, which is usually set into a building's façade.

Narthex: an enclosed room which led straight into the body of a church; a porch. ❺

Nave: the central part or aisle of the church where the congregation usually gathers. ❸

Presbytery: see chancel.

Synthronon: the area to the east of the bema where the higher clergy priests used to sit during the liturgy.

Transept: a rectangular space inserted between the apse and nave in the early Christian basilica. ❷

FIG. 2.6 Basic church floor plan, with a key to its features.

Byzantine Christianity continued to thrive in some parts of Jordan in the early Islamic period.

It must be kept in mind that the majority of the sites are multi-period ones. This means that they contain more than just early Christian/ Byzantine and ecclesiastical architectural remains. For this reason, the Christian architectural features at these sites are put in context by presenting some background information on the site as a whole, so that the visitor to the site will be able to appreciate the site not just as a place of pilgrimage but as one that frequently had a history before and/or after the early Christian/Byzantine period.

The holy places located in Jordan need to be seen in context. It must be emphasized at the outset that the principal sites in the Holy Land are those associated with the Nativity (Bethlehem) and the death and resurrection of Jesus (Jerusalem). Following these sites in importance would have been the sites associated with the ministry of Jesus in Galilee. Once these sites were visited, the pilgrim may have added on visits to holy places east of the Jordan River.

The focus of present-day pilgrims is no different. Christian pilgrims come first to Bethlehem and Jerusalem; they also visit Galilee! In addition, a small percentage of these pilgrims visit Mount Nebo and the Site of the Baptism on the east bank of the Jordan. There are fewer who make their way to Machaerus/Mukawer, the site of one of Herod's desert palaces and the beheading of John the Baptist, and even fewer travel to the sites associated with Lot and his daughters – in Ghor as-Safi – and the burial place of Moses' brother Aaron at Jabal Haroun to the southwest of Petra. Fewer still visit the village of Listib/al-Istib, which is said to be Tishbe, the home of Elijah, and nearby Tall Mar Elyas. However, as the sites described in this work become better known, they too will attract greater numbers of both pilgrims and tourists.

The pilgrimages to the Land of the Bible by Popes John Paul II and Benedict XVI in 2000 and 2009, respectively, were not confined to sites west of the Jordan. Their visits included stops at two holy sites east of the Jordan – Bethany Beyond the Jordan and Mount Nebo. In addition, Benedict XVI visited Madaba. These pilgrims were thus following a tradition that has gone on for almost two thousand years.

A Note on Iconoclasm

Iconoclasm, meaning "image breaking," refers to the extreme opposition to the representation of the human figure and the veneration of images. In its Christian context, it is especially associated with the Byzantine Empire and the first centuries of the Early Islamic period (seventh and eighth centuries). The interest here, of course, is in iconoclasm in Jordan that involved damage to the images of ordinary people and animals, not just icons, as manifested by the iconoclastic movement during the Byzantine Empire (Schick 1995: 213).

What we do know is that sometime during the first two centuries of the Early Islamic period in Palestine, the images of people and animals depicted in the mosaic floors of churches were deliberately damaged

FIG. 2.7   Iconoclastic damage to mosaic in the Church of Saint Stephen at Umm ar-Rasas (photo by Sherry Hardin).

(Schick 1988: 219; 1995: 207–9). Scholars have traditionally attributed this damage to the Muslim opposition to images in art as manifested in Umayyad government policies. However, many today think that this policy was not responsible, at least solely, for the damage to mosaics in Jordan.

Most of the damage done to mosaic floors was executed with considerable care and concentrated on the removal of the offensive images; the rest of the mosaic was left intact. The damage was usually carefully repaired, often by mixing up the tesserae – the stone cubes – that had been taken out of the mosaic and then putting them back in without apparent order. Schick (1988: 218–19) postulates that the careful way in which these alterations were made indicates that it was Christians who damaged and repaired these mosaics (fig. 2.7).

What was the motivation for this damage to mosaics? Perhaps Christians damaged the images themselves due to social pressure and criticism from their Muslim and Jewish peers of the Christian practice of venerating images (Schick 1995: 218–19). The deliberate damage to the mosaics of the churches of Umm ar-Rasas happened after AD 718. It would seem, therefore, that the iconoclastic movement in Jordan was contemporary with that elsewhere in the Byzantine Empire, but with its own local character. As the damage indicates, iconoclasm in Jordan was so radical that not even figures of fish and other animals were spared.

Throughout this work there will be many occasions to indicate the damage to mosaics at the early Christian pilgrimage sites of Jordan. Some of this damage is due to the iconoclasm movement, but not all! Other damage to church mosaics can be attributed to development, erosion, looting, and/or vandalism.

Literary Sources

Throughout this work, references are made to the literary sources of our information on the practice of pilgrimage to Jordan during the early Christian period. A brief overview of these sources is presented here in chronological order. They will be referred to in more detail as the various sites are considered in the following chapters.

The Bible

The primary literary source for the information on the topics treated in this book is the Christian Bible, which consists of the Old Testament/ Hebrew Scriptures and the New Testament. The texts from this source are presented using the English translation found in the *New Revised Standard Version with the Apocrypha* (NRSV), copyright 1989 by the Division of Christian Education of the National Council of the Churches of Christ in the United States of America.

The traditional manner in English versions of the Bible of rendering the Divine Name, the "Tetragrammaton," and the practice of the reading of the Hebrew Scriptures in the synagogue, relative to the name YAHWEH, is followed in this work. When the name appears in the Hebrew text, it is written as LORD, with four uppercase letters, in English. This distinguishes the Divine Name from the Hebrew *Adonai*, meaning "Lord," or *Elohim*, meaning "God," in translation.

Josephus

Josephus (AD 37/38–ca. 100) was a Jewish general, historian, and apologist. He was born in Jerusalem and was educated among the priestly circles as well as the various Judaic sectarian movements of his day. He went to Rome in 64 to obtain the release of Jewish priests and returned to Judaea on the eve of the First Jewish Revolt against Rome (AD 66–73). During the revolt, Josephus commanded the Jewish forces in Galilee but surrendered when the Romans defeated them in 67. He was imprisoned for a short time, but after his release he accompanied the Roman general Titus during the siege and destruction of Jerusalem in AD 70. After the war, Josephus lived in Rome under the patronage of the emperor and wrote four major works: *The Jewish War*, published shortly after the fall of Jerusalem; *Jewish Antiquities*, recounting Jewish experiences from earliest times to AD 66 and published in 93/94; *Against Apion*, quoting and refuting many anti-Semitic works from the Hellenistic age; and *The Life*. Thanks to the Christian church, Josephus' works have been preserved.

Eusebius

Eusebius Pamphili (ca. AD 260–339), Bishop of Caesarea Maritima on the Mediterranean coast, the capital of Roman Palestine, was the father of church history, a friend and confidant of the Emperor Constantine the Great, and a leader at the Council of Nicaea (AD 325). He is the author of the *Onomasticon* ("collection of names"), a dictionary of biblical topography. In the work, Eusebius maps out the Land of the Bible for students of the Bible and pilgrims. Not only does he list the cities and towns mentioned in the Bible, the work also includes rivers, hills, wadis (river/stream beds that are dry for most of the year), and other geographical features. It appears that Eusebius himself may have walked the land and visited many of the sites that appear in his work. The *Onomasticon* became a great help to biblical scholars and Christian pilgrims and may have influenced the creators of the Madaba Mosaic Map (see below).

There is no certainty as to just when Eusebius composed the *Onomasticon*. However, Taylor et al. posit that "the final form of the work must be dated between 313 and mid-325, but no later" (2003: 3).

Jerome

Jerome (ca. 342(?)–420), of Balkan origin, first traveled to Syria in AD 373, where he lived as a hermit studying Hebrew until 379 and was ordained a priest. He then went to Constantinople, where he studied Greek under St. Gregory Nazianzus. Pope Damasus called him to Rome in 382 and it was there that Jerome translated the Gospels of the New Testament into Latin. When Pope Damasus died in 385, Jerome found it expedient to leave Rome. He traveled to Palestine and Egypt and then settled in Bethlehem. His contacts persuaded him that he should translate, with the aid of Jewish scholars, the entire sacred texts into Latin. The result was the *Vulgate*, the official version of the Bible in the western world for more than a millennium and a half. In addition, he translated and made notes on Eusebius' *Onomasticon* some 70 years after its origin. Jerome retitled the work *Book on the Sites and Names of Places of the Hebrews;* it is cited throughout this work in conjunction with Eusebius' *Onomasticon*.

Egeria

The text of Egeria's *Travels* was lost for 700 years. When in the late 19th century a manuscript was found in Italy, the only part left was the middle of the book. Either at the beginning or the end the name of the pilgrim may have appeared, but it was lost. However, today there exists what seems to be solid evidence for the name Egeria.

Opinions differ relative to the date of Egeria's visit to the Levant, but most scholars date it between AD 381 and 384. Her so-called *Travels* consist of one or perhaps two letters to her "sisters." The "sisters," who received the manuscript of her *Travels* towards the end of the fourth century, may be either Egeria's name for her Christian acquaintances or a title for fellow-members of a religious society. No further information is provided.

The *Travels* describe Egeria's pilgrimage to visit holy sites and people in Egypt, the Sinai, Palestine, Transjordan, Syria, and Cappadocia. In addition, it recounts what she did once she arrived at a site of interest and the liturgy she found on her travels. The work is therefore of great value, since we must depend on her information alone for the answers to many topographic and liturgical problems of that time. The account is, indeed, unique!

In the seventh century, a monk called Valerius wrote a letter to his brethren at El Vierzo in northwestern Spain praising her travels. He refers to her as a courageous pilgrim whom he deliberately called "the most blessed Egeria." Valerius' letter is especially valuable, since it tells of Egeria's visits to several places that are missing from the incomplete manuscript. Unfortunately, the letter makes no attempt to quote Egeria verbatim, so it does not enable us to reconstruct her text.

Egeria writes that she has come "right from the other end of the earth." However, she does not say precisely where her home was; she may have come from the same part of Spain as Valerius.

On her visits east of the Jordan River, Egeria traveled from Jerusalem, crossed over the river, visited Livias (Tall ar-Ramah in the plains of Moab), and then began her ascent to Mount Nebo, probably in January or February of AD 384, according to Wilkinson (1999: 43). She visited Moses' Springs (*Khirbat 'Uyun Musa*), nearby Mount Nebo, and then Moses' mountain. From there she returned to Jerusalem. Later she journeyed to Carneas in Syria, where she believed the home of Job was located. On the way, she wrote that she visited King Melchizedek's city, the place of John's baptizing at Aenon, in the northern Jordan Valley, Tishbe (modern-day Listib/al-Istib), the home of Elijah (1 Kings 17.1), the tomb of Jephthah in Gilead (Judges 12.7), Wadi Cherith (1 Kings 17.3, 5), where Elijah was fed by ravens (1 Kings 17.5–6), and Uz, where Job was buried (Job 1.1; 42.17).

John Rufus and Peter the Iberian

What we know of Peter the Iberian (ca. AD 413/417–491), who came from what is now the eastern part of the modern Republic of Georgia, comes from the writings of John Rufus, one of his disciples and traveling companions on his trips around Palestine. Around AD 500, within a decade or two after Peter's death, Rufus wrote *The Life of Peter the Iberian*, a hagiographical biography. From this work, we are informed among other things that Peter was a revered monk and bishop who made his home in the area of Gaza on the Mediterranean coast.

According to Rufus, shortly after his initial arrival in Jerusalem in the late 430s or early 440s, Peter undertook a pilgrimage to Mount Nebo. There he discovered Moses' tomb. The trip could be counted as Peter's first journey to *Arabia*.

In the later part of his life (ca. 481), Peter had different reasons for going into the territory of *Arabia* a second time, namely his poor health. Describing the second journey, Rufus says that, "[o]nce it pleased the blessed one also to go to the areas of Arabia on account of his weakness namely, so that he would bathe in the hot spring, which is in Livias, the one which is called 'of Saint Moses'" (Horn 2005: 142). On this occasion, he not only visited Mount Nebo but also the nearby village of Nebo (Khirbat al-Mukhayyat). In addition, he made at least two visits to Madaba, where he performed miracles. Peter also visited the hot springs at Baarou/Baaras (Hammamat Ma'in) along the northeastern shore of the Dead Sea, not far from the town.

Theodosius

Theodosius, who seems to have been an archdeacon from North Africa, wrote *The Topography of the Holy Land* at the beginning of the sixth century. The work is a collection of passages from various sources – guidebooks, liturgical works, and perhaps exegeses – with the aim to guide pilgrims to the holy places. Although the work, as we now have it, is incomplete, it is a valuable historical source and mentions a large number of places of pilgrimage (Wilkinson 2002: 9–10).

Petra Papyri

In 1993, during the excavation of the fifth-century basilica of St. Mary (now generally referred to as the "Petra Church") located in the center of the ancient city of Petra, the excavators, working under the auspices of the American Center of Oriental Research (ACOR) in Amman, found carbonized Byzantine papyrus scrolls. The scrolls cover a period of some 50 years between AD 528 and 578 (or perhaps 582), during the reign of Emperor Justinian and his successors. These documents, presently referred to as the "Petra Papyri" or "Petra Scrolls," needed extensive conservation work before they could be read. They are written mainly in Greek, but there are two lines of Latin text in one of the scrolls and Latin "loan words" are frequently used. The scrolls consist of economic documents dealing with possessions, dispositions, and acquisitions of real estate and other types of property. They contain sworn and unsworn contracts, agreements and settlements of disputes concerning loans, sales, divisions of property, cessions, registrations, marriages, and inheritance. The documents make reference to Petra as well as other settlements and places around Petra. They refer to churches, such as the "Church of our All-Holy Mistress and Glorious God-bearing Ever Virgin Mary" in Petra, probably the one in which the scrolls were uncovered, and the "Monastery (Holy House) of the Saint High Priest Aaron" (Inventory 6a; see Gagos and Frösén 1998: 477). Moreover, they mention other buildings, like "the Hospital/Hostel of the Saint Martyr Cyricus in the city of Petra" (Inventory 6a; see Gagos and Frösén 1998: 477). Among the key figures in the texts are men of administrative ranks – ecclesiastical, civilian, and military (Bikai 1996).

The Piacenza Pilgrim

The author of this work, whose name we do not know, came from Piacenza in northern Italy. He wrote during the second half of the sixth century, around 570. He passed on to his readers a variety of experiences and wrote about places and practices for which we have no other evidence (Wilkinson 2002: 12). He visited a number of holy places east of the Jordan.

Madaba Mosaic Map

In 1884, during exploratory work for the construction of a new church for the Orthodox community in Madaba, remnants of what later became known as the Madaba Mosaic Map were discovered. In the 1890s, the Greek Orthodox Patriarchate of Jerusalem gave orders to examine the ruins upon which the church, now the Orthodox Church of St. George, was going to be built and cover any archaeological ruins under the roof of the new church. In 1896, the year that the new church was erected over the remains of an older church from the Byzantine period, the map – originally created as the floor of a sixth-century church – was recognized as a unique geographical mosaic map of Palestine, and study of it was undertaken the following year (fig. 2.8).

The mosaic panel enclosing the map was originally 15.60 × 6 m, or 94 square meters, of which 25 square meters are preserved, corresponding only to about a quarter of the total; only eight percent of the eastern part versus thirteen percent of the western part are extant. The map covers the

FIG. 2.8   Segment of the Madaba Mosaic Map in the Church of Saint George, Madaba (photo by Jerzy Strzelecki, 2001).

entire area from the south wall to the north wall of the church leaving only a little space for a frame, of which no remains have been recovered. The Jordan River and the Dead Sea appear to have divided the map into two equal parts. The map shows an area extending from Egypt to the Phoenician coast, and from the desert to the Mediterranean Sea. The cities and buildings on the map, as well as the captions, are oriented to the east. There are 157 such captions, and most of the sites on the map have been identified.

According to Wilkinson (1976: 98), the Madaba Mosaic Map was specifically concerned with holy places likely to be visited by pilgrims. Thus, its artist tried to represent as precisely as possible the nature of Palestine on both sides of the Jordan River and to establish the locations of Palestinian sites. The Madaba Mosaic Map is, however, probably more than just a geographic text of the time. It appears to be principally a re-reading of the story of salvation as narrated in the Bible in its geographic context. The Holy City of Jerusalem, in its remodeled appearance during the time of Hadrian (AD 117–138), is placed at its center (fig. 2.9) and the principal building is that of the Holy Sepulchre, constructed on the Rock of Calvary, thought of as being the center of the world, but above all, as the place where the most dramatic actions in the history of salvation took

FIG. 2.9   Jerusalem. Detail of the Madaba Mosaic Map in the Church of Saint George, Madaba (photo by David Bjorgen, 2005).

place. Since the map was placed between the priest and the people during a liturgical celebration, it reminded them of this story (Shadid 1998).

According to Piccirillo (1999: 22), the Madaba Mosaic Map may be dated from the sixties of the sixth century to the first decade of the seventh century AD. Today, although damaged and missing some of its segments, it continues to form part of the floor of the Greek Orthodox Church of St. George. It is a major tourist attraction.

The map is an important source for biblical and historical topography. In addition, it provides information on the location of a number of pilgrimage sites east of the Jordan that are relevant to this study. Thus, it will be referred to frequently.

John Moschus' Pratum spirituale / "Spiritual Meadow"

John Moschus (ca. AD 550–619) came from Damascus in Syria and entered monastic life at the Monastery of Saint Theodosius near Bethlehem. After his formation there, he withdrew to a more remote monastery, Paran (Pharôn) in the Judaean desert, where he stayed for ten years, possibly 568/9–578/9. It is possible that it was at this place that he was joined by Sophronios, his inseparable friend, disciple, and companion for the rest of his life.

As a monk, John Moschus felt that the holiness of the Desert Fathers was being eroded by the slackness of the new generation of monks and ascetics. Thus, he and Sophronios, who later became the Patriarch of Jerusalem (633/634), journeyed to Egypt to collect the lore of the great monastic elders. After making the rounds of monastic communities there, John went to Mount Sinai, where he stayed for ten more years. He returned to Palestine and spent some time traveling around and staying at various Palestinian communities in search of examples of great holiness such as the Desert Fathers describe. However, civil discord and Persian raids caused him to wander again. This time he traveled up the coast through Phoenicia (modern-day Lebanon) and Syria Maritima to Antioch and Cilicia, in modern-day Turkey, from where he sailed, sometime before 607, to Alexandria in Egypt. Finally, he traveled to Rome around 615, where he put the finishing touches to his *Pratum Spirituale,* or "Spiritual Meadow." The work, written in Greek, is a collection of stories and anecdotes gathered during his travels. It is a valuable source for the history of monasticism in the Judean desert and beyond during the last half of the sixth and the early seventh century.

John Moschus died, at the earliest, in 619. Sophronios fulfilled his companion's wishes and brought his remains to Saint Theodosius to be buried (Moschus 1992: xvi–xx).

Arculf

In the seventh century, a bishop from Gaul by the name of Arculf went on pilgrimage to the Holy Land. Some time later, he was entertained by Adomnan, the Abbot of Iona in Scotland, from AD 679–704. The abbot asked Arculf questions about his journey, did further library research, and eventually wrote *The Holy Places* (*De Locis Sanctis*) about Arculf's pilgrimage.

Epiphanius the Monk

In the late seventh–early eighth century, Epiphanius the Monk wrote a guidebook called *The Holy City and the Holy Places.* Although the guidebook is geographically confused, Epiphanius' description of his journey beyond the Jordan is of interest to this study.

Willibald (AD 700–781)

Willibald was a native of Wessex, England. After studying in a monastery in Waltham, Hampshire, he went on pilgrimage to Rome in 721. From there he went by way of Naples to Sicily, Greece, Asia Minor, Cyprus, and Syria. In the latter country, he was captured and imprisoned by the Saracens who thought him a spy. Upon his release he continued on through Damascus to the Holy Land, where he wandered from site to site. He visited Jerusalem on four separate occasions. Altogether his journey lasted seven years, including two years in Constantinople. Saint Boniface ordained him in AD 741, and twelve months later consecrated him a bishop of a new diocese in Bavaria. An account of his journeys in the Holy Land was written by one of his relatives, a nun of Heidenheim, where he had founded a double monastery – one for men and another for women (Colgrave 2003: 761). Among the places he visited in the Holy Land was the Monastery of John the Baptist east of the Jordan.

Saint Stephen the Sabaite

The Life (*Vita*) of Saint Stephen the Sabaite appears to have been written some years prior to the sack of Jerusalem in AD 797. The work shows that monasticism was still thriving at that time, although well below the level prior to the Sasanian invasion 150 years earlier. Stephen and other monks used to wander in the Wilderness of Judaea and walk around the Dead Sea during Lent and at other times without fear of attack by Arab tribesmen. Among the places where they stopped during their walks, and which are of interest to this study, are Zoar (Ghawr as-Safi), Mar Lot (Saint Lot, probably Dayr 'Ayn 'Abata), and Mar Aaron (possibly on Jabal Haroun).

Abbot Daniel

The Russian Abbot Daniel, a member of the Russian Orthodox Church and the head of a monastery, made an extensive trip to the Holy Land in AD 1106–1107. He visited most of the holy places and monasteries, using good guides and writing down in great detail what he saw and nothing that he did not see with his own eyes. When he was unable to visit a place, he admits that he relied on others for the information he included. He was accompanied on his travels by a monk of the Greek Laura of St. Sabbas in the Judean desert (Wilson 1895: vii–viii). The interest here is in his visits east of the Jordan River.

Various Inscriptions

In addition to the Madaba Mosaic Map (above), there are hundreds of other inscriptions, many of them parts of mosaics, associated with the pilgrimage sites of interest in this work. All these are important as sources of historical information for the early Christian through Early Islamic periods of Jordan. These inscriptions will be considered in conjunction with their associated sites.

FIG. 3.1   Gadara / Umm Qays (© David L Kennedy, APAAME, APA98_19980516_DLK-0632).

3 CASTING OUT DEMONS
GADARA (UMM QAYS) AND GERASA (JERASH)

THE Gospels according to Matthew (8.23, 28–34; 9.1), Mark (5.1–21), and Luke (8.26–39) tell the story of Jesus' "Casting out Demons." This exorcism is considered here in its biblical context and the relevant biblical passages for the expulsion are cited and explained. Other ancient texts that mention the exorcism are also considered.

The relevant biblical passages indicate two places, namely, Gadara (Umm Qays)[1] and Gerasa (Jerash) in Jordan, where the "Casting out Demons" incident is said to have taken place. The former site has archaeological evidence for pilgrimage activity and some of its excavators posit a relationship between the incident and its early Christian ecclesiastical structures. The latter site has many churches and chapels. However, none of them are linked, either by extra-biblical literary or archaeological evidence, to the story of "Casting out Demons." Nevertheless, since Gerasa (Jerash) is present in ancient biblical manuscripts that narrate the incident, it must also be treated.

THE BIBLICAL TEXTS

According to Matthew's account, Jesus turns to healing following his teaching of "The Sermon on the Mount" (5.1–7.27). After some healings in Galilee and especially at Capernaum on the northwest side of the Sea of Galilee, Jesus gets into a boat and goes to the other side (Matthew 8.23,

---

1   There are various opinions on the meaning of "Umm Qays." One opinion is that during the Ottoman period the site was a center for the collection of taxes from the surrounding villages. Tax in Arabic is *makis* (s. *maks*, pl. *mukoos*). The site was thus called Umm Makis, Umm Maks, or Umm Mukoos. Through time, the inhabitants changed the name to Umm Qays.

28), or the eastern shore, of the sea. In Mark's and Luke's account of the incident, however, Jesus is teaching in parables beside the sea and then decides to cross to the other side (Mark 4.35; Luke 8.22). Then, in all accounts, the incident of the "Casting out Demons" takes place.

Matthew 8.23, 28–34; 9.1

> And when he got into the boat his disciples followed him.... When he came to the other side, to the country of the Gadarenes, two demoniacs coming out of the tombs met him. They were so fierce that no one could pass their way. Suddenly they shouted, "What have you to do with us, Son of God? Have you come here to torment us before the time?" Now a large herd of swine was feeding at some distance from them. The demons begged him, "If you cast us out, send us into the herd of swine." And he said to them, "Go!" So they came out and entered the swine; and suddenly, the whole herd rushed down the steep bank into the sea and perished in the water. The swine-herders ran off, and on going into the town, they told the whole story about what had happened to the demoniacs. Then the whole town came out to meet Jesus; and when they saw him, they begged him to leave their neighborhood. And after getting into a boat he crossed the sea and came to his own town.[2]

Mark 5.1–21

> They came to the other side of the sea, to the country of the Gerasenes. And when he had stepped out of the boat, immediately a man out of the tombs with an unclean spirit met him. He lived among the tombs; and no one could restrain him any more, even with a chain; for he had often been restrained with shackles and chains, but the chains he wrenched apart, and the shackles he broke in pieces; and no one had the strength to subdue him. Night and day among the tombs and on the mountains he was always howling and bruising himself with stones. When he saw Jesus from a distance, he ran and bowed down before him; and he shouted at the top of his voice, "What have you to do with me, Jesus, Son of the Most High God? I adjure you by God, do not torment me."

---

2 "Gadarenes" is probably the original reading in Matthew 8.28. In the parallel texts, Mark 5.1 and Luke 8.26, the best reading seems to be "Gerasenes." Other texts have "Gergesenes." Each of the readings points to a different territory connected with Gadara, Gerasa, and Gergasa, respectively.

For he had said to him, "Come out of the man, you unclean spirit!" Then Jesus asked him, "What is your name?" He replied, "My name is Legion; for we are many." He begged him sincerely not to send him out of the country. Now there on the hillside a great herd of swine was feeding; and the unclean spirits begged him, "Send us into the swine; let us enter them." So he gave them permission. And the unclean spirits came out and entered the swine; and the herd, numbering about two thousand, rushed down the steep bank into the sea, and were drowned in the sea. The swineherds ran off and told it in the city and in the country. Then people came to see what had happened. They came to Jesus and saw the demoniac sitting there, clothed and in his right mind, the very man who had had the legion; and they were afraid. Those who had seen what had happened to the demoniac and to the swine reported it. Then they began to beg Jesus to leave their neighborhood. As he was getting into the boat, the man who had been possessed by demons begged him that he might be with him. But Jesus refused, and he said to him, "Go home to your friends, and tell them how much the Lord has done for you, and what mercy he has shown you." And he went away and began to proclaim in the Decapolis how much Jesus had done for him; and everyone was amazed. When Jesus had crossed again in the boat to the other side, a great crowd gathered around him; and he was by the sea.

Luke 8.22–23, 26–39

One day he got into a boat with his disciples, and he said to them, "Let us go across to the other side of the lake." So they put out, and while they were sailing he fell asleep…. Then they arrived at the country of the Gerasenes, which is opposite Galilee. As he stepped out on land, a man of the city who had demons met him. For a long time he had worn no clothes, and he did not live in a house but in the tombs. When he saw Jesus, he fell down before him and shouted at the top of his voice, "What have you to do with me, Jesus, Son of the Most High God? I beg you, do not torment me" – for Jesus had commanded the unclean spirit to come out of the man. (For many times he had seized him; he was kept under guard and bound with chains and shackles, but he would break the bonds and be driven by the demon into the wilds.) Jesus then asked him, "What is your name?" He said, "Legion;" for many demons had entered him. They begged him not to order them to go back to the abyss. Now there on the hillside a large herd of swine was feeding; and the demons begged Jesus to let them enter these. So he gave them permission. Then the demons came out of the man and entered the swine, and the herd rushed down the steep bank into the lake and was drowned. When the swineherds saw what had happened, they ran off and told it in the city and in the country. Then people came out to see what had happened, and when they came to Jesus, they found the man from whom the demons had gone sitting at the feet of Jesus, clothed and in his right mind. And they were afraid. Those who had seen it told them how the one who had been possessed by demons had been healed. Then all the people of the surrounding country of the Gerasenes asked Jesus to leave them, for they were seized with great fear. So he got into the boat and returned. The man from whom the demons had gone begged that he might be with him; but Jesus sent him away, saying, "Return to your home, and declare how much God has done for you." So he went away, proclaiming throughout the city how much Jesus had done for him.

COMMENTARY ON THE TEXTS

The *New Revised Standard Version* (1989), the *Revised English Bible* (1989), the *New American Bible* (1986/1991), and the *New Jerusalem Bible* (1985) all agree in reading "the country of the Gadarenes" for Matthew 8.28 and "the country of the Gerasenes" for Mark 5.1 and Luke 8.26 as the place where the incident of the "Casting out Demons" took place. There also is support for the reading "Gergesenes" in the manuscript tradition lying behind the three accounts of this story. That tradition, however, is not followed in any of the four modern translations listed above. It is for this reason that we will concentrate on Gadara and Gerasa as the location for the exorcism.

Mark and Luke give greater precision than Matthew relative to where the incident took place. Both add that it happened on the other side of the sea, that is, the Sea of Galilee. Luke, moreover, adds the topographic note that the place is opposite Galilee, while Mark notes that the man from whom the demons had been expelled "went away and began to proclaim in the Decapolis how much Jesus had done for him" (5.20).

The Decapolis, literally "ten cities," was a group, not necessarily always ten in number, of Greek cities that were differentiated from the Semitic world among which they were located in northern Transjordan, southern Syria, and northern Palestine. This differentiation came from the fact that their city plans, individual buildings, tombs, divinities, and sculpture were Greek or Roman, although many traces of Near Eastern influences could be found. Most of them claimed to have been founded as Macedonian colonies by Alexander the Great (reigned 336–323 BC) or one of his successors during the late fourth century BC. Jesus, according to the biblical texts quoted above and others, visited the Decapolis region.

If the correct reading is "Gadarenes," then the district is to the east and south of the Sea of Galilee, since Josephus speaks of the villages of Gadara and Hippos as being on the borders of Tiberias and belonging to the region of Scythopolis: "At that time, when he had persuaded the citizens to take up weapons and compelled many who did not so desire, Iustus came out with all of these men and set fire to the villages of the Gadarenes and also of the Hippenes, which happened to lie on the frontier between Tiberias and the territory of the Scythopolitans" (*Life* 9.42; see Mason 2001: 46–47). Scythopolis (modern-day Beth-shan), which became the largest city of the Decapolis, was located south of the Sea of Galilee on the western side of the Jordan River. It was at the junction of two important roads: the north–south road through the Jordan Valley and the northwest–southeast road that joined the cities on the coast with the cities on the other side of the Jordan, especially Pella (=Tabaqat Fahl), Gadara, and Gerasa (Mason 2001: 192). In the district of the Gadarenes, the main city was Gadara, modern Umm Qays, located around 10 km southeast of the Sea of Galilee/Lake Tiberias (fig. 3.1).

Gadara was built on a fertile spur of land high above the Jordan and Yarmuk Valleys – 378 m above sea level[3] – in what today is northwest Jordan. The site occupies a sharp saddle of land on the south side of the Yarmuk River, looking across to the Golan Heights (Gaulanitis). The Greek poet Meleager (first century BC) described the city as "my first city, famous Gadara, Attica in the land of the Assyrians." It appears to have been one of the most cultured of the Decapolis cities, known for its schools of philosophy and rhetoric (Mason 2001: 187).

Matthew's account of the story may indicate the difficulty posed by the distance between Gadara and the Sea of Galilee by indicating in verse 30 that "a large herd of swine was feeding at some distance from them," that is, the two demoniacs.[4]

If the reading "the country of the Gerasenes" is correct, then the reference is to the city of Gerasa, modern-day Jerash, the main city in

---

3   The Sea of Galilee is 210 m below the sea level of the Mediterranean.

4   This brings out the point that in Matthew's account there are two demoniacs, while in Mark's and Luke's there is but one possessed man.

that territory, which is located around 55 km (33 miles), or at least a two-day journey, to the southeast of the Sea of Galilee. This would be a great distance for the herd of swine to run before drowning in the sea. Thus, from a geographical point of view, "the country of the Gadarenes" would appear to be the better reading. Moreover, Gadara would be closer to the site of Jesus' activity around the Sea of Galilee than Gerasa, and the readings seem to indicate that the incident took place near the sea.

EXTRA-BIBLICAL TEXTS

Relative to Gadara, Eusebius and Jerome (in the *Onomasticon* and *Book on the Sites and Names of Places of the Hebrews,* respectively) do not specifically associate the site with the story of the "Casting out Demons:"

> **Gadara** (Matt. 8:28). A city beyond the Jordan, opposite Scythopolis and Tiberias, in the east in the mountains, where hot spring baths lie in the foothills (74); and **Gadara**. A city across the Jordan opposite Scythopolis and Tiberias on the eastern side, situated in the mountain, in whose foothills hot springs well up, with baths built above (75) (Taylor et al. 2003: 45).

The same can be said, however, for their comments on Gergasi/Gerasa, where Mark and Luke place the story:

> **Gergasi** (Deut. 7:1). A city of Galaad lying beyond the Jordan which the tribe of Manasseh took. The same is said to be Gerasa, an important city of Arabia. Some say it is Gadara. The Gospel mentions the Gerasenes (64); and **Gergasi**. A city across the Jordan adjoining Mount Galaad, which the tribe of Manasseh held. Now it is called Gerasa, an important city of Arabia. Some people think it is Gadara, but the Gospel mentions the Gergasenes (65) (Taylor et al. 2003: 40).

It appears from Eusebius that Gergasi may be identified with Gerasa or Gadara. Jerome comments similarly but adds that the Gospel mentions Gergasenes. Thus, there is some confusion as to whether Gergasi is Gerasa or Gadara, or a district in the country of the Gergasenes, distinct from the two.

Gergesa may be a site other than Gadara (Umm Qays) or Gerasa (Jerash) located on the eastern shore of the Sea of Galilee (Lake Tiberias). This seems to be favored in both the *Onomasticon* and the *Book on the Sites and Names of Places of the Hebrews:*

> **Gergesa** (Matt 5:1). There the Lord healed the demoniacs. Now a
> village is pointed out beside Lake Tiberias, into which the swine
> rushed down headlong. See above. (74); and **Gergesa**. Where the
> Saviour restored those possessed by demons to health. Today, too,
> a small village is shown on the mountain beside the Lake of Tiberias,
> into which the swine fell headlong. We spoke of this above (75)
> (Taylor et al. 2003: 45).

Tzaferis, who excavated a church, monastery, and chapel at Kursi on the
eastern shores of the Sea of Galilee, sees it as the Gergesa of the ancient
manuscripts. He dates the original church and the monastery at Kursi to
the late fifth/early sixth to mid-sixth century AD. Alterations were made
to the settlement in the late sixth–early seventh century. Following the
Persian invasion in AD 614, the settlement went into decline. The church
was destroyed and abandoned at the end of the seventh century (Tzaferis
1983: 3–4). Tzaferis suggests that the site was the location of a monastery
that also acted as a hospice for pilgrims on their way through the Galilee
(1983: 43).

The name "Gergesa" and the "land of the Gergesenes" is found only
in the Christian sources. Nevertheless, Tzaferis concludes that

> the large church and the impressive settlement of religious char-
> acter founded in this region, serve as further evidence that here
> was the site which Christians chose to identify with the story of the
> healing of the demoniac and the drowning of the swine. The topo-
> graphical features of the valley of el-Kursi, in addition to the new
> archaeological finds, show how well the elements of the story fit the
> characteristics of the terrain… (1983: 48).

Despite Tzaferis' position, the area where the incident took place would
probably lie outside strictly Jewish territory. This conclusion is based on
the fact that there were swine in the area – an animal whose flesh Jews
do not eat and which should not be associated with a Jewish territory of
the time.

THE ARCHAEOLOGY OF GADARA / UMM QAYS
DURING THE BYZANTINE PERIOD

Gadara (fig. 3.2) first appears in the historical records shortly after the
conquest of the region by the forces of Alexander the Great in 333 BC.
Alexander's successors, the Ptolemies, made the site a frontier or border –
the meaning of the toponym – with their perennial rivals, the Seleucids,

FIG. 3.2   Aerial view of Gadara/Umm Qays. The Church Terrace
(© David L Kennedy, APAAME, APA98_19980516_DLK-0637).

who were based in Antioch, north Syria. The Roman general Pompey conquered the region of south Syria in 63 BC. Shortly afterward, Gadara minted its own coins and was one of the leading cities of the Decapolis. Most of the standing Roman architecture at Gadara was built in the second century AD. At this time, the baths of Hammath Gader, located below and to the northeast of the city, were also built.

Christianity spread slowly among the people of Gadara in the first three centuries AD. During the reign of Diocletian (AD 284–305), Zacharias, together with Alpheios, suffered martyrdom in AD 303. By the early fourth century, however, Christianity was firmly rooted in the city and Bishop Sabinus of Gadara participated in the Council of Nicaea in AD 325. The victories of Islamic armies over the Byzantine forces in the first half of the seventh century brought north Jordan under Muslim control. In their wake, there was a peaceful transition from Byzantine to Islamic rule at Gadara. The city continued to prosper until earthquakes destroyed many of its structures in the seventh and eighth centuries.

The site was rediscovered in the 19th century, and the Department of Antiquities of Jordan, established in 1928, began excavating there in the 1930s. Major excavations on the part of the German Protestant Institute for Archaeology in cooperation with other foreign groups began in 1974.

The ruins of ancient Gadara (fig. 3.3) cover an area of ca. 1600 m from east to west and ca. 450 m from north to south. The area of the Greco-Roman acropolis now lies beneath the late-19th-century Ottoman village. It is from this location that the best views of the site and the surrounding regions are possible.

There is much for the pilgrim and/or tourist to see in the ancient city. For example, there is the Eastern Necropolis, the two theaters, the vaulted shops and the colonnaded main street (the *decumanus maximus*),[5] the public baths and the nymphaeum, the remnants of the western gates with their towers, and the north mausoleum, at which a Greek inscription, dated to AD 355/356, reads: "To you I say, passerby: As you are, I was; as I am, you will be. Use life as a mortal."

The *decumanus* divided Gadara into a small northern and a large southern sector. Smaller roads would have intersected with this main street to form rectangular city blocks. The main north–south street of the city (*cardo*) has not been identified to date but it is thought that it

---

5   In ancient Roman cities, the *cardo maximus* was a north–south oriented street. See, for example, the *cardo maximus* in Gerasa/Jerash (see also note 7, below). Most Roman cities had a *decumanus maximus*, an east–west street that served as a secondary main street. However, due to varying geography, in some cities the *decumanus* is the main street and the *cardo* is secondary. Such is the case at Gadara/Umm Qays.

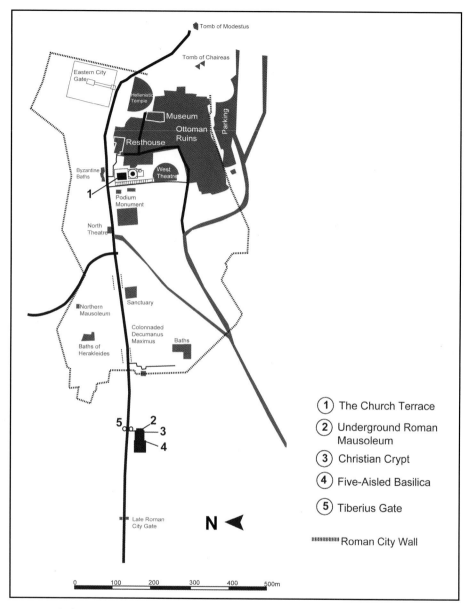

FIG. 3.3   Gadara/Umm Qays – General plan of the site (adapted from site plan provided by Ministry of Tourism and Antiquities of Jordan).

intersected with the *decumanus* near the nymphaeum. Beneath the street was an extensive subterranean drainage system that supplied the city with fresh water. The street itself was flanked by sidewalks and paved with

FIG. 3.4   The Church Terrace with its two churches (photo by Sherry Hardin).

basalt slabs. At least in the western part of the city, the street was lined with columns.

Our main interest here is in the ecclesiastical structures on the Church Terrace and the Roman Mausoleum, Christian Crypt, and Five-Aisled Basilica. Both areas seem to be associated with pilgrimage activity.

The Church Terrace

A large colonnaded terrace (UTM coordinates: 0751197 E/3616545 N; elev. 360 m)[6] is located north of the western theater (figs. 3.2, 3.4–5). There are two churches on it. They replaced an earlier Roman public building, probably a colonnaded hall or market basilica.

One of the churches is square with an octagonal interior and a large courtyard. A square, stone-lined depression in the eastern section of the interior of the octagon was the church's altar area, or bema. It was originally set off from the central domed octagonal room (the nave) by marble screen slabs or a chancel screen. A stone-lined tomb was found within the altar area. The corners of the square church are in the form of semi-circular apses. Its roof was probably in the form of a semi-circular dome.

6   The Universal Transverse Mercator (UTM) coordinates used throughout this publication are those of European Datum 1950 (ED 1950). This is the coordinate system upon which the Jordan Map Series K737, Scale 1:50,000, is based.

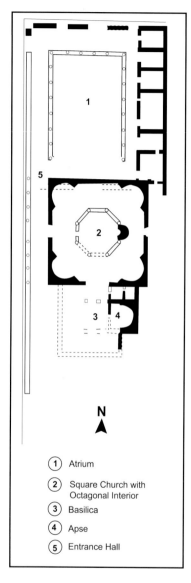

N
▲

1. Atrium
2. Square Church with Octagonal Interior
3. Basilica
4. Apse
5. Entrance Hall

FIG. 3.5 Ground Plan of the Church Terrace with its two churches (adapted from plan provided by Ministry of Tourism and Antiquities of Jordan).

The church had three entrances. It was built in the first half of the sixth century and destroyed by an earthquake, perhaps in the eighth century (Schick 1995: 478).

The second church, located immediately to the south of the square one, is smaller. It is a three-aisled basilica with a single apse. It is later than the square church and was built in the middle or the second half of the sixth century AD.

The excavators found four tombs and five reliquaries, containers in which relics were placed, in the churches. These finds indicate the importance of the complex from a Christian viewpoint. They may indicate that the site was one to which pilgrims came; in fact, the tomb in the square church may have been the grave of a venerated martyr.

Roman Mausoleum, Christian Crypt, and Five-Aisled Basilica

A five-aisled basilica (UTM coordinates: 0750575 E/3616513 N; elev. 336 m) is located in the lower city of Gadara, west of the acropolis (figs. 3.6–7). It covers the area on top of a Roman underground mausoleum and a Christian crypt extending towards the east. On the basis of the structural layout of the plan, one must consider that the Roman underground burial chamber and the crypt were deliberately adopted by the early Christian community of Gadara in their worship. The whole complex lies close to the main street to the southwest of the southern circular tower of the Tiberias Gate.

The early Christians of Gadara built an underground crypt adjacent to and east of the Roman mausoleum. This burial place was dedicated to a prominent local saint, maybe the Gadarene Deacon Zacharias, who suffered martyrdom in the years of the Diocletian persecutions (Al-Daire 2001: 553). His apse-

FIG. 3.6   The Roman Mausoleum, Christian Crypt and Five-Aisled Basilica (photo by Sherry Hardin).

framed tomb was considered a holy place and became a focus of early Christian pilgrimage. For this reason, one would assume that the whole complex, including the Roman mausoleum and the superstructures of the underground sepulchral buildings, had a memorial character. The rest of the crypt was used for the burials of other notables of the early Christian Gadarene society, who were buried close to the venerated corpse.

Weber, the excavator of the complex, concludes that the basilica, together with the underlying crypt, was constructed in the first half of the fourth century AD (1998: 449; see also Al-Daire 2001: 560). The last burials in this privileged area were put there in the late fourth or the first half of the fifth century AD.

The five-aisled basilica, which is almost square, measures 21.50 (E–W) × 20.10 (N–S) m. It is oriented east–west with an entrance hall and a large open air colonnaded courtyard (atrium) in the west, which is almost square as well, measuring 26.47 × 26.00 m. The complex was framed by paved passageways along its southern and western façades. The northern wall of the complex was located ca. 30 m from the east–west running main street. A minor, perpendicular roadway would have connected the complex to the main street on the west.

The apse of the basilica (fig. 3.8) was constructed on top of the semi-circular base of the crypt, where a local saint had been buried. Its purpose

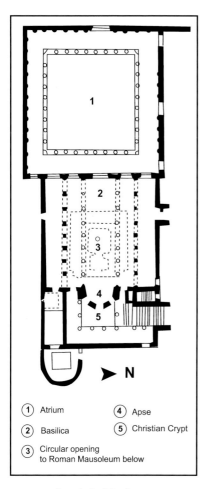

① Atrium   ④ Apse

② Basilica   ⑤ Christian Crypt

③ Circular opening
   to Roman Mausoleum below

FIG. 3.7 Five-Aisled Basilica, Roman Mausoleum, and Christian Crypt (adapted from plan provided by Ministry of Tourism and Antiquities of Jordan).

was to frame the central tomb of the early Christian cemetery. The apse was framed by a chancel screen, of which the remaining walls were found in situ.

The central nave of the basilica is situated exactly atop the Roman mausoleum. A circular opening in the center of the nave looks down into it. The church's nave was separated from the lateral aisles on both long sides by an arcade consisting of seven columns each. The adjacent areas to the south and north were subdivided by one row of pilasters corresponding to the colonnades of the central nave. Thus, the northern and the southern sections of the church hall were divided on both sides into two lateral aisles. The main entrance to the church was from the west and gave access to the church's central aisle. On both sides of the apse, two doors gave access to the aisles immediately to the north and south. The baptistery was located in the south-eastern corner of the complex.

The original fourth-century-AD church was converted into a smaller chapel after its sixth-century renovation. The existing mosaic floor, now in the Umm Qays museum, dates to the sixth century AD.

The church was used over a long period for Christian liturgy. The first substantial alteration of the architecture was most likely executed when the basilica was partially destroyed by an earthquake in the Late Byzantine or Early Islamic periods. Despite its condition, Christian liturgy continued inside the building during the Early Islamic rule. It was probably transformed into a mosque during or shortly after the time of the Crusades.

Weber thinks that the entire complex, including the integration of the Roman mausoleum into the early Christian cult, "may perhaps be connected with details in the New Testament about the miracle of Gadara (Matthew 8.28)" (1998: 452; see also Al-Daire 2001: 559). Furthermore, he writes,

FIG. 3.8
Apse of the
Five-Aisled
Basilica and
Stairway to
Christian Crypt
and Roman
Mausoleum
(photo by
Sherry Hardin).

... that the Gadarene structure must have been dedicated for an outstanding event or person of the Bible or early church history. Despite the lack of inscriptions or other striking evidence, it should not be excluded, that a pilgrim church of this size was built on the spot, where Byzantine tradition recalled that Jesus had performed the miracle of the Gadarene swine (1998: 452).

GENERAL OVERVIEW OF GERASA / JERASH'S ARCHAEOLOGICAL HISTORY

As indicated in the opening paragraph of this chapter, the texts from both Mark (5.1) and Luke (8.26) place the "Casting out Demons" incident in "the country of the Gerasenes," that is, in the area of Gerasa (Jerash). Thus, this site must be treated here, even if there are no indications, either in extra-biblical literary or archaeological evidence, that in the early Christian period the city of Gerasa was a pilgrimage site related to this incident. It does, nevertheless, have many churches and chapels.

Before turning, however, to a description of Gerasa's many churches, some general background relative to the city's history and archaeology is necessary. This ought to help put its ecclesiastical structures in context.

Gerasa/Jerash (figs. 3.9–10), one of the best-preserved Roman cities in the Near East, is located on both the west and east banks of the River Chrysorhoas, which lies to the north of the Wadi az-Zarqa/River Jabbok

FIG. 3.9   Aerial View of Gerasa/Jerash, looking north, with Hippodrome in lower-right corner, Temple of Zeus and South Theatre in left center, and Oval Plaza and cardo maximus in left-top quarter (© David L Kennedy, APAAME, APA _2005-10-03_DLK-33).

and flows into it.[7] Due to the fact that the modern town of Jerash is located on the river's east bank, most of the explorations and excavations of the ancient city have been carried out, by necessity, on the west bank.

The city, which lies along major north–south routes joining Syria in the north to the Red Sea in the south, depended upon trade for its prosperity. In addition to the north–south routes, major east–west ones connected the city with Mediterranean ports. The ruins of the city attest to its prominence during the Hellenistic and Roman periods. However, excavated materials indicate that people lived in the area as early as the Lower Paleolithic era (maybe as long ago as one million years). The Temple of Zeus probably dates to the Hellenistic period. However, excavators have not uncovered a great deal of the city's Hellenistic remains. The city came under the control of Rome with the arrival of Pompey in the area in 63 BC, which led to renewed prosperity for the city and the renovation of the Temple of Zeus in both the first and second centuries AD. Major urban

---

7   The River Chrysorhoas would have been "active" during the time of the Greco-Roman-Byzantine city. It was to the east and parallel to the main colonnaded north–south street (*cardo*) of the city. It is now no more than a depression that is dry except for periods of heavy rains.

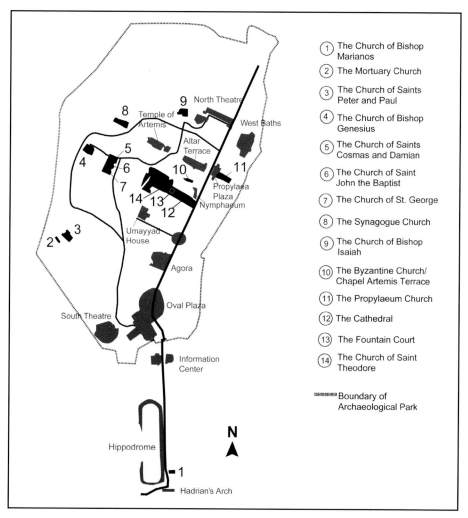

FIG. 3.10 Gerasa/Jerash - General plan of the site, with the location of the churches indicated (adapted from plan provided by Ministry of Tourism and Antiquities of Jordan).

development of the city began in the early Roman period. Plans were laid for the city's orthogonal plan, its streets, and a uniform wall around the city, the first built in AD 70. Six gates intersected the walls of Gerasa. Within the city, the 12-m-wide Ionic-colonnaded *cardo maximus* extends for more than 800 m to the settlement's northern and southern extremities and intersects two 8–9-m-wide main streets, one in the southern and the other in the northern segment of the city. The *cardo* conceals the city's sewer system and parallels the course of the River Chrysorhoas, which was traversed by three bridges.

CHRISTIAN PRESENCE AND CHURCHES IN GERASA / JERASH

It is not known how and when Christianity first came to Gerasa. However, the city sent a bishop to the Council at Seleucia in AD 359. Thus, there would have been Christian presence in the city as early as the latter half of the fourth century.

According to present dating, the earliest of the churches, the so-called "Cathedral" (see below), dates to the early fifth century on the basis of recently excavated coins,[8] rather than any inscription. It is thought that the Cathedral was built in front of a miraculous fountain, believed to be the one mentioned in a text written about AD 375 by Bishop Epiphanius of Salamis (Jäggi et al. 1997: 314) and often identified with the fountain in the structure's atrium. The fountain is thought to have become the center of the greatest complex of Christian buildings at Gerasa. The latest church at Jerash, dated to AD 611, is the one built by Bishop Genesius (Kraeling 1938: 172).

The Joint British-American Expedition, working in 1928–1930 and 1931–1934, investigated the sites of eight churches, six on the west side of the river that flows through the city and two on the east. One site on the west contained three churches, another two; thus, the total number of churches explored was eleven, besides two large chapels and several smaller buildings, though the precincts in general and three of the churches were only partially cleared. On two of the sites further clearances were made in 1931 and 1934. Two other churches, which have not been examined, are known to exist, one in the Circassian cemetery outside the walls on the east bank and one under a house in the village. The expedition realized that there may well be others that they did not record (Kraeling 1938: 171). In the late 1920s and early 1930s, when these churches were excavated, little attention was paid to the contribution of stratigraphy and pottery to dating such structures. The dates assigned to the churches thus come, for the most part, from inscriptions within them.

The Joint British-American Expedition dated the churches it investigated from the late fourth to the early seventh century, with the majority built in the sixth century. Some of them continued in use for another century or two, or at least into the eighth century and thus well into the Umayyad period.

Khouri (1986) lists thirteen churches and one chapel: Church of Bishop Marianos (AD 570); Church of Bishop Isaiah (AD 559); Byzantine

---

8 The coins were found under the original floor of the cathedral and the foundation trench of the stepped platform on which the columns of the temple were placed.

Church; Propylaeum Church (sixth century; mosaic floor dates to AD 565); "Cathedral" (ca. AD 365, according to Kraeling; but early fifth century according to Jäggi et al. [1997: 314]) and southwest chapel (added in the second quarter of the sixth century); Church of Saint Theodore (AD 494–496); the Procopius Church (AD 526–527); Church of Saints Cosmas and Damian (AD 533); Church of Saint John the Baptist (AD 531); Church of Saint George (AD 529–530); Synagogue Church (AD 530–531); Church of Saints Peter and Paul (ca. AD 540); Mortuary Church (end of the sixth century); Church of Bishop Genesius (AD 611). To this list may be added the Church of the Prophets, Apostles and Martyrs, the Chapel of Elia, Mary and Soreg, and the Roman villa/church.

All these churches, with the exception of the Church of the Prophets, Apostles and Martyrs, the Chapel of Elia, Mary and Soreg, the Procopius Church, and the Roman villa/church are located in the western segment of the city and their vast majority dates to the sixth century. It is evident that excavators have discovered a number of churches at the site during the past number of years, and there could be yet more to discover! For now, there are a total of thirteen churches and/or chapels on the west bank of the River Chrysorhoas, plus an octagonal one to the north of the city, east of the road leading to Birketein (see Clark 1986: 321). In addition, there is the Shrine of Saint Mary, built against the eastern external wall of the Cathedral no earlier than the second quarter of the fifth century AD. On the east bank of the river there are four churches and/or chapels. A glance at the map of Gerasa (fig. 3.10) shows that several of the churches are situated centrally. Many of them, however, are on the site's periphery. Our description of the churches on the west bank will begin with the one closest to Hadrian's Arch at the southern extremity of the archaeological site.

The Church of Bishop Marianos (AD 570)

The Church of Bishop Marianos (UTM coordinates: 0772370 E/3574513 N; elev. 570 m) is located 50 m to the north of Hadrian's Arch and 10 m east of the wall of the Hippodrome. It was built when the Hippodrome was already in ruins. It is a small church with one apse, measuring 13.50 (E–W) × 8.10 (N–S) m on the exterior. The church's nave is entirely covered by a mosaic carpet. The raised chancel and apse also contain mosaics. The foundation inscription, located in front of the chancel screen, reads:

> Under your most holy and God-guarded bishop Marianos, this holy
> temple was built and completed from the foundations, in the year

FIG. 3.11   The Mortuary Church (photo by Sherry Hardin).

> 632, in the month of Xanthicos, in the third indiction (Gawlikowski
> and Musa 1986: 143).

The date corresponds to April AD 570.[9] A second inscription is located
at the western extremity of the church, where the church's small porch
is completely paved with mosaics, with an inscription at its center. A
small room, a sacristy, along the church's northwest side also has a mosaic
floor. Schick posits that the church was destroyed around the end of the
Umayyad period, if not later (1995: 321).

---

9   The date given on the inscription in the Church of Bishop Marianos is 632 of the Roman
calendar. This date corresponds to our year AD 570. This is due to the fact that Gerasa "dated its
numerous official documents and coins according to an era also inaugurated after its liberation
by Pompey or one of his officers.... Inscriptions dated by the era of Gerasa and simultaneously
by indiction and month…, or by the year of tribunician power and consulship of a Roman
emperor … have established year 1 of the Gerasene era definitely in the fall of 63 BC" (Meimaris
1992: 89). "Indiction" is a term applied to a period of 15 years. It is also used for each single year
within this period. Only the years within the cycle are numbered, while the cycles themselves are
not. "Initially indiction (= declaration) was associated with the announcement of the obligatory
delivery of cereals to the state for use by the population of Rome and the Roman army"
(Meimaris 1992: 32). For a different dating system, that is, according to the Byzantine Creation Era
see Chapter 7, note 2. In addition, this note may be helpful in understanding the dating of sites
in the southern part of Jordan, based on some inscriptional material.

The Mortuary Church (end of sixth century)

This church (UTM coordinates: 0771989 E/3575238 N; elev. 607 m) is located in the southwest quarter of the city (fig. 3.11). It lies ca. 15 m south–southwest of the Church of Saints Peter and Paul, close to the city wall. It is a "single hall" building, that is, one without aisles, terminating in an apse. The floor of the church was at one time covered by mosaics, which suffered from iconoclasts and time. An arch on the south side opens into a cave that was used as a burial place, giving the church its name (Kraeling 1938: 254–55). There is a plaque on the church's south wall, just east of the cave's entrance. It reads, "Gerald W. L. Harding 1901–1979. A Great Man & Archaeologist who loved Jordan." Harding was a former Director of the Department of Antiquities of Jordan; his cremated remains are buried in the church.

The Church of Saints Peter and Paul (ca. AD 540)

This church (UTM coordinates: 0772025 E/3575244 N; elev. 608 m), like the Mortuary Church, is located on high ground. It is over 31 m long and was a triapsidal basilica. A mosaic inscription in the middle of the nave gave the dedication and the name of Bishop Anastasius, the church's founder. A series of floor mosaics covered the body of the nave and both aisles. The church's main entrance is in its west wall. Its ground plan, the three apses, and the size of the chancel are like those in the Church of Procopius (see below) (Kraeling 1938: 251–54). The church continued in use beyond the iconoclastic period (Schick 1995: 318).

A single-apsed chapel is located along the northwest side of the Church of Saints Peter and Paul. Doors lead to it from both the church proper and its western porch.

The Church of Bishop Genesius (AD 611)

This church (UTM coordinates: 0772092 E/3575515 N; elev. 601 m) is located ca. 50 m west of the Church of Saints Cosmas and Damian (see below). An inscription within it dates its mosaic floor to AD 611, during the episcopate of Bishop Genesius. It is thus the latest church built at Jerash. There is no indication as to whom the church was dedicated. The church was a basilica with a single external apse. Both its nave and its aisles were paved with mosaics (Kraeling 1938: 249). A rectangular room, also with a mosaic floor, is located along its southwest side. It is unknown for how long the church continued in use after 611 (Schick 1995: 318).

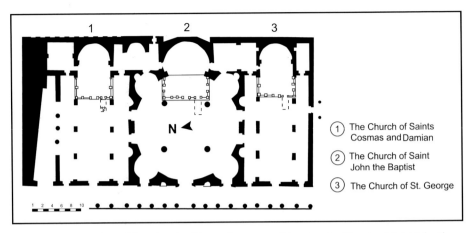

FIG. 3.12 Ground Plan of the Church of Saints Cosmas and Damian, the Church of Saint John the Baptist, and the Church of Saint George (adapted from Kraeling 1938).

Three churches at Jerash shared a common courtyard on the west and were conceived as one unit (fig. 3.12). The central one is the Church of Saint John the Baptist. It is flanked on the north by the Church of Saints Cosmas and Damian and on the south by the Church of Saint George.

The Church of Saints Cosmas and Damian (AD 533)

The church (UTM coordinates: 0772162 E/3575476 N; elev. 597 m) was built against the north wall of the Church of Saint John the Baptist. It is dedicated to twin-brother doctors, Cosmas and Damian, who were martyred in the fourth century. An inscription dates the mosaic within the church to AD 533. It reads:

> Pray now, while venerating the beautiful pair of victors. In truth, they are saints who own the art allaying suffering. From now on those who make offerings will benefit through the elimination of misadventure in their lives.

The church has the most splendid floor mosaics to be seen in Gerasa (fig. 3.13). Moreover, it contains the only representational floor in the city that was not visited by iconoclasts (Crowfoot 1941: 132). The mosaics have been recently restored.

A baptistery, located between the apses of the Church of Saints Cosmas and Damian and the Church of Saint John the Baptist, appears to be shared by both buildings.

FIG. 3.13   Interior of the Church of Saints Cosmas and Damian (photo by Sherry Hardin).

The Church of Saint John the Baptist (AD 531)

This church (UTM coordinates: 0772164 E/3575459 N; elev. 597 m), as indicated above, had a basilica on each side of it. It measures ca. 29.50 (E–W) × 23.80 (N–S) meters. Its floor was paved with interesting mosaics, and glass tesserae from its walls were found in the apse and exedrae – semicircular recesses, often crowned by a half-dome, which are usually set into a building's façade (Crowfoot 1941: 97–99). The floor mosaic, now damaged, included images of the four seasons, plants and animals, and the holy cities of Alexandria and Memphis in Egypt. The church went out of use by the early eighth century (Schick 1995: 317).

The Church of Saint George (AD 529)

According to an inscription in front of its chancel, this church (UTM coordinates: 0772158 E/3575444 N; elev. 597 m) was roofed, paved, and decorated with mosaics in AD 529. It was the first of the three churches to be built, and it opened onto a common courtyard. The other two were completed shortly afterward. The Church of Saint George continued in use after the earthquakes of AD 749.

FIG. 3.14 The Church of Bishop Isaiah (photo by Sherry Hardin).

The Synagogue Church (AD 530–531)

This church (UTM coordinates: 0772191 E/3575608 N; elev. 620 m) is a single-apsed, three-aisled building. It stands on very high ground overlooking the Temple of Artemis. It was built only a few centimeters above the floor of a former synagogue. The distinctively Jewish elements at the west end of the synagogue were removed, the floor level was raised over the rest of the building, and the eastern end of the building was adapted to Christian liturgical ritual. The nave was repaved with mosaics in the same style as other churches of the period (Kraeling 1938: 234–41).

The Church of Bishop Isaiah

The Church of Bishop Isaiah (UTM coordinates: 0772398 E/3575628 N; elev. 600 m) is located on a terrace immediately to the west of the North Theater (fig. 3.14). It is a triapsidal building, measuring 27.25 (E–W) ×18 (N–S) m externally. The floor of the nave, side aisles and chancel area, but excluding the apses, was completely covered with mosaics made, for the most part, of locally available stone (Clark 1986). The excavators uncovered fifteen inscriptions while working on the church. One of them reads:

> At the time of the most holy and blessed Thomas the Metropolitan, and Isaiah the Bishop. This place of prayer was consecrated, and

built from the foundations, covered with mosaics, and beautified through the offerings of the most illustrious Beroios and Eulampia, salvation to them, and their children. In the year 621, in the month of Daisios, in the seventh indiction (Bowsher 1986: 319).

The church thus dates to AD 559.[10] It continued in use beyond the icono-clastic period and was destroyed in the earthquake of AD 747.

The Byzantine Church/Chapel Artemis Terrace

This church/chapel (UTM coordinates: 0772434 E/3575424 N; elev. 599 m) is located on the terrace of the Temple of Artemis, as the name indicates. It appears to be a single-apsed building. It has not yet been excavated.

The Propylaeum Church (ca. AD 565)

The Propylaeum Church (UTM coordinates: 0772538 E/3575419 N; elev. 584 m), built in the sixth century, is on the site of a colonnaded square that formed part of the processional way. The columns of the way were used as part of the church. Its mosaic floor dates to AD 565. Otherwise, the history of the church is unknown (Schick 1995: 316).

The So-Called Cathedral of Gerasa

The Joint British-American Expedition to Jerash dated the so-called "Cathedral" of Gerasa (UTM coordinates: 0772389 E/3575369 N; elev. 594 m), built on the ruins of a temple, to ca. AD 365. The temple seems to have been built on a podium with an eastern staircase flanked by antae – the posts or pillars on either side of a doorway or entrance of a temple. From a typological point of view it must have been similar to the neighboring Temple of Artemis, but considerably smaller and most probably some decades earlier. Recent excavations at the Cathedral, however, have led to a terminus post quem for the church of the year AD 404 (Jäggi et al. 1998: 429). This discrepancy in dating indicates the importance of follow-up work on earlier excavations.

According to the Cathedral's most recent excavators, in the late fourth or early fifth century (in any case after AD 404), the Christians of Gerasa dismantled a Roman temple (to Dionysus?) down to the base

---

10 See note 9 as to why the date on the inscription of 621 of the Roman calendar corresponds to our calendar date of AD 559.

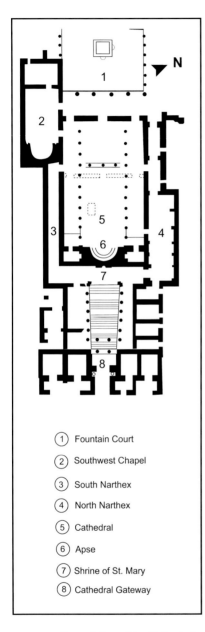

1. Fountain Court
2. Southwest Chapel
3. South Narthex
4. North Narthex
5. Cathedral
6. Apse
7. Shrine of St. Mary
8. Cathedral Gateway

FIG. 3.15 Ground Plan of the Cathedral (adapted from Kraeling 1938).

of its podium. They erected on this site a huge church, the Cathedral of Gerasa (figs. 3.15–16).[11] The earlier building determined the size of the Cathedral, since the width of the nave and the aisles was determined by the width of the podium of the temple and its ambulatory (Jäggi et al. 1997: 427). Thus, the temple served not only as a base (in the strictest sense of the word) for the width of the church but also for its floor level as a whole, as the floor slabs in the nave lay more or less directly on the remains of the podium. Only in the aisles and in the east and west of the podium high fillings were necessary. From the beginning there was a choir screen on the line of the later bema, the altar area, but still without a difference in the floor level between the choir and the nave.

The walls and the apse of the cathedral were, at least in their upper sections, decorated with mosaics. This decoration seems to have been heavily damaged by a fire in the late sixth or seventh century. During the succeeding repairs, the workers removed the stone pavement of the nave, shortened the church by building a new west wall on the line of the fifth pair of columns and (from there) recovered the remaining mosaics. They replaced the existing choir screen by two steps to the altar area and reached the new floor level in the choir by filling in masses of debris. A mortar floor was put in the new nave (Jäggi et al. 1997: 316).

The Cathedral has a south and a north porch, or narthex. In addition, there is a chapel along its southwest side.

The building was approached by a large staircase ascending directly from the

---

11 Although called a cathedral, there is no evidence that this church was any more important than others in the city.

FIG. 3.16 The Cathedral Church with Fountain Court (photo by Sherry Hardin).

west side of the main north–south street (*cardo maximus*) of the city. The staircase passed the Shrine of Saint Mary, located against the Cathedral's outer east wall (fig. 3.17). The shrine bears a painted inscription to Mary and the archangels Michael and Gabriel.

The main door of the Cathedral opened to the west onto a colonnaded courtyard or paved plaza with a square fountain. The courtyard and the fountain in its center are often referred to as the Fountain Court. It is this fountain that has been associated with the story of Bishop Epiphanius in which he related, in AD 375, the annual miracle of the fountain spouting wine instead of water. This association gave rise to an initial earlier date for the Cathedral.

FIG. 3.17 Shrine of Saint Mary (photo by Sherry Hardin).

The Church of Saint Theodore (AD 494–496)

The Church of Saint Theodore lies to the west of both the Cathedral Church and the Fountain Court (figs. 3.18–19). It is situated ca. 5 m above the latter feature. The church (UTM coordinates: 0772317 E/3575401 N; elev. 599 m) was almost the same size as the Cathedral and measured ca. 42 × 22 meters. It appears to have been built out of the remains of a single, heavy-classical building. Its apse was semicircular inside and polygonal on the outside. The aisles were slightly less than half the width of the nave. The apse, as usual, spanned the full width of the nave (Kraeling 1938: 219–25; Crowfoot 1941: 64–66). It has both a north and a south porch, a baptistery along its southwest side, a northwest and a southwest chapel, and a courtyard to its west. Schick thinks that it was destroyed in an earthquake before the beginning of the Ummayad period (1995: 316).

An inscription in the church reads:

> I am in the resplendent abode of the victor, Theodore, immortal martyr, holy man, whose glory has flown upon the earth and in the deep abyss of the oceans. His body has been returned to the earth but his soul, in the immense heavens, shares forever the life of an-

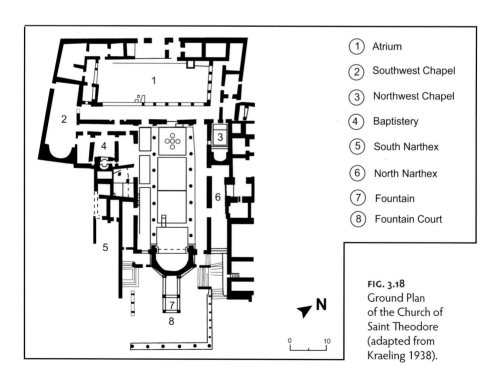

1. Atrium
2. Southwest Chapel
3. Northwest Chapel
4. Baptistery
5. South Narthex
6. North Narthex
7. Fountain
8. Fountain Court

0   10

N

FIG. 3.18
Ground Plan of the Church of Saint Theodore (adapted from Kraeling 1938).

FIG. 3.19   The Church of Saint Theodore (photo by Sherry Hardin).

gelic choirs. He is an everlasting bastion, an invincible defense of
the city and its present and future inhabitants.

Another inscription, carved on the lintel of the outer door of the church,
reads:

> I am the wonder and admiration of passers-by, because all traces
> of disorder have disappeared from here. In place of the dirt of
> the olden days, the grace of God has surrounded me on all sides.
> Once, animals tortured by sufferings were thrown here and gave
> out an unpleasant odor. Often the passer-by covered his nose, held
> his breath and escaped the nasty smell. Now, those who pass near
> this sweet-smelling place raise the right hand to their forehead and
> trace the sign of the cross.

The church is built right next to the Temple of Artemis, the city's main
deity. As the Christians of Gerasa naturally were opposed to the pagan
gods worshiped at the temple, the inscription proudly advertises the
changes to the city, now that God was worshiped instead of Artemis.

Four churches are located to the east outside the Jerash Archaeological
Park. They are the Church of the Prophets, Apostles and Martyrs, the

Chapel of Elias, Mary and Soreg, the Procopius Church, and a Roman villa/church.

The Church of the Holy Prophets, Apostles and Martyrs (AD 464–465)

This church, built in the shape of a Latin cross and the only one of this architectural form in Gerasa, was dedicated to the Holy Prophets, Apostles, and Martyrs. Like other churches in the city, it was oriented towards the east and ended in an external semicircular apse. It measures ca. 37 (E–W) × 31 (N–S) meters. There was a nave and two aisles in each arm of the cross. Doors led into the building from every side. It was richly appointed (Kraeling 1938: 190–91, 256–60; Crowfoot 1941: 85–87). The church, built in AD 464–465, was located at the north end of Gerasa on the east bank of the River Chrysorhoas. One corner of the site is now occupied by a house and the rest has been planted with trees. However, it was mentioned by many of the early travelers to the area. Apart from the date of building, the church's history is unknown (Schick 1995: 319).

The Church of Elias, Mary and Soreg

No evidence is available for dating this church. It probably went out of use before the iconoclastic period (Schick 1995: 319).

The Procopius Church (AD 526–527)

This church was built by a certain Procopius and its date has fortunately been preserved. It lies on the east bank of the River Chrysorhoas on very high ground close to the southeast corner of the city walls. It was a basilica with a nave and two aisles ending at the east in three parallel internal apses, a chapel at the northwest corner, and an atrium probably at the west end. The date comes from an inscription within the church. It gets its name from an officer named Procopius under whose name it was built. Good mosaic floors were laid in both of its side apses (Kraeling 1938: 260–62; Crowfoot 1941: 70). According to Schick, "the church continued in use beyond the iconoclastic period (1995: 319).

CONCLUSIONS

On the basis of the biblical texts, both Gadara and Gerasa are candidates for the location of Jesus' actions towards the man/men possessed by demons to the east of the Sea of Galilee. The text from Matthew favors Gadara, while those from Mark and Luke favor Gerasa.

As is clear from the archaeological findings in the form of ecclesiastical structures and their associated inscriptions, both Gadara and Gerasa became Christian Decapolis cities beginning in the fourth century. However, of the two, Gadara is the better candidate for the setting of the story of the "Casting out Demons." Geographically it makes more sense; Gerasa is too far removed from the Sea of Galilee to be a serious contender for the location of the exorcism. Moreover, Gadara has two areas that appear to have been places of pilgrimage in the early Christian period. The two churches on the Church Terrace, close to the ancient center of the city, have archaeological remains in the form of tombs and reliquaries that appear to be associated with pilgrimage activity. In addition, the Christian Crypt and the Five-Aisled Basilica, in association with the Roman underground mausoleum in the western part of the city, are probably related to pilgrimage activity. That activity could indeed be related, at least in part, to the "Casting out Demons" story.

SUGGESTIONS ON REACHING AND VISITING THE SITES

Umm Qays

Take the Jerash–Irbid Highway north of Amman. Upon reaching the city of Irbid (a one hour drive), follow the signs through the city that will take you to the site. The latter part of the drive from Irbid to Umm Qays also takes about one hour.

A visit to Gadara/Umm Qays may begin with the West Theater. From there, proceed along the street with the vaulted shops; this will lead to the Church Terrace. After a visit to the two churches there, continue on to the main colonnaded street and make your way along it to the west. Once you come to the remnants of the Tiberias Gate, turn south (or left) to visit the Roman Mausoleum, Christian Crypt, and Five-Aisled Basilica. You may then wish to visit the archaeological ruins farther to the west. Some of the mosaics that were once in the Five-Aisled Basilica can now be seen in the Umm Qays archaeological museum.

Jerash

Take the northbound Amman–Jerash Highway. Jerash is about 45 minutes away from Amman. Take the South Jerash turnoff for the site.

A visit to Gerasa/Jerash can begin at the site's entrance at Hadrian's Arch. Immediately, you will come to the Church of Bishop Marianos, which is just east of the Hippodrome. Proceeding north, you can visit the Temple of Zeus and the Southern Theatre. From here you may wish to continue through the oval plaza and then proceed up the main colonnaded street. In the center of the city you may visit the Cathedral Church, the Church of Saint Theodore, the Byzantine Church/Chapel Artemis Terrace, and the Propylaeum Church. From there you may proceed north to the Church of Bishop Isaiah, which is close to the Northern Theater. You then can continue to the west and south to visit all the churches on the periphery of the present archaeological park.

Another way to visit the churches at the site is to begin with the Church of Bishop Marianos; pass the Temple of Zeus and the Southern Theater and then turn northwest to visit the many churches on the site's periphery. After visiting these churches, you can proceed to the Church of Bishop Isaiah. From here, you can begin your way southward along the cardo maximus and visit the several churches in what is the ecclesiastical center of the site.

4 ELIJAH THE TISHBITE
LISTIB/AL-ISTIB, WADI CHERITH AND TALL MAR ELIAS

ELIJAH whose name means "my God is YAH(WEH)," is one of the greatest Israelite prophets after Moses. He is frequently associated with the area of Transjordan and specifically the mountainous region of Ajloun to the north of the modern capital city of Amman. However, his ministry takes place, for the most part, in northern Israel and the area of what is now generally referred to as Samaria on the west bank of the Jordan River.

Elijah, a ninth-century-BC prophet, was active in the time of Ahab (reigned between ca. 875–850 BC) and his son Ahaziah (who reigned little more than a year), kings of the northern state of Israel. In 1 Kings 17–19, Elijah is presented as the champion of the LORD against the royally-patronized worship of Baal. For this reason, Ahab refers to him as "you troubler of Israel" (1 Kings 18.17).

During the time of Ahab and his Phoenician queen, Jezebel of Tyre, the religion of the LORD is persecuted, while that of Baal is promoted. Elijah, in this situation, is the one who speaks the word of the true God. He is the new Moses who withstands royal oppression and keeps the faith alive. Elijah speaks a word of power to withhold rainfall. Thus, he is a threat to Baal, the god of storms and fertility. As a result, the beginning and end of the drought, which is referred to in 1 Kings 17.1, 7 and 18.41–45, is traced to Elijah. The contest between the LORD and Baal on Mount Carmel is intended to prove who is the greatest, the LORD or Baal (1 Kings 18.17–40). Elijah represents the LORD; the prophets of Baal stand in for their god. The LORD wins a resounding victory and the assembled Israelites help in Elijah's execution of the 450 prophets of Baal.

In Judaism, Elijah is often identified as a precursor of the Messiah (see below). He is associated with combating social ills by caring for the poor and punishing the unjust. He is identified with the "Wandering Jew" of medieval folklore, and a place is always set for him at the Seder table. He is protector of the newborn, and the "Chair of Elijah" is a fixture at circumcisions.

Elijah is listed in the Koran among the "righteous ones" (8:85). Moreover, the Koran recalls his mission as a staunch opponent of the cult of Baal (37:123–30).

In the Hebrew Bible, Elijah is referred to as the "messenger" (Malachi 3.1). He is the one who would precede the coming of the Messiah (Malachi 4.5–6). In two accounts of the Gospel the belief is expressed that John the Baptist was Elijah (Matthew 17.10–13; Mark 9.11–13; and see also Luke 1.17). Moreover, in the story of the "Transfiguration" (Matthew 17.1–8; Mark 9.2–8; Luke 9.28–36), Moses and Elijah talk with Jesus. This incident shows the continuity of Jesus and his teaching with Israel's pre-eminent lawgiver and prophet, respectively.

SPECIFIC BIBLICAL TEXTS ON ELIJAH THE TISHBITE, OF TISHBE IN GILEAD

While references to Elijah appear throughout both the Old Testament/ Hebrew Scriptures and the New Testament, what is of interest here are those texts that deal with Elijah and his relation to Tishbe in Gilead. In the next chapter, which introduces Bethany Beyond the Jordan, the biblical texts that deal with Elijah's departure from this earth will be considered.

1 Kings 17.1–7

> Now Elijah the Tishbite, of Tishbe in Gilead, said to Ahab, "As the LORD the God of Israel lives, before whom I stand, there shall be nei-ther dew nor rain these years, except by my word." The word of the LORD came to him, saying, "Go from here and turn eastward, and hide yourself by the Wadi Cherith, which is east of the Jordan. You shall drink from the wadi, and I have commanded the ravens to feed you there." So he went and did according to the word of the LORD; he went and lived by the Wadi Cherith, which is east of the Jordan. The ravens brought him bread and meat in the morning, and bread and meat in the evening; and he drank from the wadi. But after a while the wadi dried up, because there was no rain in the land.

COMMENTARY ON THE TEXT

In six biblical passages, Elijah is identified as "the Tishbite" (1 Kings 17.1, 21.17, 21.28; 2 Kings 1.3, 1.8, 9.36). In addition, the first of these texts informs us that he comes from "Tishbe in Gilead." However, some commentators follow the Hebrew Text and read "Toshbite," that is, "the settler" or "the sojourner" in Gilead. We will locate Gilead first, then turn our attention to Tishbe, and finally consider the location of Wadi Cherith, which the text states is also "east of the Jordan."

Gilead

What appears to be evident is that Elijah comes from Gilead, east of the Jordan. However, it is not easy to locate the region of Gilead with great precision, since the biblical texts refer to "Gilead," "the hill country of Gilead," and "the land of Gilead." These terms can have both a narrow and a broad meaning depending on the context. Moreover, there are places called Jabesh-Gilead, Mizpah-gilead, and Ramoth-gilead in the texts. This indicates that Jabesh, Mizpah, and Ramoth were located in Gilead, wherever it may be (MacDonald 2000: 199–204).

The term "Gilead" sometimes refers to the land north or south of the Jabbok River (modern Wadi az-Zarqa). In the Jephthah story (Judges 11.1–12.6), "Gilead" signifies an autonomous entity in the mountain zone of the western segment of the Transjordanian plateau to the north of as-Salt and south of the Jabbok. However, during the time of Saul, the term "Gilead" included territory north of the Jabbok, since reference is made to Jabesh-Gilead (see 1 Samuel 11.1, 31.11), traditionally located north of this river. In the list of Solomon's administrative districts (1 Kings 4.7–19), an administrator has his "residence" in Ramoth-gilead (1 Kings 4.13), which is also located north of the Jabbok. There are many other texts that can be cited to show that the term is used both in a narrow and a broad sense (MacDonald 2000: 195–99). Thus, in 1 Kings 17.1 there is no certainty whether land north or south of the Jabbok is meant.

In any case, Gilead is described as a hill country. The regions both north and south of the Jabbok fulfill this topographical requirement. In addition, Numbers 32.1–5 describes the land of Gilead as a desirous place that is good for cattle.

Tishbe

No town called Tishbe, in the area of Gilead, is attested in ancient sources. However, early Christian tradition sanctified the site of Listib/al-Istib,
13 km north of the Jabbok in the northwest Ajloun mountains, as the
location of the hometown of Elijah. Some see such an identification as
possible, based on the suggestion of the metathesis between the Hebrew
Tishbe and the Arabic *al-Istib* (MacDonald 2000: 204).

One difficulty with locating Tishbe at Listib/al-Istib is that the site
was not occupied before the Roman–Byzantine period and thus long
after the time of Elijah. However, some suggest that the name could have
moved to Listib/al-Istib from Khirbat Umm al-Hedamus, 2 km to the
east. This latter site was occupied in the ninth century BC (MacDonald
2000: 204–5).

EXTRA-BIBLICAL VISITS AND ATTEMPTS TO LOCATE THE SITE

In the late fourth century AD, Egeria visited Tishbe, which she calls the
town of Elijah. She saw there the cave in which the prophet is said to
have dwelt:

> We traveled through the Jordan valley for a little, and at times the
> road took us along the river-bank itself. Then Tishbe came in sight,
> the city from which the holy prophet Elijah gets his name "the
> Tishbite." To this day they have there the cave in which he lived, and
> also the tomb of Jephthah of whom we read in the Book of Judges.
> So we gave thanks to God there in our usual way, and set off once
> more (*Travels*, ch. 16:1-2; Wilkinson 1999: 128).

Egeria also indicates that Jephthah's tomb (Judges 12.6) was located in
Tishbe, which would identify it with Mizpah of Gilead (Judges 11.34).
However, this appears unlikely, since, as indicated previously, the site of
Tishbe (Listib/al-Istib) was not occupied at such an early date.

The best that Eusebius and Jerome can do in the *Onomasticon*
and *Book on the Sites and Names of Places of the Hebrews* is to state,
respectively:

> **Thesba** (1 Kgs. 17:1). Where Elijah the Tishbite was (102); and **Thesba**.
> Where the Prophet Elijah the Thesbite came from (103) (Taylor et
> al. 2003: 59).

Wadi Cherith

1 Kings 17.3 indicates that Wadi Cherith is located "east of the Jordan." It was to this wadi that the ravens brought Elijah bread and meat in the morning, and bread and meat in the evening. And Elijah drank from the wadi, until it dried up.

The wadi in question, with its name meaning "cutting," has been located at many places. One suggested location is Wadi Yabis, an imposing watercourse to the north of Listib/al-Istib in northern Gilead. However, most commentators can do no better than repeat the generalized location of the verse itself. In this case, Elijah, a Gileadite, returned to what was for him familiar territory.

The place shown as the "Cherith" to Egeria is thought to have been Wadi Yabis, one of the wadis that flows westward from the hills of Gilead towards the Jordan Valley. The reason for this is that after leaving Tishbe, Egeria continued her journey and writes:

> So we gave thanks to God there in our usual way, and set off once more. As we went on we saw a very well-kept valley coming down towards us on the left. It was very large, and had a good-sized stream in it which ran down into the Jordan.

> In this valley was the cell of a brother, a monk. You know how inquisitive I am, and I asked what there was about this valley to make this holy monk build his cell there. I knew there must be some special reason, and this is what I was told by the holy men with us who knew the district: "This is the valley of Cherith. The holy prophet Elijah the Tishbite stayed here in the reign of King Ahab; and at the time of the famine, when God sent a raven to bring him food, he drank water from this brook. For Cherith is the watercourse you can see running down the valley to the Jordan." So we set off again – as indeed we did every single day – giving renewed thanks to God for his goodness in showing us all the things we wanted to see, and so much more than we deserved (*Travels*, ch. 16:2-4; Wilkinson 1999: 128).

Eusebius, *Onomasticon*, and Jerome, *Book on the Sites and Names of Places of the Hebrews*, are not much help in locating Wadi Cherith. They state, respectively:

> **Chorra** (1 Kgs. 17:3). A torrent on the other side of the Jordan (174);
> **Chorath**. A torrent on the other side of the Jordan. Elijah hid in the region of that river (175) (Taylor et al. 2003: 97).

FIG. 4.1   Aerial view of Tall Mar Elyas (© David L Kennedy, APAAME, APA2006-09-11_DLK-86).

Eusebius and Jerome's location of the wadi in question is very general and thus not very helpful. For, indeed, there are many "torrents" (wadis) on the east side of the Jordan River.

John Moschus, however, is evidently not thinking of Wadi Yabis when he says that the wadi is located "to the left of Sapsas," probably indicating Wadi al-Kharra (Wilkinson 2002: 293). Thus, the location of Wadi Cherith will be considered again when dealing with "Bethany Beyond the Jordan" and the place of Elijah's being taken up into heaven.[1]

In conclusion, the story of Elijah's flight from Ahab seems to indicate that he fled out of the king's jurisdiction. An area to the east of the Jordan River would be suitable for one fleeing the king's wrath.

THE ARCHAEOLOGY OF TALL MAR ELYAS

The village of Listib/al-Istib and the nearby archaeological site of Tall Mar Elyas ("Tall of Saint Elijah") have long been identified with Tishbe, mentioned in the Bible as the home town or region of the prophet Elijah. The village of Listib is the site of a mosque dating from the Ayyubid–Mamluk

---

1   It appears that Wadi Cherith may indeed be Wadi al-Kharra, a wadi farther to the south of both Listib/al-Istib and Wadi Yabis and close to the Jordan River (see Chapter 5).

period. However, archaeological remains at the site date mostly to the Roman–Byzantine period; thus, the site was likely a village dating to that time. Tall Mar-Elyas (fig. 4.1) is located around one-half kilometer to the east of the village and ca. 9 km to the northwest of the town of Ajloun. Because of its elevated location and the preservation of trees on the site, it is an especially lovely place to visit.

Personnel from the Department of Antiquities of the Ajloun region began excavations at the site in 1999. They have uncovered the remains of two churches, a number of tombs associated with each, a baptistery, and a series of rooms, especially along the south side and to the southwest of the larger of the two churches (fig. 4.2).

The smaller of the two churches (fig. 4.3), excavated in 2003, is located close to the entrance of the restored site (UTM coordinates: 0756172 E/3484038 N; elev. 922 m). It is at a lower elevation than the larger one and to the southwest of it. Its apse is now its most distinctive feature. The excavators think that it is the older of the two and that it probably dates to the sixth century. Moreover, they posit that the tombs along its west side are from the same date. A niche in the center of the apse

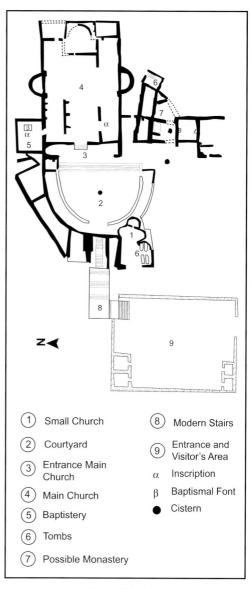

1. Small Church
2. Courtyard
3. Entrance Main Church
4. Main Church
5. Baptistery
6. Tombs
7. Possible Monastery
8. Modern Stairs
9. Entrance and Visitor's Area
α Inscription
β Baptismal Font
● Cistern

FIG. 4.2 Ground Plan of Tall Mar Elyas (adapted from site plan provided by Ministry of Tourism and Antiquities of Jordan).

shows signs of burning, probably from candles placed there by pilgrims. There is a rectangular room associated with the church off its north side.

A newly-constructed stairway to the north of the small church leads to a courtyard/atrium measuring 30 m long by 3.50 m wide. A well-pre-

FIG. 4.3   The small church at Tall Mar Elyas (photo by Sherry Hardin).

FIG. 4.4   The main church, looking northeast (photo by Sherry Hardin).

served cistern, 9 m deep and 7 m wide at its bottom, is located within the courtyard. Under the floor of the courtyard are pipes that bring water to the cistern.

Continuing to the east, one approaches a raised area. Here are located the two main entrances to the church. The remnants of a Roman-period winepress are found near the church's southwest entrance.

The main church (UTM coordinates: 0756223 E/3584035 N; elev. 946 m) at the site is at a still higher elevation to the east (fig. 4.4). It is a cruciform, or cross-shaped, structure that stands on the summit of a high hill overlooking the mountains of northern Gilead and the hills and plains that lead down to the Jordan Valley to the west. The hill itself has been revered for centuries as a holy place by local inhabitants of the area as well as by pilgrims; people come to this area to pray, especially on July 21, Elijah's annual commemoration day. The large church is now known in Arabic as *Kneeset Mar Elyas*, or the "Church of Saint Elijah."

The church measures 33 × 32 m and has one apse with columns dividing it into three aisles. Some of the column bases and drums are still in their original positions. The floor of the church was completely covered by a multi-colored mosaic of floral and geometric designs. Rooms

FIG. 4.5 The dedicatory inscription in the main church (photo by Sherry Hardin).

to the north and south of the apse are also covered with mosaics. Parts of the marble chancel screen that separated the sanctuary from the nave are still visible. One of the square rooms, immediately to the north of the apse, appears to be from an earlier phase of the site's use. It is now linked to it, but its mosaic floor is made of large, white stone cubes that are different from the mosaic floor within the main body of the church. The Roman pottery associated with this room probably indicates that it predates the church.

An inscription on the mosaic floor of the church faces its west entrances (fig. 4.5). It is in white letters on a red background and displays an invocation to Saint Elijah. It asks the saint to bless Saba, the presbyter, and his wife. The year of the dedication of the church is AD 622, which indicates that the mosaic floor was put down at this time. Such a date for the dedication is of interest, since it was during a turbulent time in the

FIG. 4.6   The baptistery associated with the main church (photo by Sherry Hardin).

FIG. 4.7   The baptistery inscription (photo by Sherry Hardin).

area. The Byzantine Empire was retreating from the region, the Persian invasion of Jordan had just occurred in 614, and it was just before the arrival of the Islamic armies from the south. Another mosaic floor lies below the one of the inscription. This suggests an even earlier date for the building of the church, possibly dating to the sixth century.

A small room off the northwest of the main church is a well-preserved baptistery (fig. 4.6). Its floor is completely covered with mosaics. A Greek inscription is located on the mosaic floor immediately below and to the west of the baptismal font (fig. 4.7). The inscription indicates that the child (being baptized) is an offering to God for the absolution of sins and for a long life (on earth). The excavators believe that the baptistery is dated later than the main church. The reason for this conclusion is that the walls of the baptistery are not bonded to the north wall of the church.

Several plastered, stone-built water channels have been excavated around the church. Moreover, a total of seven wells and cisterns have been identified to date in its immediate vicinity; the church and its associated buildings would have depended on cisterns for their water supply.

The excavators uncovered a total of seven graves just outside the main church, towards the southwest. Three of the graves are reached by a staircase consisting of nine steps. The stairs are cut from the bedrock and the graves were covered with stone slabs. Four additional graves were located in a subterranean chamber or cave immediately to the west.

The church appears to have been used for around two centuries. An earthquake may have been responsible, at least in part, for its abandonment. Repairs to the floor mosaic indicate that it may have undergone refurbishment during its lifetime.

The main church building was surrounded by other structures besides the cisterns, graves, and the courtyard. Wall remains identified to its north, east, and south probably belonged to structures associated with the

FIG. 4.8   Rock-cut tombs just outside the south wall of the main church (photo by Sherry Hardin).

church. Rooms to the southwest of the main church have mosaic floors. Did these rooms at one time belong to a monastery associated with the church? Even before the church was identified and excavated, local lore always identified the area around the church as the residence of "the nuns."

The Tombs at Tall Mar Elyas and Pilgrimage

As indicated above, several tombs have been excavated in the area of both the small and the large church at Tall Mar Elyas (fig. 4.8). In light of what we know about the goals of pilgrims, one of the places they would have visited would have been the tombs of martyrs and/or holy persons. Such seems to have been the case at Gadara/Umm Qays (see Chapter 3).

Although the archaeological evidence has not been presented to date, one can only wonder whether the two sets of tombs at Tall Mar Elyas were those of holy men and/or women. Did these tombs play a role in bringing people to the site? This, of course, does not deny the fact that many people came to the site to honor and to pray to Elijah; but there are often multiple motives that bring people to pilgrimage sites.

LOCAL TRADITION AND THE SACRED NATURE OF TALL MAR ELYAS

Local traditions attest to the sacred nature of the site. They include stories of shepherds bringing sick goats and sheep to it. The shepherds then walked the animals around Tall Mar Elyas, shot guns in the air, prayed to God and Elijah, and asked them for healing and rain. Shortly thereafter, the animals were, allegedly, always cured.

Another example of the sacred nature of the site relates to tribal justice practices in the Ajloun area. Local residents say that if two people had a dispute, the aggrieved party would take the accused to Tall Mar Elyas and ask her or him to swear by the Prophet Elijah that they did not commit the crime of which they were accused. If the accused swore to Elijah that he or she did not commit the crime, then that was sufficient proof of the person's innocence.

To this day, people of the area visit Tall Mar Elyas to pray, light candles, sacrifice animals, and tie strips of cloth to the branches of nearby trees (fig. 4.9). Thus, the many pieces of cloth tied to the site's trees have been left by pilgrims who came to the site to ask for the assistance of God and Elijah.[2]

FIG. 4.9   Tree with prayer ribbons near the apse of the main church (photo by Sherry Hardin).

SUGGESTIONS FOR GETTING THERE

Tall Mar Elyas is located around 80 km to the northwest of Amman and around 9 km from Ajloun. To get to the site from Amman, take the Jerash–Irbid highway north. A short distance south of Jerash turn north, following the signs to Ajloun. Once in Ajloun, follow the signs for Ajloun Castle. About 1 km south of the castle turn right at the sign for Tall Mar Elyas.

---

2 "The Abraham Path" is an initiative designed to follow the footsteps of Abraham. When completed, it will stretch for 1200 km, from Sanliurfa and the nearby ruins of Harran in Turkey, where Abraham is believed to have heard the call of God to go forth, to Hebron in Palestine, where he is believed to be buried. The path will pass cultural and historical sites in southern Turkey, Syria, and Jordan and serve as a route of cultural tourism and a long-distance walking trail. In June of 2008, the initiative began in Jordan with a walk through the Ajloun area by university students from Leeds Metropolitan University in England and Yarmouk University in Jordan. They followed a 12-km stretch of the path through the villages of Rasoun and Baoun to Tall Mar Elyas. General information on the path can be found at http://www.abrahampath.org. The length of the Abraham Path in Jordan is about 120 km, from the Syrian border to the Jordan River. Some of the places of historical interest through which it will pass include: Tall Mar Elyas, Ajloun, Anjara, Tulul adh-Dhahab, Salt, Iraq al-Amir, Mount Nebo, and Bethany Beyond the Jordan. Three of the sites are treated in this work.

FIG. 5.1   The Jordan River (photo by David Bjorgen, 2005).

5 THE SITE OF THE BAPTISM AND ELIJAH'S ASCENSION

BETHANY BEYOND THE JORDAN

THE region of "Bethany Beyond the Jordan" is associated with a number of biblical events: 1) the possible location of Wadi Cherith, to which Elijah fled to escape from Ahab at the time of the drought; 2) the setting for the ascension of Elijah into heaven; 3) the site where John lived across the Jordan and where he baptized; 4) the place to which Jesus came to be baptized by John; and 5) where Jesus came when opposition against him by the religious authorities in Jerusalem increased.

The previous chapter presented background information on Elijah, specifically his opposition to King Ahab of Israel because of Ahab's promotion of the worship of the storm and fertility god Baal. It also treated Elijah's place of origin at Tishbe in Gilead, traditionally identified with the village of Listib/al-Istib in the region of Mount Ajloun. The churches at the nearby site of Tall Mar Elyas commemorate the prophet. Moreover, the chapter considered the position that some commentators identify Wadi Cherith, the place to which the prophet fled from Ahab, as being Wadi Yabis.

The present chapter considers Bethany Beyond the Jordan as another possible location for the place to which Elijah took refuge and where ravens fed him in the morning and in the evening (1 Kings 17.1–7). The area is, in any case, associated with Elijah's ascension into heaven (2 Kings 2.11).

The New Testament's association of Elijah with John the Baptist as the precursor of the Messiah (Matthew 17.10–13; Mark 9.11–13; and see also Luke 1.17) was also set forth in the previous chapter. It is certainly not inappropriate to have one place where both a prophet of the Old Testament/Hebrew Scriptures and one from the New Testament are commemorated. This especially applies to Bethany Beyond the Jordan because of the close relationship between Elijah and John.

The Gospel according to John locates one of the places where John the Baptist carried out his ministry as being at Bethany Beyond the Jordan (1.28). And it is to John that Jesus came from Nazareth in Galilee to be baptized.

According to Matthew (4.1–11), Mark (1.12–13), and Luke (4.1–13), after his baptism, Jesus fasted for forty days and was tempted by Satan in the nearby "wilderness." In the Gospel according to John, however, there is no temptation of Jesus. Instead, "the next day," that is, the day after the baptism, John saw Jesus coming toward him and declared, "Here is the Lamb of God who takes away the sin of the world!" (1.29). The following day, when he saw Jesus walk by, John again exclaimed, "Look, here is the Lamb of God!" (1.35). Two of John's disciples heard him say this and they followed after Jesus (1.35–42). This took place at "Bethany Beyond the Jordan" (John 1.28). Only then did Jesus leave for Galilee (John 1.43).

The biblical texts related to John's baptizing in general and John's baptizing of Jesus in particular are considered first. Next, texts related to Elijah and his flight from Ahab as well as his ascension to heaven are considered. Finally, the archaeological ruins at Bethany Beyond the Jordan, especially Elijah's Hill on the eastern end of Wadi al-Kharrar and the John the Baptist Church Area on a former course of the Jordan River, are discussed.

BIBLICAL TEXTS ON THE PLACE OF JOHN'S BAPTIZING

A number of biblical texts (John 1.24–28, 10.40, 3.23, 3.26; Matthew 3.13; Mark 1.9; and Luke 3.3) deal with the place of the baptizing activity of John. In relation to this activity, the place where Jesus was baptized by John also needs to be considered. Finally, a text dealing with Jesus' coming to the place "beyond the Jordan," when persecuted by the religious authorities in Jerusalem, is treated (fig. 5.2).

John 1.24–28

> Now they had been sent from the Pharisees. They asked him, "Why then are you baptizing if you are neither the Messiah, nor Elijah, nor the prophet?" John answered them, "I baptize with water. Among you stands one whom you do not know, the one who is coming after me; I am not worthy to untie the thong of his sandal." This took place in Bethany across the Jordan where John was baptizing.

FIG. 5.2   Bend in the Jordan River at Bethany Beyond the Jordan, taken from the east side (photo by Sherry Hardin).

This text occurs not only at the beginning of the Gospel according to John, but it also treats the beginning of John the Baptist's ministry. According to the text, the first recorded day of John's activity closes with a reference to "Bethany across the Jordan," where John fulfills his prophetic mission of announcing the Messiah's coming. This site is mentioned again in John 10.40, since it is to this place that Jesus goes after the death of the Baptist and as opposition against him grows in Jerusalem.

The majority of texts from the second and third centuries propose the reading "Bethania(i)," that is, "Bethany." There is no general agreement, however, on the meaning of the toponym. Some dictionaries have it meaning "house of dates or figs," others understand it to mean "house of depression or misery." Riesner, on the other hand, sees the place name as derived from *bêt 'anniyâ*, "house of the boat" = ford (1992: 704). Such a meaning would place Bethany at one of the ferry crossings/fords of the Jordan. This location would fit well the ministry of John who would have been at a place where he could meet people as they crossed from one side of the river to the other.

Origen (ca. AD 200), although admitting that *almost all* the manuscripts read "Bethany," preferred another reading, namely, "Bethabara," "the place of the crossing over." He chose this reading because he could find no place called Bethany in Transjordan. His alternative reading would also place John's baptizing at one of the fords of the Jordan River and thus agrees with that of Riesner.

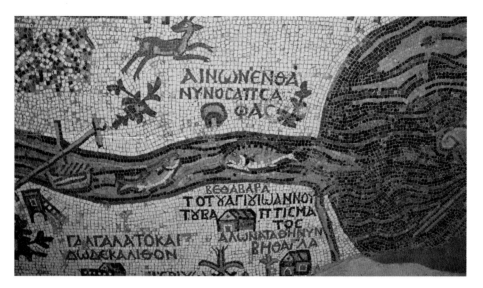

FIG. 5.3   Portion of the Madaba Mosaic Map showing 'Aenon, where now is Sapsaphas' (immediately east of the Jordan River), and 'Bethabara, the place of baptism of John' (below it and west of the river). (Photo by M. Disdero.)

Eusebius in the *Onomasticon* and Jerome in the *Book on the Sites and Names of Places of the Hebrews*, respectively, place Bethabara across the Jordan:

> **Bethabara** (John 1:28). Where John was baptizing across the Jordan. The place is shown in which also many of the brethren even now are eager to take a bath (58); and **Bethabara**. Across the Jordan, where John baptized unto repentance, whence even today very many of the brethren, that is, of the number of believers, desire to be born again there and are baptized in the life-giving torrent (59) (Taylor et al. 2003: 38).

The Madaba Mosaic Map (fig. 5.5) follows Origen and locates Bethabara west of the Jordan (Alliata 1999: 51, 55). Origen's reading, however, is generally dismissed today.

John 10.40-42

> He went away again across the Jordan to the place where John had been baptizing earlier, and he remained there. Many came to him and they were saying, "John performed no sign, but everything that John said about this man was true." And many believed in him there.

In this text, the place is once again indicated to be "across the Jordan," that is, at Bethany, where, as in John 1.28, John had been baptizing. Jesus came to this place and remained there. The people who came to Jesus could have very well been followers of John the Baptist. Could a colony of John the Baptist's disciples have remained in the area?[1]

Jesus left the hostile land and people of Palestine and crossed to Jordan. There he found the faith that was lacking in his own land. Moreover, while the retirement of Jesus to the region beyond the Jordan had the practical purpose of seeking shelter from the hostility aroused in Jerusalem, it also served the Gospel writer's theological purpose: Jesus was not to die by mob violence – he would die only when he was ready to lay down his life.

The Bethany in the text is not the town by the same name near Jerusalem (John 11.18) in which Mary, Martha and their brother Lazarus lived. It is a site "across the Jordan," where recent archaeological explorations have uncovered extensive remains that commemorate John's activity and Jesus' presence in the area. Here also Elijah's ascent into heaven is memorialized.

The Gospel according to John provides geographical information about John the Baptist not found in the other three accounts. These geographical details lend color to the theory that the Fourth Gospel preserves an independent tradition about John the Baptist. For example, there is a report concerning John the Baptist's ministry at Aenon near Salim:

John 3.23

> After this Jesus and his disciples went into the Judean countryside, and he spent some time there with them and baptized. John also was baptizing at Aenon near Salim because water was abundant there; and people kept coming and were being baptized.

While Jesus and his disciples are in the Judean countryside baptizing, John is at *Aenon*, which is said to be near *Salim*. *Aenon* is the Aramaic plural of the word for "spring," while *Salim* reflects the Semitic root for "peace."

There are a number of traditions for localizing *Aenon* and *Salim*. One of these locates *Aenon* in Transjordan, since we know from John 1.28 that John the Baptist was active in this region. Support for this comes

---

1   A colony of Essenes, a Jewish group living a monastic type of existence, would have been at Qumran, across the Jordan River to the southwest at the northwest side of the Dead Sea, at the time.

from the Madaba Mosaic Map, which has an *Aenon* just northeast of the Dead Sea: "Aenon, where now is Sapsaphas," which Alliata identifies with Wadi al-Kharrar (1999: 54), the place where recent archaeological explorations have found extensive early Christian remains (see below).

Another tradition locates *Aenon* in the northern Jordan valley, on the west bank, and some eight miles south of Scythopolis (Bethshan). This is the *Aenon* that Egeria appears to have visited:

> Then I remembered that according to the Bible it was near Salim that holy John baptized at Aenon. So I asked if it was far away. "There it is," said the holy presbyter, "two hundred yards away. If you like we can walk over there. It is from that spring that the village has this excellent supply of clean water you see." Thanking him I asked him to take us, and we set off. He led us along a well-kept valley to a very neat apple-orchard, and there in the middle he showed us a good clean spring of water which flowed in a single stream. There was a kind of pool in front of the spring at which it appears holy John Baptist exercised his ministry of baptism. "This garden," said the holy presbyter, "is still known in Greek as *Cepos tu Agiu Iohanni*, or in your language, Latin, 'Holy John's Garden.'" A great many brothers, holy monks from different parts, travel here to wash at this place. So once more we had a prayer and a reading at this spring as we did in the other places. We said a suitable psalm, and did everything which was usual when arriving at a holy place (*Travels* 15.1–4; Wilkinson 1999: 127).

This location of *Aenon* in the north Jordan Valley is supported by Eusebius in the *Onomasticon* and Jerome in the *Book on the Sites and Names of Places of the Hebrews*, respectively:

> **Ainon** (John 3.23). Near Saleim, where John baptized, as in the Gospel of John. And the site is pointed out even until today 8 milestones south of Scythopolis near Saleim and the Jordan (40); and **Aenon**. Near Salim, where John was baptizing, as is mentioned in St. John's Gospel. It is now shown as a place eight milestones from Scythopolis to the south between Salim and the Jordan (41) (Taylor et al. 2003: 29).

The Madaba Mosaic Map has a second *Aenon* south of Scythopolis (=Bethshan): "Aenon near Salem which is also Saloumias," which Alliata locates at Khirbet Khisas al-Dayr (1999: 50–51; see also Kopp 1963: 129–37).

On the basis of the biblical texts and the traditions relative to the place of John's baptizing, it would appear that John carried out his activities both at "Bethany across the Jordan" (John 1.28) and at "Aenon near Salim" (John 3.23) in the northern Jordan Valley, west of the river. However, as we will see, it is "Bethany Beyond the Jordan" that became a place of pilgrimage and the location of monasteries and churches in the Byzantine period.

John 3.26

> They came to John and said to him, "Rabbi, the one who was with you across the Jordan, to whom you testified, here he is baptizing, and all are going to him."

This text deals with John's disciples coming to him and informing him of the baptizing activity of Jesus. The disciples identify Jesus as "the one who was with you across the Jordan."

Unlike the Gospel according to John, the Gospels according to Matthew, Mark, and Luke do not specify where John was baptizing other than at the Jordan River. In Matthew we read: "Then Jesus came from Galilee to John at the Jordan, to be baptized by him" (3.13). Likewise, Mark reads: "In those days Jesus came from Nazareth of Galilee and was baptized by John in the Jordan" (1.9). Mark adds "from Nazareth" to the information provided by Matthew. Luke, however, is more general as far as the geography of the place of John's baptism is concerned. He states that "He went into all the region around the Jordan, proclaiming a baptism of repentance for the forgiveness of sins" (3.3); of Jesus' baptism, Luke states: "Now all the people were baptized, and when Jesus also had been baptized and was praying, the heaven was opened" (3.21). Luke depicts John as an itinerant desert preacher, addressing his message to all who would come to listen to him in the Jordan Valley.

Specific references are made in Matthew, Mark, and Luke to the Jordan River where the baptism took place. However, early rabbinic tradition explicitly disqualifies the River Jordan for purification. Only Josephus (*Antiquities* 18.5.2) associates John's baptism with purification (cf. John 3:25), but he makes no reference to the Jordan.

BIBLICAL TEXTS ON ELIJAH'S ASCENSION

One biblical text deals with Elijah's being taken up to heaven. This text has parallels to the Israelites' crossing of the Jordan River under their leader Joshua. Both incidents appear to have taken place in the same general region of the Jordan, close to Jericho. In addition, pilgrim texts locate Elijah's ascension in the area where John was baptizing.

2 Kings 2.5–15: Elijah taken up to heaven

> The company of prophets who were at Jericho drew near to Elisha, and said to him, "Do you know that today the LORD will take your master away from you?" And he answered, "Yes, I know; be silent." Then Elijah said to him, "Stay here; for the LORD has sent me to the Jordan." But he said, "As the LORD lives, and as you yourself live, I will not leave you." So the two of them went on. Fifty men of the company of prophets also went, and stood at some distance from them, as they were standing by the Jordan. Then Elijah took his mantle and rolled it up, and struck the water; the water was parted to the one side and to the other, until the two of them crossed on dry ground. When they had crossed, Elijah said to Elisha, "Tell me what I may do for you, before I am taken from you." Elisha said, "Please let me inherit a double share of your spirit." He responded, "You have asked a hard thing; yet, if you see me as I am being taken from you, it will be granted you; if not, it will not." As they continued walking and talking, a chariot of fire and horses of fire separated the two of them, and Elijah ascended in a whirlwind into heaven. Elisha kept watching and crying out, "Father, father! The chariots of Israel and its horsemen!" But when he could no longer see him, he grasped his own clothes and tore them in two pieces. He picked up the mantle of Elijah that had fallen from him, and went back and stood on the bank of the Jordan. He took the mantle of Elijah that had fallen from him, and struck the water, saying, "Where is the LORD, the God of Elijah?" When he struck the water, the water was parted to the one side and to the other, and Elisha went over. When the company of prophets who were at Jericho saw him at a distance, they declared, "The spirit of Elijah rests on Elisha." They came to meet him and bowed to the ground before him.

2 Kings 2 tells the story of the last event in the life and ministry of Elijah and the succession of Elisha ("[my] God saves"), his servant and follower. The two embark upon a journey from Gilgal to Bethel and thence to the Jordan River near Jericho, where they cross. On the east bank of the river Elijah departs in a spectacular way in a whirlwind.

A point of note in this chapter is an overt reminder of the traditions connected with Moses and Joshua. The similarities are quite extensive between this narrative, the narrative of the Israelites crossing the Reed Sea/Red Sea under the leadership of Moses (Exodus 14), and the narrative of the Israelites crossing the Jordan River under the leadership of Joshua (Joshua 3). The similarities extend beyond the use of common words:

the relationship of Elijah to Elisha is like that of Moses to Joshua, and both successors are appointed in similar fashion (Numbers 27:18–23; 1 Kings 19:15–21). Furthermore, the location of the crossing of the Jordan is identical, and the cities of Bethel, Gilgal, and Jericho are common to both narratives.

EARLY CHRISTIAN WITNESSES TO THE PLACE OF JOHN'S BAPTIZING AND ELIJAH'S ASCENSION

A number of early Christian writers have left information on the place of John's baptizing. Moreover, some of these writers locate Elijah's ascension in the same general area.

The Bordeaux Pilgrim (ca. AD 333) states,

> It is nine miles from Jericho to the Dead Sea… Five miles from there in the Jordan is the place where the Lord was baptized by John, and above the far bank at the same place is the hillock from which Elijah was taken up to heaven (597–98) (Wilkinson 1999: 33).

The Bordeaux Pilgrim would have approached the River Jordan from the southwest. It does not seem that he crossed the river. Thus, he placed John's baptism of Jesus in the Jordan five Roman miles (7,400 m) from the Dead Sea. Moreover, he places the hill from which Elijah was taken up to heaven above the far bank of the Jordan.

Theodosius (ca. AD 518) writes,

> At the place where my Lord was baptized is a marble column, and on top of it has been set an iron cross. There also is the Church of Saint John the Baptist, which was constructed by the Emperor Anastasius. It stands on great vaults which are high enough for the times when the Jordan is in flood. The monks who reside at this Church each receive six shillings a year from the Treasury for their livelihood. Where my Lord was baptized there is on the far side of the Jordan, the "little hill" called Hermon – Mount Tabor is in Galilee – where Saint Elijah was taken up. The tomb of Saint Elisha is there at the place where he blessed the spring, and a church has been constructed over the tomb. It is five miles from the place where my Lord was baptized to the point where the Jordan enters the Dead Sea… (Wilkinson 2002: 112).

Like the Pilgrim of Bordeaux, Theodosius places the baptism of Jesus in the Jordan River five Roman miles north of the Dead Sea. A marble column marked the spot. Moreover, Theodosius locates the Church of John the Baptist, built by the Emperor Anastasius (reigned AD 491–518), on the east bank of the Jordan. The church was built on pillars to protect it at times of flooding. Also like the Pilgrim of Bordeaux, Theodosius places the location of the ascension of Elijah on the far side of the Jordan. In addition, Theodosius places a church over the tomb of Elisha at the place where Elisha blessed the spring.

Piacenza Pilgrim (ca. AD 570)

The Piacenza Pilgrim has several comments on the location of the site of the baptism and Elijah's ascension:

> …and from there we arrived at the place where the Lord was baptized. This is the place where the children of Israel made their crossing, and also where the sons of the prophets lost their axe-head, and where Elijah was taken up. In that place is the "little hill of Hermon" mentioned in the Psalm. At the foot of the mountain at seven o'clock in the morning, a cloud forms over the river, and it arrives over Jerusalem at sunrise, about the basilica on Sion and the basilica at Christ's Tomb, the basilica of Saint Mary and Saint Sophia (once the Praetorium where Christ's case was heard). Above these places the dew comes down like showers, and sick people collect it. In the hospices all the dishes are cooked in it, and in the places where this dew falls many diseases are cured. For this is the dew of which the Psalmist sings, "Like as the dew of Hermon which fell upon the hill of Sion." In that part of the Jordan is the spring where Saint John used to baptize, which is two miles from the Jordan, and Elijah was in that valley when the raven brought him bread and meat. The whole valley is full of hermits (9; Wilkinson 1999: 135).

> I kept Epiphany at the Jordan, and on that night special miracles take place at the spot where the Lord was baptized. There is an obelisk there surrounded by a screen and in the water where the river turned back in its bed, stands a wooden cross. On both banks there are marble steps leading down to the water (11; Wilkinson 1999: 136).

> On the bank of the Jordan there is a cave in which are cells for seven virgins…. We went in with great reverence to pray there, but we

did not see the face of a single one of them. It is said that the cloth is there which the Lord wore on his face. By the Jordan, not far from where the Lord was baptized, is the very large Monastery of Saint John, which has two guest-houses…. (12; Wilkinson 1999: 137).

The Piacenza Pilgrim came to the place where the Lord was baptized. An obelisk, surrounded by a screen, marks the spot. Thus, he agrees with Theodosius on this point. In addition, a wooden cross indicates the spot where the river turned back its bed and the children of Israel made their crossing (Joshua 3.1–17). The anonymous pilgrim notes that on both banks there are marble steps leading down to the water. The Monastery of Saint John is nearby, along with its hostel. He also identifies it as the place where Elijah was taken up to heaven (2 Kings 2.11). He refers to the latter as the "little hill of Hermon" mentioned in Psalm 133.3. Moreover, the Pilgrim of Piacenza refers to the spring, two miles from the Jordan, where John used to baptize, and where Elijah was fed by the raven (1 Kings 17.6). This description would fit Wadi al-Kharrar.

The Georgian calendar of the church of Jerusalem (sixth–seventh century) recorded three liturgical meetings by the Jordan River on the Feast of the Epiphany: 1) on the fourth of January, on the eve of the feast of the baptism, the assembly meets on the other side of the Jordan; 2) on the fifth of January, the vigil of Epiphany, it gathers on the banks of the river; and 3) on the sixth of January, a solemn assembly is held at the Jordan, to commemorate the baptism in the Church of Saint John the Baptist, built inside the monastery (Piccirillo 2006a: 441).

John Moschus (ca. AD 615)

John Moschus relates a tale about the area where John the Baptist lived:

There was an elder living in the monastery of Abba Eustorgios whom saintly Archbishop of Jerusalem wanted to appoint higoumen [the monk in charge of a monastery] of the monastery. <The candidate> however would not agree and said: "I prefer prayer on Mount Sinai." The archbishop urged him first to become <higoumen> and then to depart <for the mountain> but the elder would not be persuaded. So <the archbishop> gave him leave of absence, charging him to accept the office of higoumen on his return. <The elder> bid the archbishop farewell and set out on the journey to Mount Sinai, taking his own disciple with him. They crossed the river Jordan but before they reached even the first mile-post the elder began to shiver with fever. As he was unable to walk, they found a small cave and went into it so that the elder could rest. He stayed in the cave for three days, scarcely able to move and burning with fever. Then, whilst he was sleeping, he saw a figure who said to him: "Tell me, elder, where do you want to go"? He replied: "To Mount Sinai." The vision then said to him: "Please, I beg of you, do not go there," but as he could not prevail upon the elder, he withdrew from him. Now the elder's fever attacked more violently. Again the following night the same figure with the same appearance came to him and said: "Why do you insist on suffering like this, good elder? Listen to me and do not go there." The elder asked him: "Who then are you"? The vision replied: "I am John the Baptist and that is why I say to you: do not go there. For this little cave is greater than Mount Sinai. Many times did our Lord Jesus Christ come in here to visit me. Give me your word that you will stay here and I will give you back your health." The elder accepted this with joy and gave his solemn word that he would remain in the cave. He was instantly restored to health and stayed there for the rest of his life. He made the cave into a church and gathered a brotherhood together there; the place is called Sapsas. Close by it and to the left is the Wadi Chorath to which Elijah the Tishbit was sent during the drought; it faces the Jordan (Moschus 1992: 4-5).

The elderly monk was going from Jerusalem to Mount Sinai by means of Transjordan and the road that went south to Ayla on the Red Sea/Gulf of Aqaba. He crossed over the Jordan River and was soon struck by a fever before going more than one Roman mile (1,480 m). The apparitions of John the Baptist took place at Sapsas (Sapsaphas), a place located on the Madaba Mosaic Map immediately to the east of the Jordan River ("Aenon, where now is Sapsaphas" [Alliata 1999: 51, 54]). The story locates both the place where Jesus came to visit John and to which Elijah fled in the area of what is now Wadi al-Kharrar. The site became a place for a brotherhood of monks on the Jordan's east bank.

Both the Pilgrim of Piacenza and John Moschus distinguish between the place where the baptism of Jesus was commemorated on the banks of the Jordan River and the place near the spring of Aenon/Sapsaphas to the east where Jesus and John stayed. The same distinction is made on the Madaba Mosaic Map: Bethabara on the river and Aenon/Sapsaphas beyond the Jordan.

Arculf (seventh century) states:

> The holy, venerable spot at which the Lord was baptized by John is permanently covered by the water of the Jordan River, and Arculf, who reached the place, and has swam across the river both ways, says that a tall wooden cross has been set up on that holy place....
>
> The position of this cross where, as we have said, the Lord was baptized, is on the near side of the river bed. A strong man using a sling can throw a stone from there to the far bank on the Arabian side. From this cross a stone causeway supported on arches stretches to the bank, and people approaching the cross go down a ramp and return up it to reach the bank.
>
> Right at the river's edge stands a small rectangular church which was built, so it is said, at the place where the Lord's clothes, were placed when he was baptized. The fact that it is supported on four stone vaults, makes it usable, since the water, which comes in from all sides, is underneath it. It has a tiled roof. This remarkable church is supported, as we have said, by arches and vaults, and stands in the lower part of the valley through which the Jordan flows. But in the upper part there is a great monastery for monks, which has been built on the brow of a small hill nearby, overlooking the church. There is also a church built there in honour of Saint John Baptist which, together with the monastery, is enclosed in a single masonry wall (Wilkinson 2002: 190-91).

Arculf's account places the baptism of Jesus within the river itself. A tall wooden cross marks the spot. From this cross, a causeway stretches to the east bank, where a ramp leads upward. Arculf recounts that a church on this bank (the eastern one), "right at the river's edge," marks the spot where Jesus placed his clothes at the time of his baptism. It is located in the lower part of the valley. Beyond, there is a monastery that overlooks the church. At the monastery, there is a church built to honor John the Baptist; together with the monastery, it is enclosed in a single masonry wall. Much of this is similar to the account of Theodosius.

Epiphanius the Monk

Epiphanius (last half of the seventh–first half of the eighth century) writes:

> ... and, about three miles beyond the Jordan a cave in which lived the Forerunner. There too is the bed on which he slept, a natural

shelf in the rock of the cave, and a small chamber. Inside the cave is the sound of water, and in the room is a spring in which holy John the Forerunner used to baptise (Wilkinson 2002: 213–14).

Epiphanius places the cave in which John the Baptist lived about three miles from the Jordan. It is also here that he places John's baptizing activity.

Willibald (first half of eighth century) relates about

> ... the Monastery of St. John the Baptist, where there are about twenty monks. One night they remained there, and then went on above a mile to the Jordan, where our Lord was baptized... (Mkhjian 2005: 403)

Willibald knew of a monastery dedicated to Saint John the Baptist. He indicates, furthermore, that the distance from this monastery to the Jordan, where Jesus was baptized, is about 1,480 meters.

Abbot Daniel (AD 1106–1107) states:

> Not far away from the river, a distance of two arrow throws, is the place where Prophet Elijah was taken into heaven in a chariot of fire. There is also the grotto of Saint John the Baptist. A beautiful torrent full of water flows over the stones towards the Jordan; the water is very cold and has a very good taste; it is the water that John drank while he lived in the holy grotto (*Pilgrimage of the Russian Abbot Daniel to the Holy Land* 33; Wilson 1895: 29).

Abbot Daniel places the site of the ascension of Elijah and the grotto of John the Baptist at a distance from the Jordan. At this location water flows towards the Jordan. The abbot appears to be describing Wadi al-Kharrar.

After the period of the Crusades, the memory of the place of the baptism was not lost. For example, Grethenios (AD 1400) writes: "It is said that beyond the Jordan one can find the grotto of Saint John; it is the place where he baptized the people. We did not go there for fear of the Arabs" (Piccirillo 1999b: 220).

From all the above it is evident that from the sixth century on, the monastery of Saint John on the east side of the Jordan River remained the place for the localization of the Sanctuary of the Baptism. Moreover, the texts tell of the existence of a second church on the eastern bank of the river in front of the monastery of Saint John.

During the Crusades, the Jordan River became a frontier line between the Latin Kingdom of Jerusalem and the Sultanate of Damascus. This political situation resulted in the abandonment of the sanctuaries on the east bank of the river, and the ceremonies were carried out on its west bank. This situation has continued until the present (Piccirillo 2006: 441).

The above texts are witness to a constant placement of the place of John the Baptist's activity "beyond the Jordan." The Fourth Gospel consistently emphasizes that his initial activity was "across the Jordan" (3:26; 10:40) and furnishes the further specification that the precise place was called "Bethany across the Jordan" (1.28). This is now supported by the recent archaeological excavations at Elijah's Hill, the Wadi al-Kharrar, and along the east bank of the Jordan where the wadi enters it.

BETHANY BEYOND THE JORDAN – THE ARCHAEOLOGY

The site called "Bethany Beyond the Jordan" (UTM coordinates: 0743979 E/ 3526317 N; elev. -304; taken at Ticket Office at the entrance to the site) is located east of the Jordan River, west of the modern village of Al-Kafrayn, and within sight of the town of Jericho west of the river. Situated at the head of Wadi al-Kharrar, it is at this place that several springs form pools that start the flow of water through Wadi al-Kharrar, eventually feeding into the Jordan River around 2 km to the west. Due to the springs, an oasis dominates the start of Wadi al-Kharrar and the site of Tall al-Kharrar. Moreover, thick and green vegetation is characteristic of the entire length of the wadi. As recent archaeological activity shows, the place of Bethany Beyond the Jordan was located at or around the natural hill called Tall al-Kharrar.

Starting in 1899, explorations in the area of the estuary of Wadi al-Kharrar identified the remains of a church on the east bank of the Jordan. These remains were located in front of the remnants of a monastery. In addition, the remains of hermits' cells near the spring of the wadi at Jabal Mar Elyas/Saint Elijah's Hill were identified. The two sites were visited until 1947 when, due to the political situation in the area, they had to be suspended. The Six-Day War of 1967 resulted in this area of the River Jordan becoming a fortified zone and thus off limits to civilians. With the peace treaty between Jordan and Israel in 1994, the area was once again opened up for explorations.

Recent archaeological activity in the area of Wadi al-Kharrar has identified remains dating from the Roman, Byzantine, and Early Islamic periods. These remains indicate that the area was inhabited during the

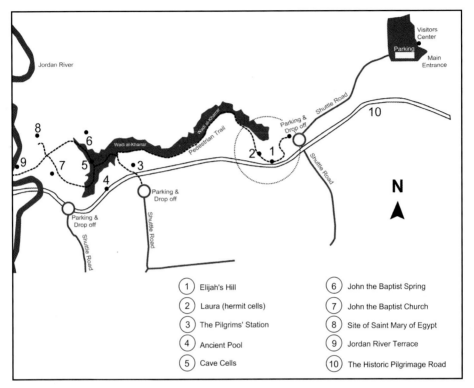

FIG. 5.4   Site Plan of Bethany Beyond the Jordan (adapted from plan provided by Ministry of Tourism and Antiquities of Jordan).

time of John the Baptist and Jesus. They also show that monks and hermits lived in the region during the Byzantine period and the beginning of Early Islamic times. Thus, a brief description of the archaeological remains is presented here (fig. 5.4).

Elijah' Hill

Saint Elijah's Hill – *Jabal Mar Elyas* in Arabic – is located at the southeastern end of Wadi al-Kharrar (fig. 5.5). The hill is associated with the Prophet Elijah's ascension into heaven (2 Kings 2.5–15). Here is located the sanctuary that attracted pilgrims into the medieval period.

Rhetorius Monastery

The Byzantine monastery called Rhetorius (fifth–sixth centuries) is located on Saint Elijah's Hill at the western edge of Wadi al-Kharrar, which connects it with the place where Jesus was baptized, a distance of ca. 1.5

km to the west (fig. 5.6). It is on the pilgrimage route from Jerusalem to Mount Nebo through Bethany Beyond the Jordan.

The name of the monastery comes from an inscription found in the apse of its northern church (fig. 5.7). The inscription reads:

> By the help of the grace of Christ our Lord. The whole monastery was constructed in the time of Rhetorius, the most God-beloved presbyter and Abbot. May God the Saviour give him mercy (Waheeb 1998: 636)

The monastery is comprised of several churches and other buildings within an enclosure wall – to protect from erosion rather than to serve

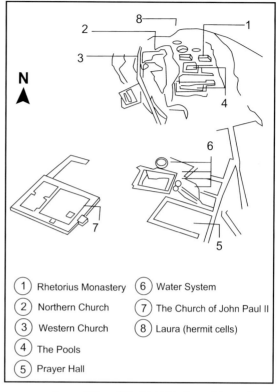

1. Rhetorius Monastery
2. Northern Church
3. Western Church
4. The Pools
5. Prayer Hall
6. Water System
7. The Church of John Paul II
8. Laura (hermit cells)

FIG. 5.5 Ground Plan of Elijah's Hill (adapted from plan provided by Ministry of Tourism and Antiquities of Jordan).

a defensive function. An entrance in the northwestern wall leads to the living quarters of the monks. The monastery and its churches were probably built to commemorate John the Baptist and Elijah. Because of the spring, the monastery had a good source of water.

In the mid-to-late Ottoman period (16th–18th centuries AD), Greek Orthodox monks established another monastery at the site, which consisted of structures for worship, residence, and accommodations for visiting pilgrims.

Northern Church

The Northern Church of the Rhetorius monastery has a typical Byzantine design of an altar area separated from the nave – the central part of the church – by a chancel screen. A colored mosaic, which included cross marks and geometric designs within a frame, covered the floor. The inscription, cited above, comes from this church. The entrances to the church are in its northern and western walls.

FIG. 5.6   Rhetorius Monastery and its modern "covering" at Elijah's Hill (photo by Sherry Hardin).

Western Church/Cave Church

The Western Church of the monastery is comprised of two parts (fig. 5.8). One part consists of a semi-circular apse cut into the natural rock. There are lamp niches carved into its southern and eastern walls. A chancel screen separates this part of the church from the second part, namely, the nave consisting of the main and two side aisles, separated by columns. Four column bases, built of well-dressed, square-cut sandstone blocks, are still in place.

FIG. 5.7   Rhetorius Monastery inscription (photo by Sherry Hardin).

The Pools

Three pools are located on Elijah's Hill. Waheeb (1998; 2001a and b), the excavator, dates the first one, located on the hill's lower, southern slope, to the third–fourth centuries AD (fig. 5.9). The pool, rectangular in shape, had an inner staircase on the eastern side, the four steps of which extend the full width of the pool. The excavator assumes that pilgrims would descend into the pool to be baptized. The other two pools, dating from the Late Roman period, are located on the top of the northern edge of the hill, overlooking the northern church. They are almost square. Large ashlars blocks

FIG. 5.8   Cave Church at Elijah's Hill (photo by Sherry Hardin).

were added to the southwestern corner of the northwestern pool at a later period; they could possibly have formed a staircase to go down into the pool. Excavations under the damaged floor of the northeastern pool revealed a well or deep cistern, dating from the Early Roman to Late

FIG. 5.9   Southern Baptismal Pools at Elijah's Hill (photo by Sherry Hardin).

FIG. 5.10   Prayer Hall at Elijah's Hill (photo by Sherry Hardin).

FIG. 5.11   Water System at Elijah's Hill (photo by Sherry Hardin).

Byzantine periods. It is built of well-cut sandstone ashlars. The pools received their water supply through channels carried over arches.

Wadi al-Kharrar

Prayer Hall

What is believed to be a Prayer Hall is located down the slope of Elijah's Hill and near its southeastern corner (fig. 5.10). It is a rectangular structure, measuring 10.70 × 7.40 m, built of undressed field stones. A plain white mosaic pavement covered its floor, while the roof was probably made of wood and reeds. The excavator thinks that based on its construction and location it may have functioned as a prayer hall or chapel. It could date from before the fourth century AD (Mkhjian 2005: 407). If so, it might be the earliest worship facility at the site.

Water System

A water system, consisting of a cistern and settling basins, is located near the Prayer Hall and the small chapel called the Church of John Paul II (fig. 5.11). It was dug out of the natural marl rock and is the largest reservoir discovered at the site. Its inner walls are built of well-cut sandstone ashlars covered by a smooth layer of plaster to prevent seepage. The excavator thinks that the system was roofed by a vault system. He dates it to the fifth–sixth centuries AD (Mkhjian 2005: 406).

The excavators have identified ceramic pipes 300 m to the southeast of the main settlement. These pipes would have brought water to the site from the nearby wadis that flow into the valley from the foothills to the east.

The Church of John Paul II

A rectangular church or chapel, measuring 13.65 × 9.45 m, is located on the saddle of land south of Saint Elijah's Hill. The excavator thinks that incoming pilgrims used it for prayer and worship. The church had a mosaic floor with cross decorations and arches supporting the roof. One of these arches has been reconstructed (fig. 5.12). The structure was probably built during the fifth–sixth centuries AD. It is presently called *The Church of John Paul II* to commemorate the Pope's visit to and blessing of the site on March 21, 2000.

Laura

Not far from Tall al-Kharrar, at a distance of ca. 300 m to the west on the southern edge of Wadi al-Kharrar, the excavators uncovered some architectural remains. These consist of small structures with foundations built from local field stones and upper courses built from mud bricks; the roofs consisted of wooden beams. Monks would have used these structures as

FIG. 5.12   Arch of the Church of John Paul II at Elijah's Hill (photo by Sherry Hardin).

their living and prayer quarters and for offering necessary services to the pilgrims visiting the site. The excavators think that these structures were part of a *laura*, or individual hermit cells, associated with the monastery.

The Pilgrims' Station

It appears that the Pilgrims' Station was built during the fifth–sixth centuries AD between the Jordan River and Tall al-Kharrar (fig. 5.13). It consisted of a number of rooms around an open courtyard, served by an adjacent water pool.

It is thought that from the fourth century onwards, Christian pilgrims visited the region east of the Jordan River on their way from Jerusalem to Mount Nebo. From the Pilgrims' Station, they would have visited the Christian facilities associated with Elijah, John the Baptist, and Jesus along the Wadi al-Kharrar, which at that time would have been known as Sapsaphas, a name that appears on the Madaba Mosaic Map. From here, pilgrims would have continued on to Livias (Tall ar-Ramah) and then on to Mount Nebo (see Chapter 6).[2]

---

2   Emperor Hadrian (reigned AD 117–138) had a road built to connect Hesban (ancient Esbus) to Livias (Tall ar-Ramah) in AD 129. He built another one to connect Jerusalem and Jericho. It is possible that Hadrian used these roads when he returned from his visit to Petra.

FIG. 5.13 Pilgrims' path to modern baptism site with Greek Orthodox Church at the upper center at Bethany Beyond the Jordan (photo by Sherry Hardin).

Ancient Pool

The excavators uncovered a large pool in the lower area of the site, just east of the Jordan River. The pool measures over 25 × 10 m and was constructed of large stones covered with plaster. It may have been used for group baptisms in the Byzantine period, since it could accommodate 300 persons. A canal directed water into the pool from a nearby spring to the north. Another canal carried water out of the pool's southern wall. On the basis of the materials recovered from the pool, the excavator dates the structure to the fifth–sixth centuries.

John the Baptist Spring

Travelers and historians describe this spring as flowing from a point near Saint Elijah's Hill. Pilgrims recount that water from the spring was used for drinking and for baptisms. Several structures and pools were built along the route of the fresh water. Ancient writers refer to this location as Aenon.

Cave Cells

Surveyors in the area found two caves just to the north of John the Baptist Spring. The caves were dug into the upper layers of the lisan marl cliffs

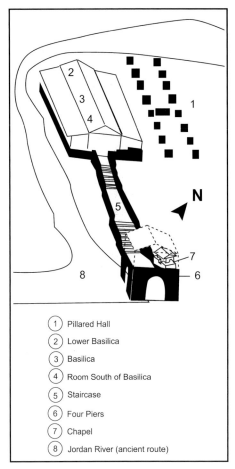

1. Pillared Hall
2. Lower Basilica
3. Basilica
4. Room South of Basilica
5. Staircase
6. Four Piers
7. Chapel
8. Jordan River (ancient route)

FIG. 5.14 John the Baptist Church Area (adapted from Mkhjian 2007).

and would have been used by monks as dwellings (cells). They have prayer niches carved into their eastern walls. The monks would have gained access to the caves by using ropes or ladders. These caves could have been part of the *laura* described previously.

John the Baptist Church Area

Three hundred meters east and 70 m north of the present course of the Jordan River, archaeologists and architects have uncovered the remains of memorial churches in an area they are calling the "John the Baptist Church Area" (figs. 5.14–15). Remnants of structures within this area are: Pillared Hall (the first church); Lower Basilica (the second church); Basilica (the third church); Room South of the Basilica (Mosaic Pavement); Staircase; Four Piers; Chapel (the fourth church); and Later Structures (Late Islamic Structures) (Mkhjian and Kanellopoulos 2003: 9).

All were built on the spot where believers located John's baptism of Jesus. Over the centuries, this series of churches was destroyed, at least in part, by floods and/or earthquakes; but they were rebuilt, because believers wished to have a memorial where they were convinced the baptism of Jesus took place (Mkhjian and Kanellopoulos 2003; Mkhjian 2007). The structures date between the fifth and 12th centuries. Had they been constructed in a less precarious location, they would probably have survived.

A comparison of the architectural remains with the historical texts cited above is enlightening: Theodosius refers to what was probably the Pillared Hall, Arculf likely mentions a structure carried on four piers and possibly the staircase, Willibald may be referring to the four piers and the presumed church above these piers, and Abbot Daniel probably

FIG. 5.15 Archaeological remains of the piers of the memorial churches at the John the Baptist Church Area (photo by Sherry Hardin).

mentions the chapel built on the ruins of the four piers (Mkhjian and Kanellopoulos 2003: 16–17).

Site of Saint Mary of Egypt

The site of Saint Mary of Egypt consists of the remains of two adjacent structures dating from the Byzantine and Ottoman periods. The site commemorates the former Egyptian prostitute's repentance and miraculous conversion at the Church of the Holy Sepulcher in Jerusalem in the fourth or fifth century. The story is told by Sophronius, the companion of John Moschus and later Patriarch of Jerusalem. According to Sophronius, the voice of the Virgin Mary told Mary of Egypt to cross the Jordan River in order to "find rest." She lived alone in this area east of the river for forty-seven years, fasting and praying. Before dying she was found by Zosima, a monk from a nearby monastery. Zosima prayed with her, listened to her story, and gave her Holy Communion shortly before she died. He buried her with the assistance of a lion.[3]

---

3   Lions and their friendly relations with monks of the Byzantine period appear frequently in John Moschus' tales.

FIG. 5.16 The Jordan River and the place on its east bank where baptisms are presently performed at Bethany Beyond the Jordan (photo by Sherry Hardin).

CONCLUSIONS

There appears to be little doubt that Wadi al-Kharrar can be associated with Prophet Elijah's ascension to heaven. It was at the eastern end of the wadi that believers placed his departure from earth by means of "a chariot of fire and horses of fire" as he "ascended in a whirlwind into heaven." The location fits well with the biblical narratives relating the crossing of the nearby Jordan by Joshua and the Israelites and the parting of the waters by both Elijah and his successor Elisha. This could also be the location of Wadi Cherith, to which Elijah fled from Ahab, and where he was fed by ravens in the morning and the evening.

John the Baptist and his connection to Elijah equally fit well in the region of Wadi al-Kharrar. Believers saw the promise of Elijah's return fulfilled in the coming of John. It was here, at "Bethany Beyond the Jordan," that John lived during the time of his ministry. Disciples, who were associated with his baptizing and preaching activities, would have been his companions. The place was convenient, since it was close to Bethabara, "the house of the crossing," one of the places where travelers would have crossed the Jordan on their way east or west.

And it was to "Bethany Beyond the Jordan" that Jesus came to be baptized by John. Believers, as archaeological investigations have shown, commemorated the place of Jesus' baptism by a series of churches and a monastery that, according to the Piacenza Pilgrim, contained two guest houses. Moreover, following John's death, Jesus retired to this area when the religious authorities in Jerusalem began to put pressure on him.

In conclusion, the biblical texts, early pilgrims' reports, the Madaba Mosaic Map, and recent archaeological work all agree in locating the place of the activity of John the Baptist and the baptism of Jesus east of the Jordan River at Bethany Beyond the Jordan.

SUGGESTIONS FOR GETTING TO AND AROUND THE SITE

To get to the site from Amman, take the Airport/Desert Highway south. South of the city, take the road to the right that says "Dead Sea." North of the Dead Sea, make a right turn at the Suwaymeh Intersection and follow the road to "Bethany Beyond the Jordan." The trip takes around 45 minutes by car.

Tour busses are permitted within certain areas of the site. They stop at various places to permit the pilgrims/tourists to walk along designated pathways to see the site's various features. Alternatively, those in private cars can park within the site and take a van, along with a guide, to visit the area. The tour begins with Elijah's Hill and continues on to the Jordan River Terrace. It lasts between 60–90 minutes.

It is possible to travel directly from "Bethany Beyond the Jordan" to Mount Nebo, Khirbat Mukhayyat, and Madaba. After leaving the baptism site, start back towards Amman. On the south side of the road at Ar-Ramah, you will see a sign that indicates Mount Nebo. The trip up through the hills should take less than one half hour. It was up through these hills that pilgrims in the Byzantine period would have traveled by foot, donkey, and/or mule on their way from Bethany Beyond the Jordan and Livias to Mount Nebo.

FIG. 6.1   The Brazen Serpent Sculpture at the Memorial of Moses on Mount Nebo
(photo by Sherry Hardin).

6 THE MEMORIAL OF MOSES
MOUNT NEBO

THE Bible associates a number of events with Mount Nebo and its immediate vicinity. These include the arrival of the Israelites in the region of Moab by the top of Pisgah (Numbers 21.20, 33.47), the Israelite encampment in the "plains of Moab" (Numbers 22.1, 33.48–49), the story of Balak and Balaam (Numbers 22–24), Moses' view of the land of Canaan, his death, and his burial (Deuteronomy 34.1–6), the dispute about the body of Moses between the archangel Michael and Satan (Jude 1.9), and the concealment of the tabernacle, the ark and the altar of incense in a cave (2 Maccabees 2.4–8). The main interest here, however, is in Mount Nebo as a place of Christian pilgrimage associated with Moses' view of the land of Canaan, his death, and his burial.

THE BIBLICAL TEXTS ON MOUNT NEBO AND MOSES

The Book of Numbers is concerned with events related to the wanderings of the Israelites from soon after their exodus from Egypt and the revelation of the LORD to Moses at Mount Sinai. Chapters 11–25 of the book tell of their travels as they make their way towards the borders of the land of Canaan. The passages in which we have an interest here deal with some of the places in the territory of the Moabites at which the Israelites stopped on their journey and specifically those related to Mount Nebo. In Numbers 21.20, the Israelites are approaching the area of Moses' view of the Promised Land and the place of his death and burial.

Numbers 21.20

> … and from Bamoth to the valley lying in the region of Moab by the top of Pisgah that overlooks the wasteland.

"The valley lying in the region of Moab" referred to in the text is associated with Pisgah. Thus, Wadi 'Uyun Musa, meaning literally "Springs of Moses," immediately north of the ridge on which Ras al-Siyagha (see below) is located, is probably the valley intended.

"The top of Pisgah" (see also Numbers 23.14; Deuteronomy 3.27, 34.1; see also "the slopes of Pisgah" in Deuteronomy 3.17, 4.49; Joshua 12.3, 13.20) is evidently a high point. Deuteronomy 34.1 indicates that Mount Nebo and "the top of Pisgah" are the same. On the basis of the texts, Pisgah can be located in that region of Moab which "overlooks the wasteland" opposite Jericho (Deuteronomy 34.1) and in a place that provides a view in all directions, including the Jordan and Gilead (Deuteronomy 3.27, 34.1). It slopes are said to be east of the Sea of the 'Arabah, that is, the Dead Sea (Deuteronomy 3.17, 4.49; Joshua 12.3). Thus, it must be a high hill or mountain east of Jericho and at the northern end of the Dead Sea, from which one can view the surrounding countryside without obstruction.

Ras al-Siyagha (elev. 710 m) and Al-Mukhayyat (elev. 790 m) to the southeast are two important peaks of the Mount Nebo ridge, which is bordered on the north by Wadi 'Uyun Musa. They provide a dramatic view of the southern segment of the Jordan Valley and the Dead Sea. Both Ras al-Siyagha and Mukhayyat are good candidates for the location of Pisgah, but the former is preferable, since the toponym Pisgah comes from the Hebrew *pasag*, which means "split/cut off" and Ras al-Siyagha has the appearance of being cut off or projecting from the plateau to the northwest of Madaba, especially when viewed from the east.

The choice of Ras al-Siyagha is in keeping with early Christian tradition. For it was on this peak that the early Christians chose to build their fourth-century church and monastery and their late sixth-century basilica as a memorial to Moses.

The Hebrew word *jeshimon* is used to designate a "desert" or "wasteland" in Deuteronomy 32.10 and Isaiah 43.19. In Numbers 21.20 and 23.28 the term may be translated either in this general sense or as a toponym. The passages in Deuteronomy and Isaiah suggest that the area or specific location must be visible from the top of Pisgah and the top of Peor, respectively, perhaps in the area northeast of the Dead Sea in what is designated as the "plains of Moab." The scant possibilities for agriculture in the area are well-described by the Hebrew word *jeshimon*.

Numbers 33.1–49 is another tradition dealing with the wilderness itineraries of the Israelites. The text probably describes an actual route widely known in ancient times. Like the previous one, it locates the Israelites in the area of Nebo and camping in the plains of Moab. From there, they make preparations to enter the land of Canaan.

Numbers 33.47–48

> They set out from Almon-diblathaim and camped in the mountains of Abarim, before Nebo. They set out from the mountains of Abarim and camped in the plains of Moab by the Jordan at Jericho.

As indicated, this text deals with the journey of the Israelites east of the Jordan on their way to the Promised Land. Some commentators understand "mountains of Abarim" as "the heights beyond" or "distant heights." Thus, the term is used as a vague and general expression for "the land over there." In Deuteronomy 32.49 (see below), the expression "mountain of the Abarim, Mount Nebo" appears to place "mountain of the Abarim" and "Mount Nebo" in apposition.

It is from the mountains of the Abarim that one can view the southern Jordan Valley, the northern end of the Dead Sea, the mountains to the north as far as as-Salt, and the eastern side of the Judean hills both north and south of Jerusalem. The mountains of the Abarim would be located on Mount Nebo, where the road passed from Dibon (modern Dhiban) in the south to the plains of Moab in the north.

The expression "plains of Moab" appears twelve times in the Bible. The plains extend from the northeastern side of the Dead Sea towards the north (see Appendix 1 – Plains of Moab).

Deuteronomy 32.48–52

> On that very day the LORD addressed Moses as follows: "Ascend this mountain of the Abarim, Mount Nebo, which is in the land of Moab, across from Jericho, and view the land of Canaan, which I am giving to the Israelites for a possession; you shall die there on the mountain that you ascend and shall be gathered to your kin, as your brother Aaron died on Mount Hor and was gathered to his kin; because both of you broke faith with me among the Israelites at the waters of Meribath-kadesh in the wilderness of Zin, by failing to maintain my holiness among the Israelites. Although you may view the land from a distance, you shall not enter it – the land that I am giving to the Israelites."

Deuteronomy 34.1, 4–6

> Then Moses went up from the plains of Moab to Mount Nebo, to
> the top of Pisgah, which is opposite Jericho, and the LORD showed
> him the whole land:…. The LORD said to him, "This is the land which
> I swore to Abraham, to Isaac, and to Jacob, saying, 'I will give it to
> your descendants;' I have let you see it with your eyes, but you shall
> not cross over there." Then Moses, the servant of the LORD, died
> there in the land of Moab, at the LORD's command. He was buried
> in a valley in the land of Moab, opposite Beth-peor, but no one
> knows his burial place to this day.

It was at the LORD's command that Moses died. However, no one knows
his place of burial. Was the death and burial of Moses a private matter
between God and Moses? Did the people not have a part in it?

While encamped in the plains of Moab, the Israelites began to
have sexual relations with the women of Moab and worshipped Baal,
the Canaanite god of storm and fertility, at the cult center of Peor[1]
(Numbers 25.1–3, 5). This place is probably the same one as the Beth-peor
of Deuteronomy 34.6, as well as Peor (Numbers 23.28, 25.28) and Baal-
peor (Hosea 9.10). The site is associated with the slopes of Pisgah (Ras al-
Siyagha). It was "in the valley opposite Beth-peor" (Deuteronomy 3.29)
that Moses provided the people with an historical review of events from
the time of their departure from Mount Sinai to their arrival "beyond the
Jordan in the land of Moab" (Deuteronomy 1.1–3.29). Moses' burial was
in a valley in the land of Moab, opposite Beth-peor. As indicated above,
that valley is probably Wadi 'Uyun Musa.

Jude 1.9

> But when the archangel Michael contended with the devil and dis-
> puted about the body of Moses, he did not dare to bring a con-
> demnation of slander against him, but said, "The Lord rebuke you!"

In the Jewish pseudepigraphical work *The Testament of Moses*, the devil
disputed with the archangel Michael for the body of Moses. The devil
accused Moses of killing the Egyptian (Exodus 2.11–12) and claimed that
for this reason Moses was undeserving of an honorable burial by Michael.
Michael did not dare rebuke the devil on his own authority. Instead, he
invoked God's authority as the only one who could judge the devil for
slander.

---

1   The toponym Peor means "opening"/"hole."

FIG. 6.2   View of the Dead Sea from Mount Nebo (photo by David Bjorgen, 2005).

2 Maccabees 2.4–8

> It was also in the same documents that the prophet, having received
> an oracle, ordered that the tent and the ark should follow with him,
> and that he went out to the mountain where Moses had gone up
> and had seen the inheritance of God. Jeremiah came and found a
> cave-dwelling, and he brought there the tent and the ark and the
> altar of incense, then he sealed up the entrance. Some of those who
> followed him came up intending to mark the way, but could not
> find it. When Jeremiah learned of it, he rebuked them and declared:
> "The place shall remain unknown until God gathers his people to-
> gether again and shows his mercy. Then the Lord will disclose these
> things, and the glory of the Lord and the cloud will appear, as they
> were shown in the case of Moses, and as Solomon asked that the
> place should be specially consecrated."

Solomon (reigned ca. 970/960–930/920 BC) brought the tent to Jerusalem
along with the Ark of the Covenant (1 Kings 8.4). There is no further
mention of the tent in the Old Testament. The Ark, however, was kept in
the first temple (built between the fourth and eleventh years of Solomon's
reign).

According to 2 Maccabees 2.4–8 Jeremiah hid the tent, the Ark, and
the altar of incense in a cave on Mount Nebo. Jeremiah's hiding of the

Ark is also taken up in the apocryphal book *Lives of the Prophets*. Also, according to Alexander Polyhistor (first century BC), Jeremiah concealed the Ark after the Babylonians destroyed the temple in 587/586 BC. In this biblical passage, however, Jeremiah hides the tent and the altar of incense along with the Ark and goes on to say that God will show himself when it is time to disclose the Ark's hiding place.

The whole story is improbable in light of Jeremiah 3.16, where it is indicated that after the return from Babylonian exile in 539 BC, the Ark of the Covenant of the LORD shall not come to mind, or be remembered, or missed – Jerusalem will replace the Ark as a symbol of the throne of the LORD.

EARLY JEWISH AND CHRISTIAN NON-BIBLICAL TEXTS ON MOUNT NEBO

Josephus, like the biblical texts, provides information on Moses' death. However, he does not explain why Moses was not permitted to enter the Promised Land. Moreover, he omits the information contained in Deuteronomy 34.1–4, namely, that God showed Moses the entire land of Israel from the top of Pisgah on Mount Nebo. He also does not include the line from Deuteronomy 34:6 about God burying Moses and no one knowing the place of his burial to this day.

Josephus

> Now as soon as they were come to the mountain called *Abarim* (which is a very high mountain, situated over against Jericho and one that affords, to such as are upon it, a prospect of the greatest part of the excellent land of Canaan), he dismissed the senate; and as he was going to embrace Eleazar and Joshua, and was still discoursing with them, a cloud stood over him on a sudden, and he disappeared in a certain valley, although he wrote in the holy books that he died, which was done out of fear, lest they should venture to say that, because of his extraordinary virtue, he went to God (*Antiquities* 4.8.48).

Eusebius and Jerome

Eusebius and Jerome, in the *Onomasticon* and *Book on the Sites and Names of Places of the Hebrews*, respectively, name both Bethphogor and Nabau. The latter is Mount Nebo, where Moses died; the former is Beth-peor, which is located across the valley in which Moses was buried:

Bethphogor (Josh 13.20). Across the Jordan, a city of the children of Reuben, near the mountains of Phogor, opposite Jericho, six miles from Livias (48); and **Bethfogor**. A city of the sons of Reuben across the Jordan beside Mount Fogor, opposite Jericho, six miles from Livias (49) (Taylor et al. 2003: 33).

Nabau [I] (Num 32.3). A mountain across the Jordan opposite Jericho in the land of Moab, where Moses died. It is pointed out even until today at the sixth milestone eastward of Esbos (136); and **Nabau [I]**. In Hebrew it is called Nebo, a mountain across the Jordan opposite Jericho in the land of Moab, where Moses died. Until today it is pointed out at the sixth milestone east of the city of Esbus (137) (Taylor et al. 2003: 75).

Egeria

Egeria provides a detailed account of her visit to Mount Nebo:

> Now we had to hurry to carry out our intention of reaching Mount Nebo. As we traveled along the local presbyter from Livias … asked us, "Would you like to see the water that flows from the rock, which Moses gave to the children of Israel when they were thirsty? You can if you have the energy to turn off the road at about the sixth milestone." At this we were eager to go. We turned off the road at once, the presbyter led the way, and we followed him. It is a place with a tiny church under a mountain – not Nebo, but another one not very far from Nebo but further in. A great many monks lived there, truly holy men of the kind known here as ascetics (*Travels* 10.8; Wilkinson 1999: 120).

> On reaching the mountain-top we came to a church, not a very big one, right on the summit of Mount Nebo, and inside, in the position of the pulpit, I saw a slightly raised place about the size of a normal tomb. I asked about it, and the holy men replied, "Holy Moses was buried here – by angels, since the Bible tells us 'No human being knoweth his burial.' And there is no doubt that it was angels who buried him, since the actual tomb where he was buried cannot be seen today. Our predecessors here pointed out this place to us, and now we point it out to you." They told us that this tradition came from their predecessors (*Travels* 12.1–2; Wilkinson 1999: 121).

Egeria's testimony takes us back to the hermitic origins of the monastic colony on Mount Nebo. She tells of a tiny church and many monks in what was probably Wadi ʿUyun Musa, and she visited a church on the summit of Mount Nebo and spoke about the place of Moses' burial there (See Appendix 2 – Livias/Tall ar-Ramah below).

John Rufus (ca. 500)

John Rufus provides information on Peter the Iberian's visits to Mount Nebo:

> On the following day we set off towards Medeba. When we were half way there we reached the holy Mountain of Moses called Abarim or Pisgah, which is where the Lord said to him, "Go up and die." A venerable and very lofty church is there, built in the name of the Prophet, and it is surrounded by a number of monasteries. We rejoiced that we had reached this place.
>
> As soon as we had prayed and performed our veneration, the venerable man [sc. Peter the Iberian] brought us into a small cell there, five cubits broad and five cubits long, and badly lit. "I remember," he told us, "How, when I was a young man, and had newly come from the Royal City, I came to visit this mountain and pray here…."
>
> Then we learned from the monks who were living on the mountain that the founders of the church were fully convinced that the body of the holy Moses had been laid in this place, and that the church had been built, and the altar and the sanctuary set up over it, and that beneath the sanctuary was a vessel of oil and ashes. Although the Divine Book says clearly that "Moses, the servant of God, died in the Land of Moab, according to the word of the Lord, and was buried in the land next to Beth Peor, and no one knows his tomb to this day," they explained to us that a shepherd of Nebo, a village located on the southern side of the mountain, was pasturing his flock, and had brought them as far as this place. When he arrived here he had a vision, and saw a very large cavern filled with brilliant light, and giving out a sweet odour. He was astonished, for never before had he seen such a thing here: but encouraged by strength from God he was brave enough to go down into the cavern. There he saw a venerable old man with a shining face, lying as if on a bed which was bright and flashing with glory and grace. He realized that it was holy Moses.
>
> The story goes on to say that the shepherd marked the spot of the cave's entrance, returned to his village and told of his vision. The

villagers returned to the marked spot but could not find the cave. Nevertheless, they believed the shepherd, and…

> The people living in that region hurried to bring there all the materials for a building, and a church was erected in the name of the great prophet and lawgiver…. It is a place of universal healing for souls and bodies, and a refuge for people from any parts who are afflicted in soul, or suffering any kind of pain (185–89; Wilkinson 2002: 99–100).

The first time Peter visited Mount Nebo, with his companion John the Eunuch, he did so as a pilgrim. On his second visit to the site, at the time when he came to Transjordan to bathe in the hot springs, Rufus attested to the presence of a sanctuary of Moses, "a venerable and very lofty church," surrounded by a number of monasteries. On this occasion, a large crowd of people from the surrounding area accompanied him and his friends (Horn 2006: 241–42).

What appears to have happened in the course of time is that although the Bible places the burial of Moses "in a valley in the land of Moab, opposite Beth-peor, but no one knows his burial place to this day" (Deut 34.6), Mount Nebo came to be seen as the place of Moses' burial. Thus, John Rufus follows Egeria in locating Moses' burial place on Mount Nebo.

The Piacenza Pilgrim (ca. 570) states:

> …. From the Jordan it is eight miles to the place where Moses departed from this life, and a little further on is Segor. There are many hermits in the neighbourhoods…. (v. 166; Wilkinson 2002: 136).

The Piacenza Pilgrim mentions the presence of many hermits in the area surrounding the place of Moses' death. He erroneously gives the distance from the Jordan River to Mount Nebo.

Master Thetmar (1217) writes:

> Then from afar I came to mount Abarim, which is very high and where Moses had died and was buried by the Lord. No human being could make out his place of burial. Around this mount, there is a valley terrifying and very deep, whose depth has terribly frightened me. The climb up and down the mount, I required a full day…. (Piccirillo 1998: 79).

FIG. 6.3   Aerial view of Mount Nebo (© David L Kennedy, APAAME, APA_2006-09-10_DLK-81).

The German traveler Master Thetmar was one of the last westerners to have reached Transjordan after the loss of the territory by the Crusaders. He climbed Mount Nebo and met there some Greek monks [with whom he spent the night?] (Piccirillo 1998: 217–18).

Pantaleào de Aveiro (1552)

The Portuguese Franciscan friar shows that there was still an interest in Mount Nebo in the 16th century. He comments:

> Having reached the other side, we started on our way to Mount Nebo, which we had in front of us, across the land of Moab which had fallen to Reuben's tribe lot. Around midday we reached the summit of the mountain, which lies between another two higher mountains: placing ourselves in the place where, more or less Moses was when he prayed and contemplated the Promised Land, as the Lord God had ordered to him which place is indicated by a church built there, very much destroyed, we could through the Lord's grace see the Promised land and contemplate it. We saw from there....
>
> I asked the abbot Caly about the whereabouts, in the area, of the church dedicated to Saint Moses, since I had heard our Father

Guardian in Jerusalem say that it had been built in the place where the body of the Holy Prophet was presumed buried: the abbot answered that he would have led us to it: descending the mountain we came to a valley lying between the mountain and another one close by, and there we saw an old church, in a much better state. We went in, prayed and recommended ourselves to the Lord, and to his servant Moses, considering ourselves very privileged to have seen that place.

.... The abbot Caly added that the people of old suspecting that that was the place, built that church dedicated to Saint Moses, that nobody might think of another burial place (Piccirillo 1998: 80).

What Pantaleào de Aveiro saw was a church on the summit of the mountain that was in ruins. However, he was able to visit a better preserved church located below in a valley. This church was believed to be situated where Moses had been buried.

THE MEMORIAL OF MOSES – THE ARCHAEOLOGY

The monastic presence at Mount Nebo extends from the second half of the fourth century to the ninth–tenth century. Egeria's account of such presence is the earliest and takes us back to the hermitic origins of the monastic colony on Mount Nebo and in the Valley of 'Uyun Musa ("Springs of Moses"), located immediately to the north of Ras al-Siyagha (fig. 6.3).

In the 19th century, early explorers visited and identified Ras al-Siyagha, 7 km to the northwest of Madaba (see Chapter 7), as the place where Moses viewed the Promised Land and then died. Archaeologists from the Studium Biblicum Franciscanum (SBF) began their excavations there in 1933. Their early work resulted in the discovery of the basilica and a large monastery that had grown up around the basilica in the Byzantine period. The SBF began the restoration of the basilica in 1963. Work at the site, now known as the "Memorial of Moses," continues (figs. 6.4–5).

On the basis of the SBF's archaeological research, the architectural history of the Memorial of Moses may be subdivided into nine main phases:
1. The pre-existing walls (4th century);
2. The *cella trichora* – a three-part structure ending at semicircles on the east, north and south sides (beginning of the 5th century);
3. The development of the monastery around the *cella trichora* (5th century);

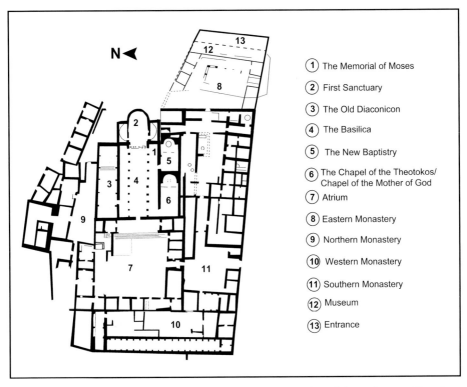

FIG. 6.4   Top plan of the Memorial of Moses at Mount Nebo (adapted from Alliata and Bianchi 1998).

4. The reconstruction of the *cella trichora* (mid-5th century);
5. The *diakonikon*-baptistery (530/31);
6. The basilica (mid-6th century);
7. The south baptistery and the north hall (end of the 6th century);
8. The Chapel of the *Theotokos* (beginning of the 7th century);
9. The final results (8th century).... (Alliata and Bianchi 1998: 151).

The first Christian building at Ras al-Siyagha consisted of the conversion of an older structure into a chapel in the fourth century. It was built as a memorial church in honor of Moses, an obvious effort to commemorate the events related in Deuteronomy 34.

A triapsidal church (a *cella trichora*) – a church with three apses – was built on the site at the beginning of the fifth century. It had semi-circles on the east, north and south sides, with a vestibule in front. Its mosaic floor covered tombs, and there were two funeral chapels, one on each side. At the same time the triapsidal church was built, a monastery adjacent to it was erected.

FIG. 6.5   The outside of the basilica on Mount Nebo (photo by David Bjorgen, 2005).

There are indications that a traumatic event occurred, resulting in the destruction of the first building (Alliata and Bianchi 1998: 162). Thus, the triapsidal church had to be reconstructed in the mid-fifth century. This work involved an open court in front of its sanctuary, which was bordered on the north by a covered passageway leading to the *diaconicon* (vestry/church service rooms) chapel that included a cruciform baptistery basin (fig. 6.6). The work of lavishly decorating the baptistery with a mosaic floor was completed in AD 531 and was carried out by a team of three mosaicists: Soelos, Daiomos, and Elias (fig. 6.7). It was made possible with offerings from officials of the Byzantine government.

FIG. 6.6   *Diaconicon* chapel with baptistery basin (photo by Sherry Hardin).

FIG. 6.7   Mosaic floor in the baptistery (photo by Sherry Hardin).

FIG. 6.8   Interior of the three-aisled basilica (photo by Sherry Hardin).

A three-aisled basilica was built during the second half of the sixth century as a memorial to Moses (fig. 6.8). As a result, the primitive church that both Egeria and Peter the Iberian had visited in the fourth and fifth centuries became its presbytery. The basilica had a long *diaconicon*, at a higher level, on its north side, and a new baptistery chapel on its south side. Its sanctuary was decorated with floor and wall mosaics. Mosaic inscriptions in the baptistery chapel of the basilica inform us that the first phase of the work was completed in AD 597/98.

At the beginning of the seventh century, the Chapel of the *Theotokos* ("the Mother of God") was added on the southern wall of the basilica. It covered two rooms of the monastery.

While the basilica was undergoing various stages of architectural development, the adjacent monastery gradually expanded, reaching its maximum size in the second half of the sixth century. The monastery, which was dominated by the memorial church of Moses, was composed of several interrelated sectors, including several rooms that opened into a central courtyard. The sectors consist of community rooms in the atrium (UTM coordinates: 0758154 E/3518119 N; elev. 711 m [taken in the courtyard to the west of the present basilica]) of the basilica and living quarters or cells to the south. The monastery was rebuilt along with the restructuring of the basilica at the end of the sixth century, when it was also enclosed

FIG. 6.9   Wadi 'Uyun Musa (photo by Sherry Hardin).

within a strong, rectangular boundary wall. It was completely abandoned in the ninth century.

The small modern monastery on the western slope of the mountain outside the Byzantine monastery is presently inhabited by the Franciscan Fathers. They are the ones who take care of the Memorial of Moses at Mount Nebo.

The monumental buildings uncovered by archaeologists at Ras al-Siyagha/Mount Nebo attest to the different forms of monastic life experienced on the mountain, ranging from the coenobitic life in the major monastery at Ras al-Siyagha to the more rigid ascetic lives as attested by the inscriptions brought to light in the small *Theotokos* monastery in the Wadi 'Ayn al-Kanisah to the south.

In 1984, archaeologists from the SBF began excavating two Byzantine churches among the vineyards in the Valley of 'Uyun Musa ("Springs of Moses;" fig. 6.9). They uncovered two churches: the Church of Kaianos, built and paved with mosaics at the beginning of the sixth century and rebuilt in the second half of the same century, and the Church of the Deacon Thomas, built and paved with mosaics possibly in the first half

FIG. 6.10 General topography of the plains of Moab (photo by Sherry Hardin).

of the sixth century. These churches would have been related to the traditional place of Moses' burial to the north of Mount Nebo. They date to around 100–150 years after Egeria's visit to the area, but neither church has any historical relationship to the one that Egeria visited in the fourth century. They do, nevertheless, testify to the occupation of the site of 'Uyun Musa in the sixth century.

Archaeological research conducted into the ecclesiastical buildings in the valleys around Mount Nebo has led the excavators to conclude that the main monastery on the top of the mountain also had jurisdiction over the monks living in the valleys near the water supply. It was in these valleys that the monastery probably had its orchards and vegetable gardens.

The SBF also excavated three churches, dating to the fifth and sixth centuries, and a monastery in the village of Nebo, Khirbat al-Mukhayyat, located to the southeast of Ras al-Siyagha. One of these churches, the Church of Saints Lot and Procopius, is of interest because of its dedication to Saint Lot, a nephew of Abraham. It will thus be considered in Chapter 10.

APPENDIX 1 – THE PLAINS OF MOAB

A number of biblical events take place in the "plains of Moab across the Jordan from Jericho" (Numbers 22.1). These plains are located south of

Wadi al-Kharrar – the "Site of the Baptism and Elijah's Ascension" (see Chapter 5) and northwest of Mount Nebo (above).

It is in the "plains of Moab" that the Israelites encamped (Numbers 22.1) before crossing the Jordan River into the land of Canaan (fig. 6.10). In this area Balak, king of Moab, called for Balaam, a soothsayer or foreteller, to come and curse the Israelites (Numbers 22.2–6). It is also here that the Israelites worshipped Baal-Peor (Numbers 25.2–3). Related to this last incident are the events at Shittim, where the Israelites began to have sexual relations with the women of Moab (Numbers 25). It was in the plains of Moab by the Jordan at Jericho that the LORD spoke to Moses (Numbers 35.1). From these plains Moses went up to Mount Nebo from where the LORD showed him the whole land, that is, the land west of the Jordan River (Deuteronomy 34.1). It was also from this area that the Israelites, led by Joshua (Joshua 1.1–2) following the death and burial of Moses (Deuteronomy 34.5–6), crossed the Jordan River and made their first encampment in Canaan at Gilgal (Joshua 3–4). The plains of Moab are also close by the place where Elijah parted the waters of the Jordan, crossed to the east side, and ascended into heaven. Following this, Elisha, who was the successor of Elijah and upon whom the spirit of Elijah rested, parted the waters of the Jordan again and crossed back to the western side (2 Kings 2.13). Finally, it was in this area that Jephthah from Gilead (see Chapter 4) seized the fords of the River Jordan during his battle against the people from Ephraim who were from west of the river (Judges 12.1–6).

The expression "plains of Moab" appears in the Bible twelve times. From the geographical information provided by these texts, it can be concluded that the plains are located "by the Jordan opposite Jericho" (Numbers 26.3, 63), "across the Jordan from Jericho" (Numbers 22.1), "by the Jordan at Jericho" (Numbers 31.12; 33.48, 50; 35.1; 36.13), and "beyond the Jordan east of Jericho" (Joshua 13.32). The "plains of Moab" thus include the area at the southern extremity of the Jordan Valley between the Jordan River and the mountains to the east. They extend from the northeastern side of the Dead Sea towards the north.

Josephus

Josephus only locates what appear to be the biblical "plains of Moab" as being opposite Jericho: "Now Moses, when he had brought his army to Jordan, pitched his camp in the great plain over against Jericho" (*Antiquities* 4.6.1; Whiston 1987: 108).

Eusebius and Jerome

Both Eusebius and Jerome provide information on the location of the "plains of Moab," which they place on the way from Livias (see below, Appendix 2) to Esbus/Heshbon. While the vast majority of Moabite territory (MacDonald 2000: 171–74) is located in the highlands of the Transjordanian plateau, the "plains of Moab" are located in "Low or Level Moab:"

> **Araboth Moab** (26:3), where the people were numbered a second time. A.: Level ground of Moab, S.: the Plain of Moab, which is beside the Jordan at Jericho. It is a place pointed out even until today near Mount Fogor, which lies opposite Jericho on the way from Libias to Esbos (12); and **Araboth Moab** where the people were numbered for the second time, which Aquila interprets as Low or Level Moab, a customary expression for the desert plateau, *homalen*, which is translated level or flat. Lastly, Symmachus translated Araboth Moab as the Plains of Moab. Even until today there is a place near Mount Fogor, on the way from Livias to Esbus in Arabia opposite Jericho which is so called (13) (Taylor et al. 2003: 16)

Mount Fogor or Phogor is Bethphogor (Taylor et al. 2003: 93), or the Mount Peor, Peor, or Beth-peor of the NRSV.

Egeria

The main road from Jericho on the west of the Jordan River to Esbus/Hesbon on the plateau to the east would have passed through the "plains of Moab." Thus, on her way to Mount Nebo, Egeria visited the area and commented on its biblical importance:

> It is a vast plain stretching from the foot of the Arabim mountains to the Jordan, where the Bible says that "the children of Israel wept for Moses in Araboth Moab at Jordan over against Jericho forty days." It is where Joshua the son of Nun "was filled with the spirit of wisdom" when Moses died, "for Moses had laid his hands upon him," as it is written. It is where Moses wrote the Book of Deuteronomy, and where he "spoke the words of this song until they were finished, in the ears of all the assembly of Israel," the song written in the Book of Deuteronomy. And it is where holy Moses the man of God blessed each of the children of Israel in order before his death. When we reached this plain, we went on to the very spot, and there we had

FIG. 6.11   Tall ar-Ramah in the plains of Moab (photo by Sherry Hardin).

a prayer, and from Deuteronomy we read not only the song, but also the blessing he pronounced over the children of Israel. At the end of the reading we had another prayer, and set off again, with thanksgiving to God (*Travels* 10.4–7; Wilkinson 1999: 119–20).

APPENDIX 2 – LIVIAS / TALL AR-RAMAH

In the *Onomasticon*, Eusebius identified Betharam with Livias, a city "near the Jordan" (48; Taylor et al. 2003: 33). Jerome, in the *Book on the Sites and Names of Places of the Hebrews*, adds that Herod, that is, Antipas (reigned 4 BC–AD 39) changed the name of the place to Livias in honor of the wife of the Emperor Augustus (49; Taylor et al. 2003: 33; see also Josephus, *Antiquities* 18.2.1). The site is now generally identified with Tall ar-Ramah (fig. 6.11; UTM coordinates: 0750394 E/3524325 N; elev. -221 m) and appears on the Madaba Mosaic Map as "Bethramphtha, now Livias" (Alliata 1999: 51, 54). It was on the main road that led from Jericho across the Jordan and on to Esbus/Heshbon, where it would have met the *Via Nova Traiana* ("Trajan's New Road"), which connected Bostra in southern Syria to al-'Aqaba on the Red Sea. Its religious significance derived from its position in the "plains of Moab," where Moses bade the children of Israel farewell before his death (Numbers 33.48–50, 36.13; Deuteronomy

1–33). It also became identified as the place where Moses struck the rock, and sweet water with curative properties came forth (see below).

Egeria states:

> …. After crossing the river we came to the city of Livias, in the plain where the children of Israel encamped in those days. The foundations of the camp and the dwellings of the Israelites are still to be seen there today (*Travels* 10.4; Wilkinson 1999: 119).

Peter the Iberian

> It was to the hot springs of Livias that Peter the Iberian came as an old man in ca. AD 481 to seek a cure from his illness(es). However, Peter found the springs too cold and found no cure there. It was also on this occasion that he visited Mount Nebo for a second time and then went on to Madaba and the hot springs at Ba'ar/Baaru (Hammamat Ma'in), along the northeastern shore of the Dead Sea (Horn 2006: 241; see Chapter 9, Appendix).

Theodosius (ca. 518)

Theodosius does not seem to have visited Mount Nebo but only came as far east as Livias at the foot of the mountain in the Jordan Valley, just to the northeast of the Dead Sea. He states:

> The city of Livias is across the Jordan, twelve miles from Jericho. This Livias is where Moses struck the rock with his staff, and the water flowed, and from that place flows a large stream which waters the whole of Livias. Livias contains the large Nicolaitan date-palm. There too Moses passed away from this world, and there also are some hot spring in which Moses washed. Lepers are healed in them (Wilkinson 2002: 111–12).

The Piacenza Pilgrim (ca. 570)

The Piacenza Pilgrim testifies to the hot springs called the Baths of Moses at Livias. He also relates that occasionally lepers receive a cure there:

> Nearby is a city called Livias, where the two half-tribes of Israel remained before crossing the Jordan, and in that place are natural hot springs which are called the Baths of Moses. In these also lepers are cleansed. A spring there has very sweet water which they drink as a

cathartic, and it heals many diseases. This is not far from the Salt Sea, into which the Jordan flows, below Sodom and Gomorrah. Sulphur and pitch are collected on that shore. Lepers lie in the sea there all through the day in July, August, and the early part of September. In the evening they wash in these Baths of Moses. From time to time by the will of God one of them is cleansed, but for most of them it brings some relief (Wilkinson 2002: 135–36).

SUGGESTIONS FOR GETTING TO THE SITES

To get to Mount Nebo from Amman take the Airport/Desert Highway south. After about 20 km, follow the signs west to Madaba. The town is about 45 minutes from Amman. At the entrance to Madaba, follow the signs for Mount Nebo, which is about ten minutes to the northwest.

After your visit to Mount Nebo, you may wish to visit Khirbat al-Mukhayyat (see Chapter 10, Appendix 2). It is to the south of the road leading from Madaba to Mount Nebo. The two places can be easily visited in a half-day.

Both the plains of Moab and Livias (Tall ar-Ramah) are in the Jordan Valley and along the road that leads to the Site of the Baptism/Bethany Beyond the Jordan (see Chapter 5). They may be seen at the same time as a visit to the latter site. To get to the area, take the Dead Sea Highway. Both the plains of Moab and Livias are located just off the highway before coming to the Suwaymeh Intersection (where you may turn northwest to visit the Site of the Baptism). They are both located about 45 minutes from Amman.

FIG. 7.1   The Church of Saint George in Madaba (photo by Jonathan Ferguson).

7 CITY OF CHURCHES AND MOSAICS

MADABA

Due to the discoveries of the past century and a half, Madaba is often referred to as both the "City of Churches" and the "City of Mosaics." Out of all Madaba's churches and mosaics, the most well-known is the Church of Saint George in which the sixth–seventh century Madaba Mosaic Map is housed (see Chapter 2 and below). It was the discovery and publication of this map in the late 19th century that turned the attention of scholars to the town of Madaba. However, the map is only one of the many ecclesiastical and other ancient attractions of this Roman and Byzantine town.

The toponym Madaba does not appear in the New Testament. Neither is it the known burial place nor home town of any biblical person. Why then is it important as a place of pilgrimage and as a city of churches and mosaics?

One answer may be Madaba's association with the person of Moses, who is intimately connected to Jesus (see especially the Gospel according to Matthew and the Epistle to the Hebrews 3) and to the area. As Moses was the leader of God's people in the Old Testament/Hebrew Scriptures, the New Testament attributes this role to Jesus. Following the death of Aaron at Jabal Haroun (see Chapter 11), Moses led the Israelites to the region of Madaba, where he died and was buried in a nearby valley (see Chapter 6). Both sites are just to the west of Madaba. Later, the Madaba area became associated with the Israelite tribes of half-Manasseh, Reuben and Gad. In addition, it was the northern segment of the holdings of the biblical Moabites. Thus, the Madaba area is one of the richest in biblical associations of all the regions of Transjordan (Shahid 1998).

As mentioned in Chapter 2, the Holy City of Jerusalem is placed at the center of the Madaba Mosaic Map. The principal building within the city is that of the Holy Sepulchre, constructed on the Rock of Calvary, thought of as being the center of the world, but above all, as the place where the most dramatic actions in the history of salvation took place. Thus, by way of the Madaba Mosaic Map, the city of Madaba is connected intimately to both Jerusalem and Jesus.

MADABA IN THE BIBLE AND OTHER EARLY TEXTS

Madaba appears for the first time in the Bible in the "taunt song against Heshbon" (Numbers 21.27–30). It is frequently associated with the *Mishor*, that is, the "tableland" or "flat country," which is generally recognized as the plain area between Heshbon (ancient Esbus) in the north, the Arnon (Wadi al-Mujib) in the south, the Dead Sea escarpment in the west, and the desert in the east. For example, "all the tableland from Madaba" is part of the allotment Moses gave to the half-tribe of Manasseh, the Reubenites, and the Gadites (Joshua 13.8–9). It was in the area of Madaba that the battle between King David's army and a coalition of the Ammonites and Arameans is said to have taken place (1 Chronicles 19.7–9).

The Mesha Inscription (a ninth-century Moabite record) credits King Omri of Israel with taking possession of Madaba (cf. 2 Kings 3.4–5). According to the inscription, the Moabite King Mesha retook Madaba and its surrounding land from the Israelites. Shortly afterward, Madaba, one of the cities of Moab, appears in a curse of Isaiah 15.2, where its future destruction is foretold: "Up goes daughter Dibon to the high places to weep; over Nebo and Madaba Moab wails. Every head is shaved, every beard shaved off."

Josephus mentions Madaba frequently. He repeats the 1 Maccabees 9.35–42 narrative about the conflict between the Maccabees and the Jambri family of Madaba that took place ca. 160 BC after the ambush of a Jewish caravan (*Antiquities* 13.1.2 and 4) in the neighborhood of Madaba. The leader of the Jewish Hasmoneans (an autonomous Jewish state in ancient Israel from 140–37 BC) captured the town in 129/128 BC (*Antiquities* 13.9.1). The Hasmoneans in time turned over the town to the Nabataeans, who are generally associated with the south of Jordan, especially Petra, and the Negev from the third century BC to the second century AD, in return for their support. It appears that Madaba remained under the influence of the Nabataeans until the Roman emperor Trajan (reigned AD 98–117) incorporated the region into the Roman Province of Arabia in AD 106.

Eusebius, *Onomasticon*, and Jerome, *Book on the Sites and Names of the Places of the Hebrews*, assign Madaba to the Roman Province of Arabia and place it near Heshbon:

> Meddaba (Josh. 13.9). Even now there is a city of Medaba in Arabia called this, near Esebon (128); and **Medaba**. Up to today, a city of Arabia which keeps its ancient name, near Esebon (129) (Taylor et al. 2003: 72).

MADABA AND CHRISTIANITY

Christianity gained a foothold in the region of Madaba during the Late Roman–Early Byzantine period. Evidence for this comes from Egeria's visit to Christian monks at Mount Nebo and nearby Wadi 'Uyun Musa at the end of the fourth century AD. Archaeological excavations have confirmed Egeria's account of such monastic presence (see Chapter 6). Madaba was the seat of a bishop from at least the mid-fifth century onwards. A bishop from the town is listed as attending the Council of Chalcedon (AD 451).

Inscriptions from Madaba, Mount Nebo (see Chapter 6), and Kastron Mefaa (Umm ar-Rasas; see Chapter 8) are important sources of historical information on the region from the first decades of the sixth through the eighth centuries AD. Specifically, inscriptions in the various churches of Madaba provide information on the bishops and other ecclesiastical leaders of the town. For example, it is from such inscriptions that we know that Bishop Sergius I of Madaba, who was bishop from AD 576–595/596, was also the church leader for Mount Nebo and Kastron Mefaa. These inscriptions also indicate the level of building activity during Bishop Sergius' episcopate and provide the dates for when the various churches in the region were built and the mosaics within them laid down. In addition, other inscriptions provide evidence for some of the work, especially the building of churches, carried out on behalf of other ecclesiastical leaders.

The remnants of the churches and their mosaics as well as archaeological remains from non-ecclesiastical structures, such as palaces of the Byzantine and Umayyad periods, bear witness to the artistic grandeur of the city during the Late Byzantine period. As the inscriptions from the churches of Umm ar-Rasas/Kastron Mefaa indicate, this flourishing of artistic output continued well into the eighth century.

The mosaic in the Church of the Virgin (see below) in the center of Madaba was repaved in AD 767. This is the last date that is available for the Christian community and for the city. There is little archaeological evidence for Madaba's occupation from then until the modern settlement in 1880, when a group of Christians from Karak in the south of Jordan settled in its ruins.

Peter the Iberian's Visit to Madaba

Peter visited Madaba ca. AD 481. According to John Rufus, his biographer, Peter's prayers there resulted in the dried-up land of the region receiving rain, ending a lengthy period of drought. The people of Madaba responded to Peter:

> … we are calling him [that is, Peter] a second Elijah and Moses, the former, on the one hand, as one who at the time of lack of rain opened the heaven[s] after three years (see 1 Kings 18), the latter, on the other hand, as one who brought forth water from solid rock for those who were in danger from thirst (see Exodus 17:1–7) (*Vita Petri Iberi* 90; Horn 2006: 242).

Rufus depicts Peter as a holy man whose prayers opened the gates of heaven and let rain pour down.

THE CHURCHES AND MOSAICS OF MADABA

The modern city of Madaba covers its ancient remains to a large degree. However, remnants of its earliest settlement are preserved in the form of a low-lying mound and an acropolis that is visible in the town's center. Archaeological work in this area has uncovered architectural remains from the end of the fourth as well as from the first millennium BC. In addition, two tombs in the necropolis area to the west date to the 13th century BC while another, from the Iron I–Early Iron II period, was found on the slopes of the hill to the south of the acropolis area. Settlement of Madaba and its surrounding area intensified during the Iron II period. During this time the town was probably within the Moabite sphere of influence. As indicated above, the Bible and Josephus provide information on the town during the Hellenistic period. Nabataean and Roman remains are present in the form of inscriptions and coins minted at the end of the second and the beginning of the third century AD. During this time, as both Eusebius and Jerome indicate, Madaba was a part of the Roman province of Arabia. The main east–west colonnaded street (*decumanus maximus*; see Chapter 3, note 5) with its flanking public structures, including a temple on which the Church of the Virgin Mary (see

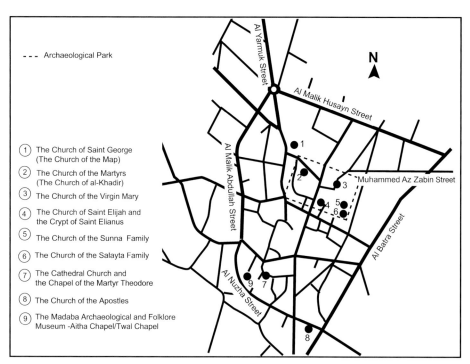

FIG. 7.2   Map of Madaba city center and the location of the churches (adapted from plan provided by Ministry of Tourism and Antiquities of Jordan).

below) was erected, dates to the Roman period. A section of the street is preserved in the Madaba Archaeological Park. However, the majority of the ancient structures excavated to date in the city date to the Byzantine and Umayyad periods. It is these architectural features that are of principal interest here.

Over the past century and a half a large number of churches and chapels have been documented within the town of Madaba (fig. 7.2). The following paragraphs describe the most important ones. The Church of Saint George, located in the center of the town, is commented on first, followed by other churches and chapels between it and the Church of the Apostles on Madaba's southern outskirts.

Church of Saint George

The Church of Saint George (figs. 7.1 and 7.3; UTM coordinates: 0764782 E/3512706 N; elev. 804 m) is the present-day Greek Orthodox Church of the town of Madaba and houses the famous Madaba Mosaic Map (see Chapter 2). The modern church itself dates to 1896 but was

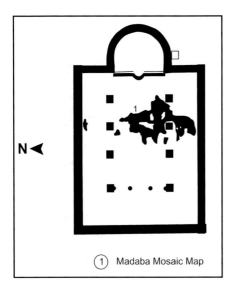

① Madaba Mosaic Map

FIG. 7.3   Ground plan of the Church of Saint George.

built over the remains of a Byzantine church from the sixth century. The mosaic map (see figs. 2.8–9), which now forms part of the floor of the Church of Saint George, is dated to the last decades of the sixth and the first decade of the seventh century AD. The early church continued in use beyond the iconoclastic period (Schick 1995: 394). Because of the map, the Church of Saint George is the one that most modern-day pilgrims and tourists visit.[1]

Church of the Martyrs / Church of al-Khadir

The Church of the Martyrs (fig. 7.4; UTM coordinates: 0764865 E/3512575 N; elev. 780 m [from extreme NW corner of the structure]) is known by the local Christians of Madaba as the Church of al-Khadir. It is now within the Madaba Archaeological Park,

FIG. 7.4   The Church of the Martyrs/Church of al-Khadir (photo by Bethany J. Walker).

1   Visitors may view it except during the times when religious services are in progress.

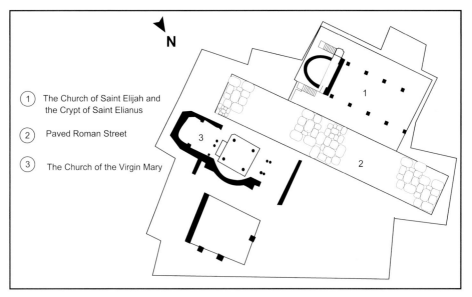

FIG. 7.5   Plan of the Archaeological Park of Madaba (adapted from plan provided by Ministry of Tourism and Antiquities of Jordan).

established in 1995 and located to the southeast of the Church of Saint George (fig. 7.5).

The church, which the German Evangelical Institute excavated in 1966, measures 32.15 × 16.10 m and consists of one apse, a nave and two aisles, three doors, and a narthex (porch). It dates to the sixth century. Although iconoclasts have damaged its mosaic floor, it is still largely legible: the central section of the mosaic consists of scenes of hunting, fowling, wine-making, and herding among rows of trees laden with fruit.

Church of the Virgin Mary

The Church of the Virgin Mary (fig. 7.6; UTM coordinates: 0764931E /3512540N; elev. 790 m) is also now located within the Madaba Archaeological Park. It is built above a Roman period temple. The church has a round nave, a vestibule, and an elongated presbytery to the east. A pulpit was located in the southeast corner of its nave. This church has the privilege of being the first church in Madaba the mosaic floor of which became known to scholars. Inscriptions on this floor identify it as the Church of the Virgin Mary. The church dates to the end of the sixth and the beginning of the seventh century, probably ca. AD 608, around the same time as the neighboring Church of Saint Elijah. Its inscriptions,

FIG. 7.6   Interior of the Church of the Virgin Mary (photo by Sherry Hardin).

however, are much later. An inscription in a round medallion within the church reads:

> If you want to look at Mary, virginal Mother of God, and to Christ whom she generated, Universal King, only Son of the only God, purify [your] mind, flesh and works! May you purify with [your] prayer the people of God.

The dedicatory inscription (fig. 7.7) in front of the church's chancel reads:

> At the time of our most pious father, Bishop Theophane, this most beautiful mosaic work was realized in the glorious and venerable house of the Holy and Immaculate Queen (Mary) Mother of God. Thanks to the zeal and ardor of the people who love Christ in this city of Madaba, for the salvation, and assistance, and remission of sins of those who have made offerings, and of those who will make offerings, to this holy place. Amen, O Lord. Finished by the grace of God in the month of February in the year 6274, of the fifth indiction.

The first line gives the name of Bishop Theophane. This ecclesiastical leader of Madaba was unknown until the discovery of the mosaic.

There is no general agreement regarding the dating of this inscription. The year given is either 6074 or 6274, that is, from the creation of

FIG. 7.7   Dedicatory inscription in the Church of the Virgin Mary (photo by Sherry Hardin).

the world.[2] This dating system is attested in Palestinian literature in the sixth and seventh centuries; it is also occasionally used in inscriptions. Di Segni chooses to read 6274; reckoning by the Byzantine creation era, this corresponds to AD 766/767 (Di Segni 1992: 256) and thus to the beginning of the Abbasid period.

A third inscription at the entrance of the church's nave reads: "Holy Mary, help Menas (your) servant." Menas was probably a benefactor of the church and the same person as the one mentioned in one of the inscriptions in the Church of Saint Elijah (see below).

Church of Saint Elijah and the Crypt of Saint Elianus

The Church of Saint Elijah (UTM coordinates: 0764922 E/3512529 N; elev. 786 m) and the Crypt of Saint Elianus (fig. 7.8) are located across the Roman street and to the west of the Church of the Virgin Mary. They are also within the Madaba Archaeological Park. Although the Church of Saint Elijah was largely destroyed by the time of its discovery, excavations, which archaeologists from the Studium Biblicum Franciscanum com-

---

2   The Byzantine Creation Era was the calendar used by the Byzantine Empire and the Eastern Orthodox Church. The Creation Era was derived from the Septuagint, the Greek version of the Hebrew Scriptures/Old Testament. It placed the date of creation at 5,508 years before the birth of Christ. The era was calculated as starting on September 1 and Jesus was thought to have been born in the year 5,509 *Annus Mundi* (AM). A somewhat similar dating system is found in Judaism. For example, Tuesday, September 30, 2008, marks the beginning of the Jewish year 5,769. The Jewish calendar is now used for predominantly religious purposes. The choice of reading the date as 6274 rather than 6074 suggests that the hundred digit was left out by mistake.

pleted in the summer of 1994, have uncovered both sections of mosaic pavement and inscriptions.

The mosaic, which formed the floor of the Church of Saint Elijah, is well preserved in places. It contains three inscriptions. The damaged dedicatory inscription within the nave of the church and near the step leading to the presbytery, reads:

> Placed beyond the corruption which has overtaken all human nature, he who has brought back the people of Israel to the only truth, the prophet Elijah … with zeal, in cooperation with prayer, has also built this beautiful temple … of Leontius, the most sweet priest, true friend of peace, who has succeeded to the labors of Sergius, the friend of God and the caretaker who had gathered some gifts. Menas, [son of] Pamphilus, and Theodose, *Aigiarian* brothers, have become benefactors to them and to this humble city. Completed in the year 502, of the 11th indiction (Piccirillo 1992: 124).

The church, which is dedicated to the prophet Elijah, was completed in the time of Bishop Leontius, a successor of Bishop Sergius of Madaba (see Chapter 8). It is dated to AD 607/608.[3]

The second inscription is a prayer to the prophet Elijah. It accompanies a medallion, once decorated with a peacock, in the center of the nave and reads:

> You who with your prayer set in motion, as is fitting, the clouds, bearers of rain, and who give mercy to the people, O prophet, remember also the benefactors and this humble city (Piccirillo 1992: 124).

This inscription commemorates the prophet Elijah who ended the drought in Israel (see 1 Kings 18.41–45 and Chapter 4). It also petitions the prophet to remember the benefactors, probably those mentioned in the dedicatory inscription, and the city of Madaba.

Finally, another inscription, located at the entrance to the nave of the church, is based on the Greek version of the Old Testament/Hebrew Scriptures Psalm 65.5–6, "Holy is your temple, marvelous in sanctity."

---

3   See Chapter 3, note 9, for the dating of churches in the north of Jordan, for example, at Gerasa/Jerash. In the south, the dating system is different. Above (note 2), one of the differences relative to the dating of the Church of the Virgin Mary is indicated. Another dating system used in inscriptions from Madaba and other sites farther to the south, e.g., Umm ar-Rasas, takes March 22, AD 106, as its starting point. It was at this time that the southern area of Jordan became part of the Roman province of Arabia, was assigned a governor and compelled to obey the laws of Trajan. As a result, the conversion rule to be followed is that "for dates between 22 March and 31 December we add 105…. For those between 1 January and 21 March we add 106" (Meimaris 1992: 148).

The church is a duplicate of the one in which the Madaba Mosaic Map formed the original floor. It probably went out of use before the iconoclastic period (Schick 1995: 394).

The Crypt of Saint Elianus is located beneath the Church of Saint Elijah and was connected to the latter by two stairways. The crypt consists of a single apse with niches to the east, north, and south. The dedicatory inscription in the crypt's nave reads:

> The Christ God has erected this house at the time of the most pious Bishop Sergius for the care of Sergius, the priest of Saint Elianus, the year 490 … was paved with mosaics with the offerings of ….

FIG. 7.8   The Crypt of Saint Elianus (photo by Sherry Hardin).

The inscription informs us that the crypt church was built in Saint Elianus' honor during the time of Bishop Sergius (see Chapter 8), a predecessor of Bishop Leontius. It was built in AD 595/596. A small room off the south wall of the crypt's nave also has a mosaic floor.

Church of the Sunna' Family

The so-called Church of the Sunna' Family (UTM coordinates: 0764972 E/3512477 N; elev. 790 m) is located about 50 m to the east of the Church of the Prophet Elijah and on the same side of the paved Roman street. Its original name has not been preserved. Although the church was known prior to 1993, the Studium Biblicum Franciscanum carried out new investigations within it at the time that the Madaba Archaeological Park was being established. Specifically, the remains of its mosaic floor were re-cleaned, photographed, and restored.

The church measures 29 × 16 meters. It has three aisles, a central apse, and a *synthronon* – a row of built seats, frequently stepped, on which the clergy sat in the sanctuary of a Christian church. Its presbytery, which is flanked by two side rooms, extends out into the nave as far as the second row of columns.

The church was paved with mosaics of fine quality that suffered iconoclastic damage. It was probably still in use during the iconoclastic period (Schick 1995: 395). It is presently closed to visitors.

Piccirillo dates the church to the first half of the sixth century. He bases his dating chiefly on stylistic affinities with other dated mosaics nearby (Piccirillo 1993a).

Church of the Salayta Family

The Church of the Salayta Family is located to the south of the Church of the Sunnaʿ Family. By the time it was excavated in 1972 most of its mosaic pavement had been destroyed, some of it by iconoclasts (Piccirillo 1992: 132). Parts of the remaining mosaics have been removed, the church has been completely reburied, and the area where it is located is now an empty lot. The history of the church is unknown (Schick 1995: 396).

Cathedral Church

The Cathedral Church (UTM coordinates: 0764743 E/3512275 N; elev. 798 m) was named after its size. Its remains are located on a plateau on the southern slope of the ancient city's acropolis, partially beneath modern houses. Although the church's western and eastern ends have been excavated, it is still a promising venture for future excavation. At present, the area where the church is located is enclosed by a cement wall. It is thus closed to visitors.

Chapel of the Martyr Theodore

The Chapel of the Martyr Theodore was built on the southern side of the Cathedral Church's western sector in AD 562, during the time when John was bishop of the diocese of Madaba. It was constructed while work continued on the cathedral. It measures 16.35 x 5.1 m and its entrance, in the north wall, opened onto the central courtyard of the cathedral. A mosaic in the central nave of the chapel displays the earth being watered by the Rivers of Paradise – Pishon, Gihon, Tigris, and Euphrates (Genesis 2.10–14).

Two other chapels, a Baptistery Chapel and a Lower Baptistery Chapel, are also associated with the Cathedral Church. The Baptistery Chapel is a rectangular hall with a traditionally oriented apse. A cruciform baptismal font is located in the hollow of the apse. The Lower Baptistery Chapel is a long and narrow room measuring 5.8 (up to the font) × 1.8 m wide. Its circular baptismal font is ca. 80 cm in diameter and nearly 1 m deep. Neither can be visited.

Church of the Holy Fathers

The Church of the Holy Fathers (UTM coordinates: 0764627 E / 3512261 N; elev. 777 m) is presently located within the Madaba Archaeological and Folklore Museum on the southern slope of the ancient town's acropolis. However, it is not *in situ*. Originally located outside the village of Khattabiyah to the north of Madaba, the church was moved from its original place to a former government Rest House in Madaba and then to the museum. It is a single-apsed church with a nave paved with mosaics. A partially damaged Greek inscription within a medallion of the mosaic reads: "Tomb of the holy fathers, Eustratius, Magnus and of the others who here repose" (Piccirillo 1992: 244).

FIG. 7.9   Aitha Chapel: Mosaic of the upper level (photo by Sherry Hardin).

FIG. 7.10   Aitha Chapel: Inscription (photo by Sherry Hardin).

Aitha Chapel / Twal Chapel

The Aitha Chapel/Twal Chapel is also located within the Madaba Archaeological and Folklore Museum; this building is *in situ*. It has a mosaic pavement, dated to the sixth century, which was the floor of a family chapel divided into two areas by a chancel screen. The areas are at different levels: the raised presbyterium is square, measuring 4 m on one side. It shows a grid of leaves with a central medallion of a lamb nibbling at a tree (fig. 7.9). There is a damaged inscription at the step. The tentative reading is, "With the offering [of] your [servant] Aitha, this holy

FIG. 7.11   Aitha Chapel: Mosaic of the lower level (photo by Sherry Hardin).

place was paved with mosaics" (Piccirillo 1992: 128; fig. 7.10). The mosaic of the second, or lower, level of the chapel has a geometric design featuring several different birds, one of which is in a cage (fig. 7.11).

Church of the Apostles

The Church of the Apostles (UTM coordinates: 0764915 E/3512059 N; elev. 765 m) is located on the south side of Madaba, a few meters to the north of the King's Highway (Numbers 20.17; 21.22). The church is a basilica, measuring 23.5 × ca. 15.3 m, with a nave and two aisles. Three doors in the facade open onto a narthex with mosaics (fig. 7.12).

A beautiful mosaic in the center of the church's nave shows a woman as *Thalassa,* a personification of the sea. The woman is surrounded by sea creatures. An inscription in the central medallion of its mosaic floor dates the church to AD 578, during the time of Bishop Sergius I of Madaba. It reads:

> O Lord God who has made the heavens and the earth, give life
> to Anastasius, to Thomas, to Theodore and to Salamanios, the
> mosaicist.

FIG. 7.12 Church of the Apostles (photo by Sherry Hardin).

The signing of the mosaic by the craftsman is highly unusual!

The body of the church's sanctuary is well preserved and it contains one of the best dated and signed decorative programs of sixth-century Madaba. Two doors in the north wall of the church lead to two chapels that also contain mosaics. One of the chapels has a mosaic floor depicting stags, sheep, and gazelles between pomegranate and apple trees. In the second chapel, one mosaic is divided by four fruit trees in a diagonal design, with pairs of animals in between. A second mosaic in the same chapel shows three pairs of animals and an inscription that reads:

> O Lord, accept the offering of those who have offered and will offer
> to the temple of Holy Apostles [built] in memory of the priest John
> for the zeal of the deacon Anastasius.

It is from this inscription that the church gets its name.

Prior to the construction of the church, a small chapel was built on the spot during the time of Bishop John of Madaba, ca. AD 562. The Church of the Apostles was later added to it.

Church of Saint John the Baptist

The Church of Saint John the Baptist (UTM coordinates: 0764747 E/3512402 N; elev. 800 m) is the modern Roman Catholic Church of Madaba. The church's designation is in keeping with the closeness of Madaba to Machaerus/Mukawer (see Chapter 9).

SUGGESTIONS FOR GETTING TO AND AROUND MADABA

To get to Madaba from Amman take the Airport/Desert Highway south. After about 20 km, follow the signs west to Madaba. The town is about 45 minutes from Amman.

The Church of Saint George is located in the center of the town. You may wish to start your visit there and then go on to The Madaba Archaeological Park. You may wish to end your visit at the Church of the Apostles. A ticket to the park is also good for entrance to The Madaba Archaeological and Folklore Museum and the Church of the Apostles.

The churches and mosaics of Madaba can be visited in a half day. Sundays and Greek Orthodox holy days are not the best days for visiting the Church of Saint George.

8 SAINT STEPHEN – DEACON AND FIRST CHRISTIAN MARTYR

UMM AR-RASAS

THE site of Umm ar-Rasas, designated a UNESCO World Heritage Cultural Site in 2004, is located on the edge of the desert 30 km southeast of Madaba. It is extensive and well preserved and consists of a rectangular fortified camp, measuring 158 × 139 m, and an open quarter, of about the same size, located outside the fort to the north. The entire site thus covers an area of around three hectares, or seven and a half acres. In addition, two towers are located to the north of Umm ar-Rasas, at a distance of ca. 1.5 kilometers (fig. 8.1). One, measuring 14 m high, is surrounded by ruined buildings, including a church. The other, square in shape and not as high, is near rock-hewn pools.

To date, most of the excavation, preservation, and restoration of the site has taken place in the open quarter to the north of the fort. In this area, a number of churches and related structures have been exposed and prepared for site visitors. In addition, two churches located within the southeast corner of the fort have been excavated. Finally, a church is associated with the tallest of the two towers to the north of Umm ar-Rasas. All of these twelve churches and two chapels are of interest in this chapter, since they point to the ecclesiastical importance of the site.

One group of churches to the north of the fortress is called the "Saint Stephen Complex." It consists of a series of four churches, a chapel, and associated buildings. One of the churches within the complex is the Church of Saint Stephen, dedicated to one of the first deacons of the Christian community in Jerusalem and its first martyr. It is the most impressive of the group.

This chapter begins with some background information on the site itself (fig. 8.2). Next, the biblical texts on Stephen as deacon and martyr

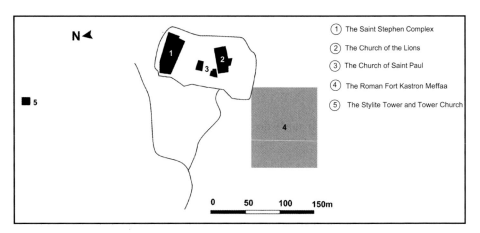

FIG. 8.1   Plan of Umm ar-Rasas and the location of the Stylite Tower and Tower Church.

are considered. Finally, the recent excavations of the churches and chapels at the site, especially the churches of the Saint Stephen Complex, are
treated in order to indicate the site's importance as a pilgrimage center.

MEPHAATH / MEFAA / KASTRON MEFFAA / MAYFAʿA – UMM AR-RASAS IN ANCIENT TEXTS

The ancient name of Umm ar-Rasas is Mephaath/Mefaa/Kastron Meffaa/
Mayfaʿa. It is attested four times in inscriptions in the mosaic floors of
two of the site's excavated churches, namely, the Church of Saint Stephen
and the Church of the Lions. Thus its identity is certain!

The place name Mephaath appears in the Bible on four occasions. In
Joshua 13.18 and 1 Chronicles 6.79 it appears among the list of cities that
the tribe of Reuben inherited on "the tableland by Madaba." In Joshua
21.37 it is cited as a Levitical town belonging to the tribe of Reuben.
Finally, in Jeremiah 48.21 the city appears among other cities of Moab
upon which judgment is rendered because of its negative attitude towards Judah. In the texts, the site is associated with other well-known
biblical sites such as Madaba, Nebo, Maʿin, and Dhiban.

Eusebius and Jerome, in the *Onomasticon* and the *Book on the Sites
and Names of Places of the Hebrews* respectively, describe the city as a
Roman military camp:

> **Mephaath** (Josh 13:18). Tribe of Benjamin. There is another be-
> yond the Jordan [Mephaath II], where there is a military garrison
> stationed beside the desert (128); and **Mefaath**. In the tribe of

FIG. 8.2 Aerial photo of Umm ar-Rasas (© David L Kennedy, APAAME, APA_2007-04-17_DLK-110).

> Benjamin. There is another one across the Jordan where there is a
> garrison of Roman soldiers on account of the neighbouring desert
> (129) (Taylor et al. 2003: 72).

It needs to be pointed out that the above comments by Eusebius and
Jerome predate the churches, which will be described below, by a couple
of centuries. Thus, the site was a Roman fort before it became an important Byzantine settlement and ecclesiastical center. Most of the Byzantine
settlement is probably located within the mostly unexcavated Roman
fort (fig. 8.3).

The *Notitia Dignitatum*, a list of all high offices in the eastern and
western parts of the Roman Empire, also locates a Roman military camp
at Mefaa. It is dated to the end of the fourth and the beginning of the
fifth century AD.

BIBLICAL TEXTS ON STEPHEN AS DEACON AND MARTYR

Following Jesus' death and resurrection, his disciples were increasing in
number in Jerusalem. As the community grew larger, some among them
were being neglected in the daily distribution of bread. With this situation
in mind, the twelve apostles called a meeting of the community and said,

FIG. 8.3   The fortress at Umm ar-Rasas (photo by Sherry Hardin).

> It is not right that we should neglect the word of God in order to wait on tables. Therefore, friends, select from among yourselves seven men of good standing, full of the Spirit and of wisdom, whom we may appoint to this task, while we, for our part, will devote ourselves to prayer and to serving the word (Acts of the Apostles 6.2–4).

The community was pleased with the apostles' decision and "they chose Stephen, a man full of faith and the Holy Spirit, together with Philip ...." (Acts 6.5). It "had those men stand before the apostles, who prayed and laid their hands on them" (Acts 6.6).

Stephen and the other six are traditionally regarded as the first Christian deacons. Their names are Greek; it is thus likely that Stephen and the others were Gentile converts to Judaism before becoming Christians. Stephen is listed first among the seven deacons and is described as "a man full of faith and the Holy Spirit."

In the Acts of the Apostles 6.8, positive comments about Stephen continue. He is described as one who is "full of grace and power" and as doing "great wonders and signs among the people." However, not all were pleased with him and some engaged him in debate. Stephen's wisdom and the Spirit with which he spoke resulted in his victory. However, this led to some in Jerusalem instigating efforts to destroy him. He was confronted, seized, and brought before the Jewish council. Like Jesus, Stephen was charged with prophesying against the temple. When asked if the charges were true, Stephen replied in a long discourse (Acts 7.2–53), in which he retold the Old Testament/Hebrew Scriptures' stories of Abraham, Joseph, Moses, and others. In his speech, he refers to the idolatrous actions of his listeners and their ancestors and says that God does not dwell in houses made by human hands. He thus implies that Solomon was wrong to build a house for God. Stephen goes on to say: "you stiff-necked people, uncircumcised in heart and ears, you are forever opposing the Holy Spirit, just as your ancestors used to do" (Acts 7.51). Furthermore, Stephen accused the people of not keeping the law that they had received (Acts 7.53).

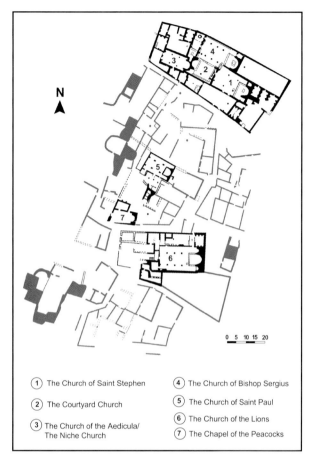

N
▲

0 5 10 15 20

1. The Church of Saint Stephen
2. The Courtyard Church
3. The Church of the Aedicula/The Niche Church
4. The Church of Bishop Sergius
5. The Church of Saint Paul
6. The Church of the Lions
7. The Chapel of the Peacocks

FIG. 8.4 General plan of the location of some of the churches in the ecclesiastical segment of Umm ar-Rasas (adapted from Piccirillo 1997a: 376).

His accusers became enraged at him, and in the ensuing chaos Stephen had a vision of the Son of Man in heaven standing at the right hand of God. His opponents dragged him out of the city and began to stone him (Acts 7.58), a traditional way of putting one to death at the time. Stephen's response is to ask God to forgive his persecutors, just as Jesus had done before him (Luke 23.34), and then he dies.[1] As a result, Stephen is recognized as the first Christian to die for his faith and is given the title of "first martyr."

---

1 Paul approved of the killing of Stephen by the people (Acts 8.1).

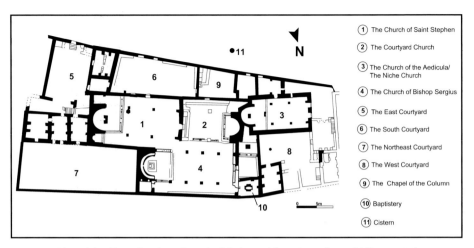

The Church of Saint Stephen
The Courtyard Church
The Church of the Aedicula/
The Niche Church
The Church of Bishop Sergius
The East Courtyard
The South Courtyard
The Northeast Courtyard
The West Courtyard
The Chapel of the Column
Baptistery
Cistern

FIG. 8.5   Plan of the "Saint Stephen Complex" (adapted from Piccirillo and Alliata 1994).

ARCHAEOLOGICAL EXCAVATIONS

Under the direction of M. Piccirillo, the Studium Biblicum Franciscanum (SBF) in Jerusalem began excavations at the site of Umm ar-Rasas in 1986 (fig. 8.4). In the beginning, the work focused on a cluster of churches, rooms, and courtyards in an enclosed area in the northeastern part of the site, north of the fort. The excavators named the cluster the "Saint Stephen Complex" after the main church of the group. The complex was enclosed by a continuous wall with its main entrances from the south (Piccirillo 1993b: 1492).

Since a considerable amount of debris covered the ruins, the archaeologists began their work on two structures with apses on the northern edge of the ruins. Here they excavated two churches, the Church of Bishop Sergius and the Church of Saint Stephen. In addition, they excavated a paved courtyard that had been subsequently converted into a chapel by the addition of an apse on its western wall; this is now called the "Courtyard Church." A fourth church excavated in the complex is called the Church of the Aedicula or the Niche Church. Finally, they excavated a paved chapel to the west, which is called the "Chapel of the Column." These five ecclesiastical buildings form a large and interconnected liturgical complex, dating to the Byzantine and Early Islamic periods and called the "Saint Stephen Complex."

The SBF also excavated other churches in the open quarter of the site, which will be indicated below. The Swiss Archaeological Mission of the Max van Berchem Foundation in Geneva excavated, beginning in

1987, inside the fort, working on two side-by-side churches in its south-east corner. In addition, personnel from the Department of Antiquities of Jordan excavated the "Church of the Priest Wa'il" in 1990.

The earliest sherds uncovered at the site of Umm ar-Rasas date to the Iron II period (1000–586 BC). Although there is some Nabataean material at the site, its majority of remains belongs to the Roman through Umayyad periods. Today, the site's pre-eminent features are, of course, the Byzantine remains. It appears that the site was abandoned, except for some minor domestic habitation, in the late eighth or early ninth century AD.

THE CHURCHES

As indicated above, a large number of churches has been excavated at the site. Discussion here will begin with descriptions of the churches and chapels of the "Saint Stephen Complex" (fig. 8.5; UTM coordinates: 0777517 E/3489026 N; elev. 760 m)[2]. Following this, descriptions of the other excavated churches of Umm ar-Rasas, as well as the one at the tower to the north, are presented.

The "Saint Stephen Complex"

The Church of Saint Stephen

The Church of Saint Stephen is located to the southeast of the Church of Bishop Sergius (see below) and is 1 m higher than the latter. It is a single-apsed basilica with three aisles and measures 13.5 × 24 meters. There is a sacristy on the south side of the presbytery and an apsed chapel on its north side. The names of the church's benefactors are given in front of the door of this northern chapel (Piccirillo 1992: 239). The plan of the church is similar to that of the Church of Bishop Sergius. On the basis of a section of a lower mosaic floor found under the base of the altar of the church, the excavators determined that the church was built above the ruins of a previous structure (Piccirillo 1992: 238). The main entrance to the Church of Saint Stephen is on the west. Two other doors are located in its south wall.

The church is completely paved with mosaics (fig. 8.6). Because of the wealth of its inscriptions and the quality of its mosaic pavement, it is one of the most important archaeological monuments in Jordan (Piccirillo 1992: 238).

---

2   Due to the shelter covering the complex, the reading was taken just to the south of the Church of Saint Stephen.

FIG. 8.6   Mosaics in the Church of Saint Stephen
(photo by Sherry Hardin).

According to dedicatory inscriptions, located on either side of the altar, the church's presbytery was paved with mosaics in AD 756, in the time of Bishop Job. The name "Mary" is written behind the altar. She is the only woman mentioned in the church (Piccirillo 1992: 238).

A second dedicatory inscription (fig. 8.7), running along the step of the presbytery, relates that anonymous mosaicists added more decorations to the church in the time of Bishop Sergius (the Second). The letters which once dated this work were repaired in antiquity; therefore, it is difficult to determine when this work was carried out (Piccirillo 1992: 238). The inscription now reads:

> At the time of the most holy Bishop Sergius the mosaic of the holy and illustrious proto-deacon and proto-martyr Stephen was completed by the care of John, son of Isaac, most beloved of God, lexou and deacon and leader of Mefaa, econom, and by the care of all the people of Kastron Mefaa who love Christ, in the month of October, the second indiction year of the Province of Arabia 680, in memory of the repose of Fidonus (son) of Acias, lover of Christ (Piccirillo 1988: 210).

The inscription indicates that the church is dedicated to Stephen, one of the earliest Christian deacons and the first of its martyrs. It also gives the ancient name of the site as Mefaa, or Kastron Mefaa. On the basis of the repaired inscription, some scholars date it to AD 785 (see Chapter 7, note 3). However, since the inscription was damaged and repaired in antiquity, the late date is questionable (Schick 1997: 279); a date of AD 718 is suggested instead (Di Segni 2006: 114).

The mosaic in the church's nave is the most interesting. Its central portion has been disfigured, but the double frame that surrounds it is

FIG. 8.7 Dedicatory inscription along the step of the presbytery (photo by Sherry Hardin).

intact and of great importance, since it contains a number of city plans, each accompanied by a Greek toponym, or place-name (fig. 8.8). The outer frame, occupying the space between columns on the north, depicts eight Palestinian cities: The Holy City (Jerusalem), Neapolis (Nablus), Sebastis (Samaria), Caesarea on the Sea, Diospolis (Lydda), Eleutheropolis (Beit Gibrin), Askalon (Ashkelon), and Gaza. In the intercolummar spaces of the south row of columns, a series of seven Jordanian cities is shown: Kastron Mefaa (Umm ar-Rasas), Philadelphia (Amman), Madaba, Esbunta (Hesban), Belemunta (Ma'in), Areopolis (Rabbah), and Charach Muba (al-Karak)

FIG. 8.8 Mosaic with Greek toponyms: Esbunta (Hesban), Belemunta (Ma'in) and Areopolis (Rabbah). (Photo by Sherry Hardin.)

(Piccirillo 1992: 238). Two additional Jordanian cities, Limbon (possibly the town of Libb, 10 km south of Madaba) and Diblaton (possibly biblical Diblataim [Num 33.46–47], today maybe the twin sites of Kh. ad-Deleilat al-Gharbiyya and Kh. ad-Deleilat ash-Sharqiyya, ca. 4 km north of Libb), are portrayed, one at the head of each aisle.

The inner frame, which depicts a river with fish, birds, flowing water, boats, and boys fishing and hunting, portrays a series of ten cities in the Nile Delta: Alexandria, Kasin, Thenesos, Tamiathis, Panau, Pilousin, Antinau, Eraklion, Kynopolis, and Pseudostomon (Piccirillo 1992: 238).

The mosaic and its depictions are of great historical importance. The name Kastron Mefaa, meaning "camp of Mefaa," suggests the military nature of the site during the Roman, Byzantine, and early Islamic periods. This information agrees with that in the *Notitia Dignitatum* to the effect that local soldiers were stationed at Kastron Mefaa as auxiliary troops.

The Greek inscriptions in the churches of Kastron Mefaa contain the names of many benefactors. The majority of the Semitic names are of Arabic origin. This supports the conclusion that the site was a camp of the Arab auxiliary soldiers who served the Roman, Byzantine, and Umayyad armies.

The late date of the mosaics within the Church of Saint Stephen indicates that people lived at the site and that the Christian community there was governed by a deacon with a bishop and local clergy well into the eighth century AD. The settlement was characterized by high artistic achievement. The eighth-century date extends the history of mosaic art in Jordan for almost a century. It also shows that Christianity continued to flourish in parts of Jordan well into the Early Islamic period.

The Church of Bishop Sergius

The Church of Bishop Sergius, located to the northwest of the Church of Saint Stephen, was built on an older structure. It is a basilica, measuring 13.1 × 23 meters. It and the Church of Saint Stephen, which are side by side, have the same basic structure: two rows of columns created a central nave flanked by aisles on the north and the south with an apse and an elevated presbytery on the eastern end, two steps higher than the nave.

The church was accessed by means of three doors, one opening into each aisle. Two rows of four pillars separated the aisles. A single sacristy is located to the north of the apse. A baptistery was added to the west side of the church and a rectangular chapel to its south wall.

The mosaic floors both within the presbytery and in the nave of the church are rich, but iconoclasts have defaced the ones in the latter area. The mosaics feature scenes of hunting, fishing, and viticulture, a depic-

FIG. 8.9 Mosaic with medallion in the Church of Bishop Sergius (photo by Sherry Hardin).

tion of a season holding a cornucopia, classical personifications of the Abyss (Sea) and the Earth, life scenes of the benefactors of the church, and more scenes from everyday life.

A rectangular panel is enclosed in a frame of squares immediately in front of the altar. The panel contains a medallion flanked by a goat and a tree on each side (fig. 8.9). The inscription within the medallion reads:

> In the good times of our lord, the most holy and most blessed Bishop Sergius, the whole work of this most holy church was paved with mosaics by the priest Procopius, in the month of Gorpiaus in the sixth indiction of the year 482 of the Province of Arabia (Piccirillo 1992: 234 and image 331; see also Piccirillo 1988: 208).

The inscription indicates that the church was built AD 587, that is, in the time of Bishop Sergius I. It also gives the name of the mosaicist Procopius. Another inscription near the step of the presbytery reads:

> The Lord has loved the gate of Zion more than the tents of Jacob (Piccirillo 1992: 234 and image 366).

The inscription is a quote from Psalm 87.2.

Names of donors are given in a medallion inside the central western door of the church. Moreover, an inscription in an intercolumnar space to the north reads:

O Lord, have mercy on all who toiled on this mosaic. Their names are known to You. [It was done] in the times of Soel, of Kasiseus, of Abdalla, of Obed, and of Elias, your faithful [ones] (Piccirillo 1992: 235).

As indicated, the two churches of Saint Stephen and Bishop Sergius suffered iconoclastic damage to their images after 718 (Schick 1995: 474). They were perhaps abandoned in the late eighth or ninth century.

The Courtyard Church and the Chapel of the Column

Piccirillo and his team excavated a paved courtyard that was later converted into a chapel by the addition of an apse on its western wall. This is called the Courtyard Church. In the latest phase, the double door of this church was blocked, and the adjoining room was converted into a poor chapel with reused materials. This is called the *Chapel of the Column.*

The church may have served a funerary purpose. This conclusion is based on the fact that multiple tombs were located beneath its floor.

The Church of the Aedicula / The Niche Church

This church (fig. 8.10; UTM coordinates: 0777492 E/3489051 N; elev. 757 m) was somewhat isolated from the other three churches in the "Saint Stephen Complex" and is named after the small niche in its southern wall. It is a basilica-style church, measuring 17.6 × 9.2 meters. It had its own entrance in the southwestern corner of the complex. On the basis of the excavated pottery, the excavators date the structure to the sixth century, without greater precision.

FIG. 8.10 The Church of the Aedicula/The Niche Church (photo by Sherry Hardin).

FIG. 8.11   The Church of Saint Paul (photo by Sherry Hardin).

Other Churches North of the Fortress

The Church of Saint Paul

The Church of Saint Paul (fig. 8.11; UTM coordinates: 0777477 E/3488999 N; elev. 760 m) is located in the center of the ecclesiastical complex between the Church of Saint Stephen to the north and the Church of the Lions to the south. It takes its name from an invocation to the apostle incised on a roof tile picked from the collapse. The inscription reads:

> Saint Paul and Germanos save the Blues and Papiona (son of) George the lector. Amen (Piccirillo 2002: 547).

The Blues are a sporting association. They later became a political faction in Constantinople. They are known from other inscriptions found in Jordan (Piccirillo 2002: 547–48). The name Papiona recurs on Mount Nebo (Piccirillo 2002: 548).

The plan of the church, which measures 16 × 7 m, is that of a normal basilica with a raised apsed presbytery (fig. 8.12). The church was completely paved with mosaics that suffered damage from the iconoclasts and later domestic use. The mosaics are probably best assigned to the time of Bishop Sergius I (AD 576–595/596) of Madaba and may be attributed to the mosaicist responsible for those found in the Church of the Bishop

FIG. 8.12   The Church of Saint Paul: Raised presbytery (photo by Sherry Hardin).

Sergius (Piccirillo 2002: 548). The church itself was probably built in the latter half of the sixth century, a time that saw extensive building activity throughout the diocese of Madaba, including at Umm ar-Rasas. It continued in use up to the first half of the eighth century. Afterwards, a Bedouin family used it domestically up until the ninth–tenth century AD (Piccirillo 2002: 548–49).

Four Greek inscriptions were uncovered during the church's excavation (one is cited above). The inscription along the step of the presbytery begins with a cross. It is destroyed at the center. It reads:

> +For the memory and the repose [of...and of....... Sergis and] of Paul his sons and for the salvation and remittance of sins of Rabbus....... through their care all the work was completed [...in the month] of July the twelfth indiction (Piccirillo 2002: 546).

The Chapel of the Peacocks

This chapel (fig. 8.13; UTM coordinates: 0777461 E/3488971 N; elev. 760 m) is located in the northwestern angle of the vast complex that is part of the area where the Church of Saint Paul is situated. It is to the southwest of the Church of Saint Paul and to the northwest of the Church of the Lions. It is comprised of an apsed prayer hall and a northern service room, both paved with mosaics. The chapel measures ca. 7 × 14 meters.

FIG. 8.13 The Chapel of the Peacocks (photo by Sherry Hardin).

The surviving parts of the mosaic floor in the sanctuary of the Chapel of the Peacocks make it possible to detect two tails and one leg of peacocks who face each other. From this, the chapel takes its name.

On the basis of the style of the mosaics within the chapel, Piccirillo dates them to the episcopate of Bishop Sergius I of Madaba, that is, to the last quarter of the sixth century (2002: 552). The structure was still used for liturgical purposes in the Umayyad period, at least until the eighth century. It was used for domestic purposes until the ninth–tenth century.

The Church of the Lions

The Church of the Lions (fig. 8.14; UTM coordinates: 0777489 E/3488948 N; elev. 760 m) belongs to a vast ecclesiastical complex located in the eastern section of the town, which developed to the north of the fortress in the Byzantine period. Archaeologists from the SBF excavated it in 1989 and 1990.

The Church of the Lions is three-apsed and measures 26 × 15 meters. It was completely paved with mosaics. The church has two entrances on both its west and north sides. In the raised presbytery, enclosed by a chancel screen, the bases of the altar are still in place. A pulpit, to the southwest of the presbytery, is the best preserved example found to date in Jordan (Piccirillo 1992: 236).

FIG. 8.14 The Church of the Lions (photo by Sherry Hardin).

An inscription within a medallion in the nave of the church refers to Bishop Sergius I. It reads:

> At the time of the most pious Bishop Sergius this holy temple was completed in the month of Desius of the seventh indiction … (Piccirillo 1992: 236).

The date is uncertain. However, it probably dates to either AD 574 or 589. As indicated previously, Sergius I was bishop of Madaba from AD 576–595/596.

Another inscription, which the iconoclasts badly damaged, gives the names of the church's donors: John the Egyptian, Salaman, son of Soban, John, son of Saol, Toemus, and Paul, son of Kassianus (Piccirillo 1992: 236). A city plan of Kastron Mefaa decorates a northern intercolumnar space.

The church was abandoned before the iconoclastic period (Schick 1995: 474–75). Later it was used as a domestic space.

A third large ecclesiastical area lies outside the northwestern corner of the wall of the fort. Here, work on three churches, namely, the Church of the Reliquary, the Church of the "Tabula Ansata," and the Church of the Priest Wa'il, has taken place. These are treated here in an east-to-west order.

The Church of the Reliquary

The Church of the Reliquary (UTM coordinates: 0777369 E/3488923 N; elev. 762 m), a single-apsed basilica, was excavated due to illicit "work" at the site. It is located outside the northern wall of the Roman fort, between the Church of the "Tabula Ansata" to the south and the Church of the Lions to the north. It is named for the stone reliquary found under its altar. However, like the remainder of the church, the reliquary had been "robbed" before the archaeologists uncovered it (Piccirillo 2006b).

The Department of Antiquities of Jordan began work on the church in the summer of 2003 with the removal of surface stones from the structure's collapse. Archaeologists from the SBF, under the supervision of M. Piccirillo, completed the excavations in 2004.

The church's main entrance was in its western wall. A door in its northern wall gave access to a series of rooms. The church's dedicatory inscription is located in its nave, adjacent to the steps leading to the elevated presbytery. It indicates that the church was paved with mosaics in AD 586, at the time of Bishop Sergius of Madaba. Thus, it dates to the same time as several of the other churches at Umm ar-Rasas. Another inscription within the presbytery gives a list of the church's benefactors.

The excavators uncovered two tombs within the church. One is located immediately north of the western extremity of the presbytery, or immediately east of the northern aisle of the church. The other tomb is positioned in the southwestern corner of the structure, that is, the southern corner of its southern aisle. The excavators recovered a number of artifacts from the tombs (Pappalardo 2006).

The Church of the "Tabula Ansata"

Piccirillo, the leading excavator of this church, named it the Church of the "Tabula Ansata" (UTM coordinates: 0777307 E/3488932 N; elev. 760 m) from an inscription framed in a tabula incised on a stone slab of the presbytery. The church is a basilica. In its first phase, it was paved with mosaics, which were later covered by stone slabs. The church was built in the sixth century and restored in the seventh.

The Church of the Priest Wa'il

This church (fig. 6.15; UTM coordinates: 0777286 E/3488947 N; elev. 760 m) is a small, single-apsed one with three aisles. It measures ca. 12 × 9 meters. Personnel from both the Department of Antiquities and the SBF excavated it. The church's mosaic floor, which at one time was completely paved, is somewhat deliberately damaged.

FIG. 8.15 The Church of the Priest Wa'il (photo by Sherry Hardin).

The dedicatory inscription in the nave of the church reads:

> At the time of the most pious Bishop Sergius, this holy temple was
> built and completed by the care of the Priest Wa'il in the month of
> Dius of the fifth indiction of the year 481. This is the priest and his
> servant (Piccirillo 1992: 242).

The inscription mentions the priest Wa'il. A dedication date of AD 586 is
also given on the mosaic. Thus, it too was built during the time of Bishop
Sergius I of Madaba. Schick (1995: 475) thinks that the church continued
in use beyond the iconoclastic period.

Churches within the Walled Enclosure

As indicated previously, the Swiss Archaeological Mission of the Max
van Berchem Foundation investigated four ecclesiastical structures inside
the walls of the fort. They excavated two of them, side-by-side or twin
churches, in the fort's southeastern corner in 1988 and 1990. The churches
are known as the Church of the Rivers and the Church of the Palm Tree
(Piccirillo 1992: 240–42). Both churches, built during the time of Bishop
Sergius I of Madaba, date to after the construction of the fort's wall.

FIG. 8.16 The Church of the Rivers (photo by Sherry Hardin).

The Church of the Rivers

The Church of the Rivers (fig. 8.16; UTM coordinates: 0777447 E/3488805 N; elev. 770 m) is the northern and earlier of the two churches. It is a single-apsed, basilica-style church with a raised presbytery. Each aisle of the church could be accessed from a separate door in its western wall.

What can be read from the mainly destroyed dedicatory inscription, which is located near the door of the church, indicates a possible date of AD 578/579 or 593/594. Both dates are within the episcopacy of Bishop Sergius I (Bujard et al. 1992).

The church's mosaic floor, which has been deliberately damaged, may have been laid by the same mosaicists who worked in the Church of Bishop Sergius, as the same patterns and style are used. Despite the damage to the mosaics within the church's nave, some figures remain intact. One figure, located in the southwest corner, is the personification of a river with a reed in his right hand (Piccirillo 1992: 241).

The church was abandoned at the end of the eighth or the beginning of the ninth century. Later, it was used for domestic purposes.

The Church of the Palm Tree

The Church of the Palm Tree (UTM coordinates: 0777445 E/3488793 N; elev. 770 m), also a single-apsed basilica, is the southern counterpart of the

FIG. 8.17 Second plan of Kastron Mefaa in the St. Stephen's Church mosaic (photo by Jonathan Ferguson).

Church of the Rivers. Only segments of its mosaics remain; however, the mosaic floor of the presbytery is mostly intact. Part of it depicts a central palm tree growing from a vase. A number of animals, including two peacocks and two lambs, face the palm.

The church does not have a dedicatory inscription and the date of its construction is unknown. However, the excavators posit that it was built after its northern twin. They thus date it toward the end of the sixth century, the time of Bishop Sergius I. It was probably abandoned in the eighth century (Bujard et al. 2002)

THE TOWER OF UMM AR-RASAS

On one of the mosaics within the Church of Saint Stephen there is a double plan of Kastron Mefaa, as depicted in the series of Jordanian cities. This second plan of Kastron Mefaa, outside of the camp proper, depicts a church with three burning lamps hanging from its arches. A courtyard, surrounded by rooms on all sides, is located behind the church. A solitary column/pillar shown against a white background is depicted within the courtyard (fig. 8.17). A kind of a parapet with a line of black tesserae in the middle is shown on the top of the column. The entire depiction may be a representation of the present tower complex (figs. 8.18–19; UTM coordinates: 0777525 E/3490227 N; elev. 740 m [ground level] and 754 [near top]) north of Umm ar-Rasas.

The Tower

The tower stands in the middle of a square courtyard in which there is a cistern in the north and a small church in its southeast corner. The wall lines of the courtyard are visible on all sides of the tower.

Some have interpreted the tower (fig. 8.20), which is located ca. 1.5 km to the north of the main site of Umm ar-Rasas, as a military structure associated with the fort guarding against military raids from the Bedouin of the desert and/or protecting the water pools hewn out of the nearby rock. Others have interpreted it as a platform for a stylite, one of the ascetics who lived on top of a pillar. Such a conclusion is not too

FIG. 8.18 The tower of Umm ar-Rasas (© David L Kennedy, APAAME, APA_2007-04-17_DLK-103).

FIG. 8.19 The tower of Umm ar-Rasas, seen from the site itself (photo by Sherry Hardin).

FIG. 8.20 The tower of Umm ar-Rasas (photo by Sherry Hardin).

far-fetched in light of the practices of the time and recent findings in Jordan at Wadi 'Ayn al-Kanisah, to the south of Ras al-Siyagha.[3]

The archaeologists working at the tower, which stands ca. 14 m high, could find no stairway and no door, except at the very top, on its south side and facing the church. The tower's roof was dome-shaped. A channel, which ran from the top to the bottom of the interior wall of the tower, may have served as part of a toilet.

Tower Church

Excavations around the tower found a simple church, the Tower Church (fig. 8.21; 0777532 E/3490211 N; elev. 744 m), which was used during the Byzantine and Early Islamic periods. It is a basilica measuring ca. 13 × 9 meters. Two rooms adjoin the church on the north side. The excavators date the church to the beginning of the sixth century.

The eastern end of the northern aisle of the church was turned into a small shrine by the addition of a small arch, which covered a stone reliquary set in the floor. The disarticulated bones of an adult were found inside the reliquary. The bones were covered with oil, a Christian practice of veneration for the bones of martyrs (Piccirillo 1993b: 1493). This find could indicate the church as a place of pilgrimage.

---

3   Stylites were individuals who retired to the top of pillars to live the religious life in solitude. Hence, they were often referred to as "pillar saints." While a hermit generally went off to some isolated place, the stylite lived on his pillar adjacent to a community. Frequently, a visitor would petition the stylite for assistance or even for a miracle. The stylite movement began in Syria and spread to Mesopotamia, Egypt, Palestine, and Greece. It was Saint Simeon the Stylite who inaugurated the practice in northern Syria. Often referred to as the "Elder," he took up residence on the top of a column in AD 423 to escape the crowds that followed him around. Saint Simeon the Younger inhabited a pillar on a mountain near Antioch in Syria for most of the sixth century. Another stylite is known to have spent ten years in a tub hanging in mid-air from poles! Piccirillo reads the name "Abba Longinus the Stylite" in an inscription, dated to the sixth century, in the chapel at the center of the Theotokos monastery at Wadi 'Ayn al-Kanisah, to the south of Ras al-Siyagha (1998b: 196–97, 217; see Chapter 6). There is, thus, epigraphic evidence in Jordan for a stylite among the monks of the area. It would appear that a stylite at the tower north of Kastron Mefaa would not be out of context.

FIG. 8.21 The Tower Church (photo by Sherry Hardin).

There is another, square-shaped tower (UTM coordinates: 0777550E/ 3490288N; elev. 738 [at base of tower]) close to the taller one. It is near rock-hewn depressions that were used to gather and hold water and probably served as a watchtower related to the water resources.

CONCLUSIONS

Umm ar-Rasas, ancient Mephaath/Mefaa/Kastron Meffaa/Mayfa'a, was an important military fort, Roman to Abassid period settlement, and Byzantine ecclesiastical center. Of all its areas excavated to date, it is the Saint Stephen Complex that is the most impressive. This complex, which possibly also included a monastery, consists of a number of important churches. The one that is most elaborately decorated in dedicated to Saint Stephen, one of the first Christian deacons and the first Christian martyr. It would have been a church to which pilgrims would have come.

The Church of the Reliquary, located between the Saint Stephen Complex and the Roman fort, housed relics of some holy person(s). It would have been one to which pilgrims would have also been attracted.

Finally, the tower and nearby church, 1.5 km to the north of the fort, appear to have been an important center for a stylite. The stylite, who lived on the tower, along with the relic(s) within the church would have attracted people who sought the assistance of the holy man and petitioned by prayer the holy person(s) whose remains were kept in the church.

SUGGESTIONS FOR GETTING TO THE SITE

The site of Umm ar-Rasas is located in central Jordan, 60 km south of Amman. To get there, follow the Airport/Desert Highway south of Amman. Follow the signs southwest to Madaba. Drive through Madaba and south along the King's Highway to Dhiban, from where you can take a road going east to Umm ar-Rasas. Alternatively, you can take the Airport/Desert Highway south, passing Qastal, the Queen Alia International Airport, Jiza, and Dab'a. Shortly after passing Dab'a, take a road to the west that leads to the site. Both routes will take about 60–90 minutes to drive. The site is located about half-way between the Airport/Desert Highway on the east and the King's Highway on the west.

There is a Visitor's Center at the site. Guides will lead you to visit the "Saint Stephen Complex."

9 THE BEHEADING OF JOHN THE BAPTIST

MACHAERUS / MUKAWER

THE story of the beheading of John the Baptist is found in the first three accounts of the Gospel (Matthew 14.1–12; Mark 6.16–29; Luke 3.19–20, 9.7–9). It does not appear in the Gospel according to John. Although the Gospel accounts do not tell us where the beheading took place, Josephus informs us that it happened at the palace-fortress of Machaerus along the eastern shore of the Dead Sea.

No ecclesiastical structures have been found in the excavated palace-fortress of Machaerus. Thus, there is no indication that the site became a place of pilgrimage. Excavators have uncovered three churches/chapels in the nearby village of Mukawer, but again, no evidence of pilgrimages to the village has been found. Nevertheless, both sites are considered here because of the importance of John as a New Testament figure.

An appendix on "The Waters of Callirhoe and Baarou/Baaras" is added to this chapter. The addition was made because of the relation between these waters and the palace-fortress of Machaerus.

BIBLICAL TEXTS AND COMMENTARY ON THE BEHEADING OF JOHN THE BAPTIST

Early in his account of the Gospel, Matthew mentions that John had been arrested (4:12). In 14.1–4 we learn the reason for the arrest.

Matthew 14.1–12

> At that time Herod the ruler heard reports about Jesus; and he said to his servants, "This is John the Baptist; he has been raised from

the dead, and for this reason these powers are at work in him." For Herod had arrested John, bound him, and put him in prison on account of Herodias, his brother Philip's wife, because John had been telling him, "It is not lawful for you to have her." Though Herod wanted to put him to death, he feared the crowd, because they regarded him as a prophet. But when Herod's birthday came, the daughter of Herodias danced before the company, and she pleased Herod so much that he promised on oath to grant her whatever she might ask. Prompted by her mother, she said, "Give me the head of John the Baptist here on a platter." The king was grieved, yet out of regard for his oaths and for the guests, he commanded it to be given; he sent and had John beheaded in the prison. The head was brought on a platter and given to the girl, who brought it to her mother. His disciples came and took the body and buried it; then they went and told Jesus.

Herod Antipas (reigned 4 BC–AD 39), one of the sons of Herod the Great and tetrarch of Galilee and Peraea – that land area east of the Jordan River between the Sea of Galilee in the north and the Dead Sea in the south – had put John in prison for his apparently public opposition to Herod's marriage to Herodias.[1] Herod would not tolerate John's condemnation and so had him arrested. Any form of opposition from an apocalyptic preacher could easily have been regarded as sedition. On the occasion of Herod's birthday and the associated party, the daughter of Herodias danced for the leader and his guests.[2] Herod was pleased and promised the girl anything she wished. After consulting with and being encouraged by her mother, the dancer asked for the head of John the Baptist on a platter, a request which Herod fulfilled. The girl gave the head to her mother. When John's disciples heard of this, they came, took the body, buried it, and went and told Jesus. This last piece of information, found only in Matthew, points to the close ties between Jesus and John (see also Luke 7:18–30); John's disciples knew that because of their association, Jesus must immediately hear about John's death. Neither the place of the imprisonment nor the place of burial is indicated in the text.

---

1 Herodias was Herod Antipas' niece but, more importantly, his half-brother Philip's wife.

2 Many commentators have pointed out the incongruity of a princess dancing at such a bawdy occasion. See, for example, Kopp 1963: 138–39.

Mark 6.16–29

> But when Herod heard of it, he said, "John, whom I beheaded, has been raised." For Herod himself had sent men who arrested John, bound him, and put him in prison on account of Herodias, his brother Philip's wife, because Herod had married her. For John had been telling Herod, "It is not lawful for you to have your brother's wife." And Herodias had a grudge against him, and wanted to kill him. But she could not, for Herod feared John, knowing that he was a righteous and holy man, and he protected him…. But an opportunity came when Herod on his birthday gave a banquet for his courtiers and officers and for the leaders of Galilee. When his daughter Herodias came in and danced, she pleased Herod and his guests….; and the king said to the girl, "Ask me for whatever you wish and I will give it."…. She went out and said to her mother, "What should I ask for?" She replied, "The head of John the Baptist." Immediately she rushed back to the king and requested, "I want you to give me at once the head of John the Baptist on a platter." The king was greatly grieved; yet out of regard for his oaths and for his guests, he did not want to refuse her. Immediately the king sent a soldier of the guard with orders to bring John's head. He went and beheaded John in prison, brought his head on a platter, and gave it to the girl. Then the girl gave it to her mother. When his disciples heard about it, they came and took his body, and laid it in a tomb.

In contrast to Matthew's account of the arrest and beheading of John the Baptist, Mark informs us that the "leaders of Galilee" were among the invitees to Herod's birthday party. Thus, one could conclude that the affair took place in the north of the country, probably at Tiberias on the west side of the Sea of Galilee, where Herod had established the residency for his court. However, there is no solid basis for assuming that Mark locates the party at Tiberias. Since he gives no precise location for the next episode, the "feeding of the five thousand" (Mark 6.30–46), we have no solid basis for assuming he associated either of the adjoining pericopes with Tiberias. Since the birthday party and the beheading seem to have taken place at the same time, the prison must have been nearby. However, John the Baptist is never associated with the area of Galilee but with Judah and Peraea.

Mark assigns the name of Herodias to the girl who danced for Herod and his guests.[3] Thus, both the girl and her mother have the same

---

3   Josephus, *Antiquities* 10.8.5.4 gives her the name of Salome, and that is often the name by which she is known.

name. The story ends when John's disciples take the beheaded "body, and laid it in a tomb."[4]

Luke 3.19–20

> But Herod the ruler, who had been rebuked by him because of Herodias, his brother's wife, and because of all the evil things that Herod had done, added to them by shutting up John in prison.

Luke 9.7–9

> Now Herod the ruler heard about all that had taken place, and he was perplexed, because it was said by some that John had been raised from the dead, by some that Elijah had appeared, and by others that one of the ancient prophets had arisen. Herod said, "John I beheaded; but who is this about whom I hear such things?"

Luke's account of the Gospel is unique in its reporting of the imprisonment of John the Baptist before Jesus is baptized (Luke 3.20). Like Matthew and Mark, he never tells us where the prison is. The baptism of Jesus is narrated in the next episode, in which John is not even mentioned. Thus, this episode of the imprisonment of John finishes off the ministry of the Baptist and serves to remove him from the scene before Jesus appears. The death of John is not mentioned in Luke 3.19–20, only in Luke 9.7–9.

JOSEPHUS AND THE BEHEADING OF JOHN THE BAPTIST

It is to Josephus and his work *Antiquities* that we must turn to find further information on the place of John's imprisonment and beheading. Josephus also provides some background that is relevant to Herod's divorce and remarriage.

The daughter of the Nabataean ruler Aretas IV (reigned 9/8 BC–AD 40/41) was married to Herod Antipas. Herod wished to divorce her and marry Herodias, his half-brother Philip's wife. Aretas IV's daughter heard of this and asked Herod to send her to Machaerus, "which is a place on the borders of the dominions of Aretas and Herod, without informing him of any of her intentions.... She soon came to Arabia ... and she soon came to her father, and told him of Herod's intentions" (*Antiquities* 18.5.1).

---

4   In a similar manner, Joseph of Arimathea will get Jesus' corpse from Pilate and place it in a tomb (Mark 15:46).

Aretas took Herod's action as a personal slight and went to war against him.[5] The people took this war, according to Josephus (*Antiquities* 18.5.2), to be God's punishment for Herod's killing of John the Baptist:

> …. Now, some of the Jews thought that the destruction of Herod's army came from God, and that very justly, as a punishment of what he did against John, that was called the *Baptist*; for Herod slew him, who was a good man, and commanded the Jews to exercise virtue, both as to righteousness towards one another, and piety towards God, and so to come to baptism; for that the washing [with water] would be acceptable to him, if they made use of it…. Herod, who feared lest the great influence John had over the people might put it into his power and inclination to raise a rebellion, (for they seemed ready to do anything he should advise), thought it best, by putting him to death, to prevent any mischief he might cause, and not bring himself into difficulties, by sparing a man who might make him repent of it when it should be too late. Accordingly he was sent a prisoner, out of Herod's suspicious temper, to Macherus, the castle I before mentioned, and was there put to death (*Antiquities* 18.5.2).

It is Josephus who informs us of John's imprisonment and death at Machaerus, the very place to which the daughter of Aretas IV had gone. The reason Josephus gives for John's arrest is an accusation of sedition.

The logistics of arranging for such a group in a festive setting has led many commentators to assume the location, though unstated in the Gospel accounts, was Tiberias, where Herod had established the residency for his court. Herod had indeed built the city of Tiberias, in honor of the Roman Emperor Tiberius, on the west shore of the Sea of Galilee in ca. AD 18. In the process, he had to remove the tombs in the area, since otherwise he would have been transgressing Jewish laws. Because the site was controversial, Herod had to force new settlers to take up residence in the city by gifts of lands and houses. Moreover, Josephus informs us that pious Jews avoided the city, because it had been built on a cemetery (*Antiquities* 18.2.3).

There is no evidence that John was ever in the area of Galilee. He originated from Judea and his missionary activities were carried out in

---

5   Aretas IV was king of the Nabataeans. His reign overlapped with that of Herod Antipas. Moreover, his territory was next to that of Herod's. It was to Aretas' kingdom in Arabia that Paul went following Jesus' revelation to him and his subsequent conversion (Galatians 1.17). King Aretas appears in 2 Corinthians 11.32 as the one ultimately in charge of Damascus when the city's governor ordered Paul to be seized. Paul escaped by being let down in a basket through a window in the city wall (2 Corinthians 11. 33).

FIG. 9.1   Aerial view of Machaerus (© David L. Kennedy, APAAME, APA _2006-09-10_DLK-30).

Judea and across the Jordan (see Chapter 5). The only evidence we have of his baptizing farther to the north is the notice in John 3.23 that "John also was baptizing at Aenon near Salim," which, according to the *Onomasticon,* is eight Roman miles south of Scythopolis, modern-day Beth-shan (see Chapters 3 and 5).

   John's imprisonment at Machaerus, on the other hand, makes geographical sense. John not only baptized across the Jordan in the Wadi al-Kharra region immediately to the north, but he resided there as well. Thus, it would make sense for Herod to seize him there and imprison him in one of his castles immediately to the south. And if the people of the time expressed unhappiness with Herod's action towards John, Machaerus, in an out-of-the-way and isolated area, would have been a good place to imprison him.

EXCAVATIONS AT MACHAERUS AND MUKAWER

The modern village of Mukawer is located 30 km to the southwest of Madaba on the south bank of Wadi Zarqa Ma'in (see Appendix – The Waters of Callirhoe and Baarou/Baaras, below). It preserves the name of the Hasmonean-Herodian fortress of Machaerus, built on the southern border of Jewish Peraea against the Nabataeans. It also has remains from the Roman-Byzantine period.

The archaeological site of Machaerus, found 2 km to the west of the village, is located on the east side of the Dead Sea and provides a spectacular view of it (fig. 9.1). It may be divided into two segments: the fortress ruins on the isolated spur of Qal'at al-Mishnaqa (figs. 9.2–3), and the associated lower town built on the steep northern slope.

According to Josephus (*War* 7), Alexander Jannaeus (reigned 103–76 BC), a Hasmonean ruler, built the fortress consisting of upper and lower segments. Gabinius, one of Pompey's generals, destroyed it in 57 BC; Herod the Great (reigned 37–4 BC) rebuilt it. After Herod's death, his son Herod Antipas inherited the fortress. Upon the latter's death in AD 39, it passed to Herod Agrippa I until his death in AD 44. After this time it came under the control of the Romans. Subsequently, during the First Jewish Revolt, Jewish rebels took control of it after AD 66. The Romans besieged the fortress in AD 72, the rebels were allowed to leave, and then the

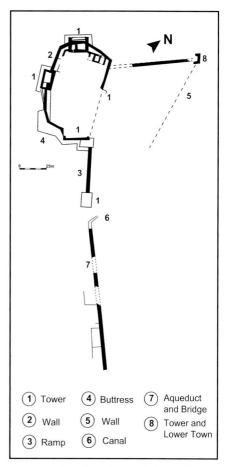

① Tower	④ Buttress	⑦ Aqueduct and Bridge
② Wall	⑤ Wall	⑧ Tower and Lower Town
③ Ramp	⑥ Canal	

FIG. 9.2 Plan of Machaerus (adapted from Piccirillo 1979: 181).

Romans tore it down, leaving only the foundations.

In the 1800s, explorers visited and recorded the ruins at the site. In 1965, the Jordanian Department of Antiquities partially excavated a church in the nearby village of Mukawer. International groups carried out further investigations at the site. The Franciscan Biblical Institute began its explorations there in 1978 and continued the work in 1979. In addition to work at the site itself, the institute excavated a second Byzantine church in the nearby village in 1989.

Throughout the fortress of Machaerus, there were two main periods of occupation, followed by a short reoccupation: 1. the Hasmonean fortress (90–57 BC); 2. the Herodian fortress (30 BC–AD 72); and a short reoccupation soon after AD 72.

FIG. 9.3   The Palace-Fortress of Machaerus (photo by Sherry Hardin).

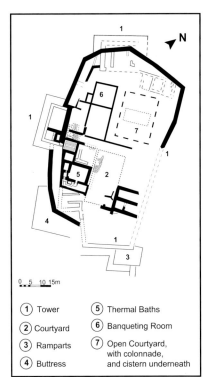

FIG. 9.4   Plan of the Palace-Fortress at Machaerus (adapted from Loffreda 1981: 88).

Palace and Fortress

The Franciscan Biblical Institute excavated the upper segment of the fortress, also called palace-fortress, on the top of Qal'at al-Mishnaqa (fig. 9.4; UTM coordinates: 0749081 E/3495658 N; elev. 695 m) (Piccirillo 1997b). This resulted in the identification of the Hasmonean fortress, the Herodian fortress, and the fortifications of the Zealots during the First Jewish Revolt (AD 66–73). Moreover, the institute also investigated the lower segment, the so-called lower town, on the mountain's north slope where the housing for the palace-fortress personnel was located.

The remains of the Hasmonean fortress consist of three towers on the crest of the mountain, part of the defensive wall on its southwest side, and some rooms that were reused as a substructure for the *thermae* – the baths – in the Herodian fortress. A tower at the northwest corner of the site's lower segment also belongs to this period.

FIG. 9.5   Courtyard with colonnade in the Palace-Fortress (photo by Sherry Hardin).

This tower was connected to a large rock-cut water reservoir of 8 m depth. The reservoir, the entrance of which was carefully masked and blocked in antiquity, is perfectly preserved.

The central Herodian palace-fortress measures 110 (E–W) × 60 (N–S) meters. A north–south running corridor divided the structure into two blocks. The eastern block has a paved courtyard in the center flanked by the *thermae* (baths) on the south; there are also additional rooms. The western block has a peristyle of columns on the north, erected on a water cistern, and a possible *triclinium* (formal dining area) on the south (fig. 9.5). There are traces of mosaics within the rooms of the fortress.[6]

Aqueduct and Bridge

An aqueduct, 15 m in height, brought rainwater from the nearby plateau to a series of hewn and plastered cisterns on the northern slope of the mountain (fig. 9.6). It also served as a bridge that connected the for-

---

6   A mosaic from the baths of the fortress dates to the first century BC, the time of Herod the Great (ruled from 37–4 BC), which makes it the most ancient mosaic found in Jordan to date. It is now in the Madaba Archaeological Park (see Chapter 7).

FIG. 9.6   The water system at Machaerus (photo by Sherry Hardin).

tress to the high plateau. A lower channel directed water from Wadi al-Mishnaqa into a lower series of cisterns.

Only a few houses have been excavated in the lower town, which was built on the site's steep northern slope. These houses are located inside the northern retaining and defensive wall surrounding the site. The wall was defended on both sides by a tower. From inside this tower, the large cistern referred to above could be reached.

CHURCHES IN THE VILLAGE OF MUKAWER

Three Byzantine churches and/or chapels have been located in the ruins of the village of Mukawer, around 2 km to the east of the palace-fortress (fig. 9.7). The northern one, with its mosaics, was built in AD 602–603. The central church, the Church of Bishop Malechios, possibly dates from the first half of the seventh century. The third church is referred to as the West Church.

The West Church

The West Church (0749935 E/3495721 N; elev. 719 m) is located at the western extremity of the modern village, immediately south of the road leading to Machaerus. It has been investigated but not excavated. The investigations revealed that it is a basilica-style church with three aisles. Piccirillo dates a strip of mosaics in it to AD 603 (1995). Presently, it is difficult to discern any traces of the church's structure.

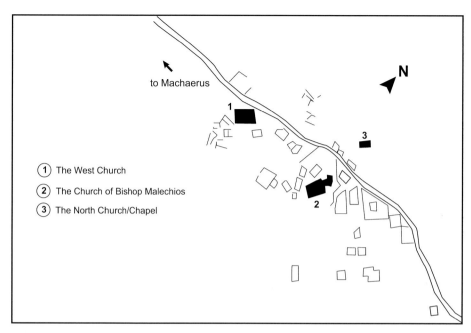

FIG. 9.7 Plan of the location of the churches in the village of Mukawer (adapted from Piccirillo 1995: plan 27).

The Church of Bishop Malechios

The Church of Bishop Malechios (figs. 9.8–9; UTM coordinates: 0750041 E/ 3495629 N; elev. 717 m) is also located to the south of the road that cuts through the modern village. It is ca. 100 m east of the West Church. It too is a basilica with three aisles, measuring 21.5 × 15 m. The bishop, after whom the church is named, was unknown until the church's discovery; he belonged to the Episcopal Seat of Madaba. A Greek inscription in the north aisle of the church mentions "Sergios and George, servants of

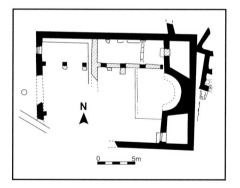

FIG. 9.8 Ground plan of the Church of Bishop Malechios (adapted from Piccirillo 1995: 297).

Christ." Both are well-known from other churches in the Madaba region. Piccirillo dates the church to the end of the fifth or the beginning of the sixth century.

FIG. 9.9   The Church of Bishop Malechios in the village of Mukawer (photo by Sherry Hardin).

The North Church/Chapel

The North Church/Chapel (fig. 9.10; UTM coordinates: 0750150 E/3495658 N; elev. 706) is located on the northern slope of the hill on which the modern village is located. It is a small church or chapel, measuring 13.65 × 6 m, with but one aisle. Its date is unknown.

APPENDIX – THE WATERS OF CALLIRHOE AND BAAROU / BAARAS

Callirhoe and Baarou/Baaras are two locations of hot/thermal springs along the northeastern shore of the Dead Sea that were of importance in antiquity. According to Josephus, King Herod the Great visited the ones at Callirhoe: "(Herod) went over the Jordan, and made use of the hot waters of Callirrhoe, which run into the lake Asphaltitis, but are themselves sweet enough to be drunk" (*War* 1.657). Lake Asphaltitis is, of course, the Salt Lake or Dead Sea (Alliata 1999: 56).

There would probably have been a harbor on the Dead Sea at Callirhoe to land boats coming across the water from Jericho. Moreover, a pathway would have gone up the mountain from Callirhoe to Herod's palace at Machaerus (Clamer 1999).

FIG. 9.10 The North Church/Chapel in the village of Mukawer (photo by Sherry Hardin).

Archaeological work at the site of Callirhoe shows that it was planned in connection with Herod the Great's building activities at Machaerus. Remains dating from the end of the first century BC to the end of the first century AD indicate that the area was a place of thermal baths and recreation centers close to the Dead Sea. Access would have been easy, even for sick guests arriving by boat. Villas and farm houses were located on the lower terraces of the site. After a gap of 300 years, the site was reoccupied during the Byzantine period in the second half of the fourth and the fifth century. However, occupation was sparse (Clamer 1999).

Josephus also describes the place called Baarou/Baaras: "In that valley which encompasses the city (of Machaerus) on the north side, there is a certain place called Baaras, which produces a root of the same name with itself" (*Wars* 7.180–81). The valley that Josephus refers to is Wadi Zarqa Ma'in. He continues: "In this same region flow hot springs …." According to Clamer (1998: 222), this description clearly refers to the hot springs of Hammamat Ma'in, situated in Wadi Zarqa Ma'in, ca. 4 km inland.

Josephus places Machaerus on the south side of Wadi Zarqa Ma'in. *Baaras* is located on its north side.

According to Eusebius and Jerome, in the *Onomasticon* and the *Book on the Sites and Names of Places of the Hebrews* respectively, the hot springs of Baarou/Baaras are near a very large village by the name of Beelmeon:

> **Beelmeon** (Num. 32:38). Beyond the Jordan, which the sons of Reuben built. It is a very large village near Baarou with hot waters called Beelmaous of Arabia, situated 9 milestones from Esbos. The prophet Elisha came from there (46); and **Beelmeon**, across the Jordan, which the children of Reuben built. It is even today a large village near Baarus in Arabia, where hot water springs spontaneously from the earth, called Beelmaus, nine miles from Esbus, whence Elisha the Prophet came (47) (Taylor et al. 2003: 32).

The toponym "meon" may be preserved in the name of the modern village of Ma'in and in the water course of Wadi Zarqa Ma'in. The ancient village is mainly from the Byzantine period (MacDonald 2000: 117–18). The given distance of nine Roman miles from Esbus (Heshbon) fits. Both Eusebius and Jerome place the home town of Elisha at Beelmeon.

On the Madaba Mosaic Map the hot springs of Baarou/Baaras are placed slightly northeast of the Baths of Callirhoe, which are depicted with date palms along the east shore of the Dead Sea (fig. 9.11). This position corresponds to the hot springs of Hammam az-

FIG. 9.11 Detail of the Madaba Mosaic Map with the Baths of Callirhoe shown (photo by Jonathan Ferguson).

Zarqa or Hammamat Ma'in (Alliata 1999: 56–57). Alliata identifies the "Waters of Callirhoe" with Zara (1999: 56–57).

Peter the Iberian

Peter the Iberian's description of the hot springs at Baarou/Baaras agrees with that of Josephus. In 481, after he found the springs at Livias too cold, the people of the area suggested that Peter visit the hot springs at Baarou/Baaras along the northeastern shore of the Dead Sea, not far from the town of Madaba (Horn 2005: 142; 2006: 241).

SUGGESTIONS FOR GETTING TO THE SITES

To get to the site of Machaerus/Mukawer, take the Airport Highway south off Amman. At the sign for Madaba turn to the southwest. Go through the town of Madaba and continue south along the King's Highway. At Libb, follow the signs to Machaerus/Mukawer. Drive through the village of Mukawer and continue on until you come to the parking lot for visitors to the site of Machaerus. It is about a ten-minute walk from the parking lot to the top of the site. You will need about one hour and a quarter to drive from Amman to the site.

Once you have visited the palace-fortress, you may wish to continue on to the churches, especially the Church of Bishop Malechios, in the village of Mukawer.

Visits to both the archaeological site and the village can be done in a half-day.

The Waters of Callirhoe are located along the east side of the Dead Sea. They are now the location of a public bathing area. To get to them, take the Airport Highway south off Amman. Follow the signs to the Dead Sea. The Waters of Callirhoe are located south of the major hotels along the northeast side of the Dead Sea. Driving time from Amman to the area is about one hour.

Baarou/Baaras, as indicated above, is identified with Hammam as-Zarqa or Hammamat Ma'in. It can be reached by following the signs from Amman to Madaba and then on to the hot springs. The drive from Amman is about one hour.

188

FIG. 10.1 View of the Dead Sea (photo by David Shankbone, 2007).

10 LOT'S CAVE, INCEST AND A PLACE OF PILGRIMAGE

DAYR 'AYN 'ABATA

THE story of Lot's living in a cave with his two daughters, their pregnancy by their father, and the resulting birth of the ancestors of the Moabites and the Ammonites follows the narratives of the separation of Abraham and Lot and the destruction of Sodom and Gomorrah. Generations after these stories were related, and specifically during the early development of Christianity, Lot was known as a "saint" and received special veneration. Evidence for this comes from the Bible, the archaeological remains unearthed at Dayr 'Ayn 'Abata, along the southeast coast of the Dead Sea, and inscriptional material from Khirbat al-Mukhayyat, close to Mount Nebo. Moreover, the cave where early Christians believed that Lot lived with his daughters and where the incest occurred became a place of pilgrimage.

BIBLICAL TEXTS

Both Abraham and his nephew Lot had large flocks and herds. As a result, the land was not able to sustain them both. Since Abraham wished to avoid strife, he offered Lot his choice of land. Lot chose the plain of the Jordan, journeyed eastward, settled in the cities of the Plain, and moved his tent as far as Sodom. But "the people of Sodom were wicked, great sinners before the LORD" (Gen 13.13).

Sometime later the LORD revealed to Abraham, who was living by the oaks of Mamre (Gen 13.18) at Hebron, that he was going to destroy the cities of Sodom and Gomorrah because of the sinfulness of their people. Abraham questioned the justice of God in allowing innocent people to be punished with the guilty (Genesis 18).

The story continues in Genesis 19. Two angels, in the form of men, arrived at the gates of Sodom in the evening at a time when Lot was sitting there. Lot, being a hospitable man, invited them to spend the night in his house. After some persuasion, they accepted and Lot made them a feast. However, the men of Sodom arrived at Lot's door and requested to have sexual relations with the visitors. Lot pleaded with them but to no avail. Then, in keeping with his responsibilities as a host, rather than giving up his visitors, Lot offered his two virgin daughters to the men. The men of Sodom refused Lot's offer and were on the verge of doing harm to Lot and breaking down the door of his house, when the angels brought Lot inside the house, shut the door, and struck the men of Sodom with blindness so that they were unable to find the door.

Lot's visitors revealed to him that they were about to destroy the city and urged him to leave the city with his wife and two daughters. Lot was reluctant to leave, but the angels seized him and the members of his family and led them out of Sodom and told them to flee for their life, not to look back, and not to stop anywhere in the Plain. Lot was, however, reluctant and thought that he could not flee to the hills, since he feared that disaster would overtake him. Instead, he wanted to flee to a "little one," that is, the small city of Zoar, where his life would be saved. The angels granted Lot's request, and Lot and his family members reached Zoar before the LORD rained sulfur and fire out of heaven on Sodom and Gomorrah. And the LORD overthrew the cities of the Plain, all their inhabitants, and all vegetation. But Lot's wife looked back and she became a pillar of salt (Gen 19.26).

Abraham saw the devastation. However, the LORD did not forget him and thus spared Lot and his family. But Lot and his daughters did not stay in Zoar!

Genesis 19.30–38

> Now Lot went up out of Zoar, and settled in the hills with his two daughters, for he was afraid to stay in Zoar; so he lived in a cave with his two daughters. And the firstborn said to the younger, "Our father is old, and there is not a man on earth to come in to us after the manner of all the world. Come, let us make our father drink wine, and we will lie with him, so that we may preserve offspring through our father." So they made their father drink wine that night; and the firstborn went in, and lay with her father; he did not know when she lay down or when she rose. On the next day, the firstborn said to the younger, "Look, I lay last night with my father; let us make

him drink wine tonight also; then you go in and lie with him, so that
we may preserve offspring through our father." So they made their
father drink wine that night also; and the younger rose, and lay with
him; and he did not know when she lay down or when she rose.
Thus both the daughters of Lot became pregnant by their father.
The firstborn bore a son, and named him Moab; he is the ancestor
of the Moabites to this day. The younger also bore a son and named
him Ben-ammi; he is the ancestor of the Ammonites to this day.

The general geographical setting for the story is the cities of the Plain and
their nearby hills. The cities consisted of Sodom, Gomorrah, Admah,
Zeboiim, and Bela (Zoar) (Gen 14.2). Four eastern kings did battle with
these cities "in the Valley of Siddim (that is, the Dead Sea)" (Gen 14.3). It
was in Sodom that Lot pitched his tent, and it was to Zoar that he fled when
the cities of Sodom and Gomorrah were threatened with destruction.

There is support in the biblical texts for locating the cities of the
Plain both north and south of the Dead Sea; however, the majority of
texts support a southern location. Extra-biblical texts are almost unani-
mous in locating the cities, particularly Sodom and Zoar, in relation to
the southern basin of the Dead Sea (see Appendix 1 – Zoar; MacDonald
2000: 45–61). Moreover, it is in the hills along the southeastern shore of
the Dead Sea that Lot's Cave is located.

Although the NRSV and other modern English translations follow
the convention and have Lot and his daughters living "in a cave," the
Hebrew text has the definite article to signify "a certain cave." Thus, it
could be that Lot lived in the hills "in a well-known cave." If such is the
case, then this story could be based on a Transjordanian legend tracing
the common ancestry of Moab and Ammon to Lot, who was worshipped
at the "cave" referred to in Gen 19.30. Did the author of the text know of
a particular cave in the hills in the vicinity of Sodom and Zoar? Was this
particular cave known to the people of the early Christian period as one
that was associated with Lot? And if so, is this the reason they built their
monastery there as a memorial to Saint Lot?

The birth of the ancestors of the Moabites and the Ammonites is the
result of incest between Lot and his daughters. Lot is excused because "he
did not know when she lay down or when she rose" (Gen 19.33, 35). He
was thus without fault and considered "saintly" by subsequent generations. The daughters are likewise found without fault, because "there is
not a man on earth to come in to us after the manner of all the world"
(Gen 19.31). They thus took the only action that was open to them to
"preserve offspring through our father" (Gen 19.32).

The Old Testament/Hebrew Scriptures are a product of first-millennium-BC Israel and were thus written by an adversary of the Moabites and Ammonites. Viewed in this light, the story could have been used to poke fun at two of Israel's enemies.

EXTRA-BIBLICAL TEXTS

Eusebius in the *Onomasticon* and Jerome in *Book on the Sites and Names of the Places of the Hebrews* provide only general information on the location of Sodom, Gomorrah, Adamah, Zeboiim, and Bela (Zoar), the cities of the Plain. Our interest here is in the first two cities. We will treat Zoar later (see Appendix 1 – Zoar).

> **Gomorra** (Gen. 10:19). One of the five cities of Sodom destroyed at the same time as the rest (60); and **Gomorra**. One of the five cities of the Sodomites, which suffered divine vengeance like the rest (61) (Taylor et al. 2003: 39).

> **Sodoma** (Gen. 14:2). A city of sinful men which was burnt near the Dead Sea (150); and **Sodoma**. A city of sinful men which was consumed by divine fire, beside the Dead Sea (151) (Taylor et al. 2003: 84).

Eusebius posits a relationship between Gomorrah and Sodom, and the latter is said to be located near the Dead Sea.

FIG. 10.2 Detail of the Madaba Mosaic Map showing the location of Lot's Church (photo by Sherry Hardin).

Madaba Mosaic Map

The Madaba Mosaic Map places a church in the hills at the southeastern end of the Dead Sea (fig. 10.2). The inscription accompanying the structure reads "the (place) of Saint Lot" (Alliata 1999: 58, 61). It is located north of Zoar, also on the map. The site is identified with Dayr 'Ayn 'Abata, the archaeological name given to the site at the time of its discovery (MacDonald and Politis 1988; MacDonald et al. 1992: 104). The archaeological name indicates that the site is a monastery located at a spring called the "spring of the Abbot." As archaeological investigations have proven, both designations have turned out to be correct.

There appears to be no doubt that the Byzantine craftsmen who designed the Madaba Mosaic Map knew of the existence of a church along the eastern side of the Dead Sea that was called "Saint Lot." They show it as being not far from Zoar (see Appendix 1).

Life of Saint Stephen the Sabaite

The Life of Saint Stephen the Sabaite mentions that the monks who walked around the Dead Sea during Lent in the mid-eighth century stopped at the caves of Saint Lot:

> He was living with them (…) in the caves of the Arnon, or of Saint Lot, or of Saint Aaron, or beyond the Dead Sea (*Vita S. Stephani Sabaitae* 17:3).

Abbot Daniel

The Abbot Daniel visited "Sigor" in the early years of the 12th century. About Lot and his cave he writes:

> Lot's sepulchre and that of his two daughters are to be seen there; they are two separate sepulchres. In this mountain there is a large cavern, in which Lot took refuge with his daughters …. (*Pilgrimage of the Russian Abbot Daniel in the Holy Land* 56; Wilson 1895: 47).

In the area of Sigor, that is, Zoar, Abbot Daniel claims to have visited Lot's cave and the two tombs in which Lot and his two daughters were interred. The cave is said to be located in mountainous terrain. Abbot Daniel goes on to say that towards the south there is a stone column that is Lot's wife. His visit reflects a tradition of venerating Lot in this area well into medieval times.

DAYR 'AYN 'ABATA – THE ARCHAEOLOGY

Since "the (place) of Saint Lot" is depicted on the Madaba Mosaic Map, researchers have attempted for centuries to locate it along the eastern shores of the Dead Sea. Beginning in the 1930s, some identified the church of Saint Lot with that of a small hermitage in the north cliffs at the mouth of the Wadi al-Hasa gorge (see Appendix 1 – Zoar). However, during the course of an archaeological survey that I conducted in the Southern Ghors and Northeast 'Arabah in 1986, survey team members discovered and reported the structures that Politis later excavated as Dayr 'Ayn 'Abata, or Lot's Cave. What caught our attention on the first day

FIG. 10.3   View from Lot's cave toward the visitors' center (photo by Sherry Hardin).

we visited the site was the discovery of a large pottery sherd, possibly a part of a communion paten, which had a cross engraved on it. Under the arms of the cross were the Greek letters *Alpha* (A) and *Omega* (Ω), the first and last letters of the Greek alphabet (MacDonald and Politis 1988; MacDonald et al. 1992: 103). Christians use these two symbols to indicate that Christ is "the first and the last, the beginning and the end" (Revelation 22.13).[1] This was our first clue that we were dealing with an ecclesiastical structure.

The site (UTM coordinates: 0738877 E/3437658 N; elev. -253 m) is located on a steep mountain slope overlooking what was once the southern end of the Dead Sea. Today, due to the shrinking of the Dead Sea, the site overlooks agricultural fields as well as the spring from which it takes its name. It is located immediately to the northeast of the modern town of as-Safi. From the site, one gets a wonderful view to the south, west, and north of the lowest land surface on the face of the earth (figs. 10.3–4).

There is material evidence for a fifth–sixth-century church and monastery at the site. However, no *in situ* structures from this period were uncovered.

Excavations of a later monastic complex at the site includes the reservoir, the church and its adjoining cave, and the living quarters for

---

1   A cistern excavated by P. Bikai in Madaba has a cross with these letters under its right and left "arms."

FIG. 10.4 View from Lot's cave toward the west (photo by Sherry Hardin).

monks and a hostel for pilgrims (fig. 10.5). The latter structures are located at the northern segment of the site, still next to the cave.

The Reservoir

The first segment of the site that the excavators worked on was the reservoir (fig. 10.6), which is located at the site's southern extremity, next to a wadi (dry river bed). It was 6 m deep and covered with arches. In antiquity, aqueducts brought water from farther up the wadi to provide the needs of the monastery's inhabitants. In addition, water would have been available from the spring at the foot of the mountain below the site.

Work in the area of the reservoir resulted in the discovery of remnants of a mosaic with a 12-line inscription dated to AD 574. The in-

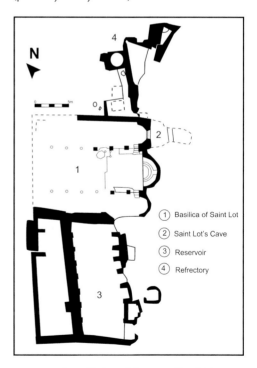

1. Basilica of Saint Lot
2. Saint Lot's Cave
3. Reservoir
4. Refectory

FIG. 10.5 Overall plan of the site of Lot's Cave /Dayr 'Ayn 'Abata (adapted from Politis 1995: 478).

FIG. 10.6   The reservoir at Lot's Cave / Dayr 'Ayn 'Abata (photo by Sherry Hardin).

scription named the mosaicist Kosmas. It is the largest of all the mosaics found at the site and may have been located at the monastery's entrance.

The Church

The triple-apsed basilica church, located immediately north of the reservoir and built directly into the hillside, is particularly well-preserved (fig. 10.7). It was paved with four mosaics, three of which had Greek inscriptions.

A mosaic within the front of the church, which contained the altar, is decorated with typical early Byzantine motifs such as birds, a lamb, and a peacock, all surrounded by vines. An inscription reads *telos kalon*, that is, "good end." Another mosaic is located in the nave of the church. It has a Greek inscription of six lines and names the country bishop and presbyter as Christoforos, the presbyter and steward as Zenon, the governor as Ioannis, son of Rabibos, and describes the site as a holy place and the church as a basilica. The construction of the mosaic is dated to May AD 691. The entire inscription is enclosed in a rectangle that has an additional diagonal inscription naming an Iannis, son of Sabinaou, who presumably was the mosaicist.

FIG. 10.7 The apse of main church at Lot's Cave / Dayr 'Ayn 'Abata (photo by Sherry Hardin).

This inscription is of particular importance. Describing the church as a basilica means that it was large enough to accommodate pilgrims, since a small monastic community would only require a chapel. As indicated above, the inscription specifically calls the basilica a "holy place," which infers an association with a biblical episode. It also attests to the existence of a local Christian community whose members have Semitic names like Rabibos and Sabinaou. Since part of this mosaic was damaged and in danger of sliding down the slope, the excavators removed it. To their surprise, they discovered another mosaic floor, belonging to AD 605, an earlier phase of the church, underneath.

A four-line inscription, in a *tabula ansata* at the eastern end of the northern aisle and just at the entrance to the cave bears the names of Bishop Jacobus and the Abbot Sozomenos. It provides a date of AD 606 (Piccirillo 1992: 336).

At the northeastern end of the nave, the excavators discovered a part of the pulpit. Once it was removed, they found traces of the pulpit that belonged to the earlier phase of the church.

From the above it is evident that the church was renovated in AD 691. The date is important, since it is well into the Umayyad period (AD 661–750), the time of the first Islamic dynasty. This indicates that

FIG. 10.8 The entrance to Lot's Cave at Dayr 'Ayn 'Abata (photo by Sherry Hardin).

there was religious tolerance and collaboration between Christians and Moslems well into the beginning of Islam. The excavators concluded that the church was peacefully abandoned.

Among the debris of columns and other architectural elements strewn around the site, the excavators uncovered a reused block with a red-painted inscription invoking Saint Lot.

The Cave

The cave, the entrance to which is actually the north aisle of the church (fig. 10.8), appears to have been central to the complex's existence. It is a natural one in the slope of the site. Its entrance is preserved to its original height. The sandstone pilaster capitals that constitute the frames of the entrance are carved with eight-cornered (Maltese-type) crosses bearing remnants of red paint; the lintel had a similarly engraved cross in the center. This cross is flanked by two rosettes, also with traces of paint. One graffiti on the plastered wall on the south side of the entrance gave the name, in Greek, of a local Christian woman called Nestasia Zenobia. Another, in Kufic Arabic script, is an Islamic invocation.

A room, measuring 2 × 2.5 m, is within the cave. It was paved with fine white marble slabs. This could indeed be the place where early Christians believed that Lot and his two daughters took refuge after their flight from Zoar.

Finds within the cave indicate that it has a long history of occupation. The most recent materials recovered date to the early ninth century AD, probably the final habitation of the cave. Under the cave's floor, which is dated to the Byzantine–Abbasid period (fourth–eighth centuries), the excavators found ceramic and glass oil lamps dating to the early Byzantine period, ca. fourth–sixth centuries AD. Beneath this, they uncovered Late Hellenistic–Nabataean vessels from the first century BC to the first century AD. Still farther down, evidence of Early Bronze and Middle Bronze "habitation" within the cave was unearthed; it consists of a fine ceramic chalice and a copper duck-bill axe-head, belonging to the Middle Bronze Age II period (ca. 1900–1550 BC). Digging deeper, the excavators found multiple burials surrounded by a stone wall and over a dozen pottery juglets and cups dating from the Early Bronze Age I (ca. 3300–3000 BC). The ceramics were in association with many burials. Flint tools, a complete jug, a dipper, and drinking cups characteristic of this period attest to an occupational phase to the west in front of the wall. Overall, the archaeological evidence indicates that the cave could have been used as a place of shelter for around five thousand years.

One inscribed architectural block located just in front of the cave bears an inscription in Greek. It asks Saint Lot to bless Sozomenou, Ulpious, and a third person whose name cannot be deciphered. Politis, the excavator, thinks that these people were probably pilgrims or monks who lived in the monastery.

The domestic quarters of the site consist of several different features. There is a communal dining room or refectory, complete with long benches, a pilgrims' hostel, and a communal burial chamber in what had once been a cistern. The chamber contained twenty-eight adult males, one adult female, and three infants. It is possible that this segment of the site also served as a hospital or infirmary for the monks and pilgrims.

The entire complex – consisting of reservoir, church, cave, and domestic quarters – dates from the Byzantine to early Abbasid period (fifth–eighth centuries). An early ninth-century Arabic inscription at the site may attest to a Muslim interest in Lot, whom the Koran describes as a prophet (*Qur'an* 37: 133–36).

Terracing

Work at Dayr 'Ayn 'Abata revealed terracing down the slope immediately to the west of the site. This could have been one of the places where the monks planted crops; the excavations have revealed, through analysis of bones and seeds, the plants and animals consumed at the monastery in the sixth–eighth centuries. A great deal of the produce and meat the monks, and most likely the pilgrims, ate would have come from of the local area; some of this food may have come from planting and harvesting or raising and eventually slaughtering at the site itself.

APPENDIX 1 – ZOAR

Zoar is one of the cities of the Plain (Gen 14.2). It was to here that Lot, his wife, and his two daughters fled at the time of the destruction of Sodom and Gomorrah. The Bible describes it as a "small place," since the word Zoar means "little" (Gen 19.20–22).

The site of Bala/Sigor/Soora/Zoar/Zogora/Zoora is of importance to Eusebius and Jerome. Both have multiple entries for it, under various names. It was a town that would have existed in their times.

> **Bala** (Gen. 14:2). This is Sigor, now called Zoora, the only one of the cities of the Sodomites to be saved. Even now it is still inhabited, lying beside the Dead Sea, and there is a garrison of soldiers there. And balsam and date-palms grow there, evidence of the ancient prosperity of the places (42); and **Bala**, that is, Segor. Now it is called Zoar, the only one of the five cities saved by the prayers of Lot. It is close to the Dead Sea, and a garrison of Roman soldiers is stationed there, manned by its own inhabitants. Balsam and dates are grown there, a proof of ancient fruitfulness. But nothing suggests that Segor is called by the same name as Zoara, when the same name is of one smaller or lesser; but it is called Segor in Hebrew, and Zoara in Syriac. Bala means swallowed up; but we have spoken at length about this in the Books of Hebrew Questions (43) (Taylor et al. 2003: 31).

> **Zogera** (Jer. 48:34). In Jeremiah. A city of Moab. The same is now called Zoora, or Sigor, one of the five cities of the Sodomites (94); and **Zogora**. In Jeremiah, a city of the Moabites. This is what is now called Zoara or Segor, one of the five cities of the Sodomites (95) (Taylor et al. 2003: 54).

Eusebius and Jerome provide a great deal of information. Both locate the site beside the Dead Sea. It was the site of a garrison of (Roman) soldiers and, Jerome adds, manned by the inhabitants of the town. Moreover, it was a prosperous place, growing both balsam and date palms. The *Notitia Dignitatum* (34.26), dated to the end of the fourth and beginning

FIG. 10.9 Detail of the Madaba Mosaic Map depicting Zoar (photo by Sherry Hardin).

of the fifth century AD, also indicates the presence of a Roman garrison at Zoar.

Madaba Mosaic Map

The Madaba Mosaic Map depicts the town of Zoar as a large walled building with an arched entrance and three towers (fig. 10.9). The town is surrounded by six date palm trees, indicating a well-watered area. It is located to the south of "The (place) of Saint Lot" on the same map. The accompanying inscription reads:

> Balak also Segor, now Zoara.

Alliata identifies the "Balak also Segor, now Zoara" of the Madaba Mosaic Map with Ghor as-Safi (1999: 58).

Abbot Daniel

The Abbot Daniel visited "Sigor" in the early years of the 12th century but did not go farther south, because he feared the people of the area (*Pilgrimage of the Russian Abbot Daniel in the Holy Land* 56; Wilson 1895: 47).

FIG. 10.10 The hermitage in the north bank of Wadi al-Hasa, near its mouth (photo by Sherry Hardin).

A number of explorers have searched for the remains of Zoar in the vicinity of the modern town of as-Safi. As a result, most locate it at Khirbat Sheikh 'Isa, on the present south bank of Wadi al-Hasa, and the modern town of as-Safi. Early Bronze, Roman, Nabataean, Byzantine, and Islamic period sherds have been collected at the site (MacDonald et al. 1992). There seems to be little doubt that Khirbat Sheikh 'Isa was Byzantine–Early Islamic Zoar/Zughar/Sughar.[2]

Recent surveys and excavations at Khirbat Sheikh 'Isa revealed part of a large structure, which could be the one depicted on the Madaba Mosaic Map. Nearby, 700 inscribed funerary stelae have been found; most have come from illicit digging. More than 400 of these stelae have been recorded (Meimaris and Kritikakou-Nikolaropoulou 2005) and date to the fourth–sixth centuries AD. Around 90 percent are in Greek, while the remainder are in Jewish-Aramaic. This find provides more evidence for the presence of a Byzantine settlement at Zoar.

A hermitage is located just north of Khirbat Sheikh 'Isa, at the mouth of the Wadi al-Hasa gorge and on its north bank (fig. 10.10; MacDonald et al. 1992). A Greek inscription scratched on a wall of the hermitage reads: "O Lord God of this holy place, come to the help of your servant" (Saller and Bagatti 1949: 195). This hermitage was at one time identified with "The (place) of Saint Lot" of the Madaba Mosaic Map. However, with the 1986 discovery of the site of Saint Lot at Dayr 'Ayn 'Abata, the place is now regarded as a hermitage that could have been associated with Lot's Cave. There are other hermitages and church/monastery sites in the area, for example, those on the Lisan Peninsula to the northwest of Lot's Cave (Holmgren and Kaliff 1997; 2005).

---

2   The name Zughar/Sughar comes from the nearby sugar mills that existed in the area in the Early and Middle Islamic periods.

APPENDIX 2 – THE CHURCH OF SAINTS LOT AND PROCOPIUS AT KHIRBAT AL-MUKHAYYAT

The site of Khirbat al-Mukhayyat, the most probable candidate for the identification of the biblical site of the village of Nebo, is located on a ridge ca. 3 km to the southeast of the Memorial of Moses (see Chapter 6) at Ras al-Siyagha (MacDonald 2000: 86–87). It is related to the veneration of Saint Lot, since one of its churches is dedicated to the "Saints Lot and Procopius" and an inscription within the church is an intercessory prayer to Saint Lot.

Nebo (Num 33.47) is the name of both a geographical feature called Mount Nebo (Deut 32.49; 34.1) and a village/town. The village is depicted in the Bible as a city of Moab. Eusebius describes it as a "deserted village" in the fourth century AD that is located eight Roman miles from Esbus (Heshbon) (*Onomasticon* 136–37; Taylor et al. 2003: 75). John Rufus, the biographer of Peter the Iberian, knew a village by that name on the mountain of Nebo, which was inhabited by Christians; the shepherd who had a vision of the dead Moses in a cave probably came from this village. Moreover, it was probably the inhabitants of the village of Nebo who built the church over the alleged tomb of Moses at Ras al-Siyagha (see Chapter 6).

Archaeologists have extensively surveyed the area of Khirbat al-Mukhayyat and have found evidence of thousands of years of occupation. The Franciscan Archaeological Institute has excavated the site itself. The results include the uncovering of three churches and a monastery, along with evidence of a Byzantine settlement at the tell and nearby. One of the churches is of interest here because of its dedication to Saint Lot.

The Church of Saints Lot and Procopius (fig. 10.11; UTM coordinates: 0760023 E/3516141 N; elev. 767 m) is at the high point of the site and measures only 16.25 × 8.65 m. It was completely paved with mosaics. A dedicatory inscription in its nave dates its construction to AD 557, during the time of Bishop John of Madaba (fig. 10.12). The inscription reads:

> At the time of the most holy and most saintly bishop John, Your holy place was built and finished by its priest and sacristan Barichas in the month of November of the time of the sixth indiction. O God of Saint Lot and of Saint Procopius, receive the offering and the present of the brothers Stephen and Elias, the children of Cometissa. O God of the holy martyrs, receive the present of Sergius and Procopius his son. For the welfare of Rabata (the daughter) of Anastasia and

FIG. 10.11 The interior of the Church of Saints Lot and Procopius at Khirbat al-Mukhayyat (photo by Sherry Hardin).

> for the repose of John [the son] of Anastasius and for those who contributed; the Lord knows their names (Saller and Bagatti 1949: 184; Piccirillo 1992: 164).

The mosaic is divided into two separate panels: the eastern panel is decorated with hunting, pastoral, and wine-making scenes, while the western one is decorated with four fruit-laden trees placed in the four corners and meeting in the center. Pairs of animals facing each other are placed among the trees. Among the animals are two bulls facing an altar. The inscription below them reads, "Then they shall offer calves upon Your altar. Lord have mercy on the lowly Epiphania." The first part of the inscription is from Psalm 51.21.

Another inscription, at the eastern end of the southern aisle of the church, reads: "O Saint Lot, receive the prayer of Rome and Porphyria and Mary, your servants" (Saller and Bagatti 1949: 192; Piccirillo 1992: 165). On the basis of the inscriptions uncovered at Lot's Cave/Dayr 'Ayn 'Abata, those within the Church of Saints Lot and Procopius at Khirbat al-Mukhayyat, and the inscription and depiction of a church dedicated to Saint Lot on the Madaba Mosaic Map, there is no doubt that the Christians of the Byzantine period believed that Lot was a saint and that he actually enjoyed a special veneration. The saintly position of Lot is supported by Wisdom 10.6, which states: "Wisdom rescued a righteous man

FIG. 10.12 Greek inscription in the Church of Saints Lot and Procopius at Khirbat al-Mukhayyat (photo by Sherry Hardin).

when the ungodly were perishing; he escaped the fires that descended on the Five Cities" (see also Wisdom 19.17). Moreover, 2 Peter 2.7–8 reads: "and if he rescued Lot, a righteous man greatly distressed by the licentiousness of the lawless (for that righteous man, living among them day after day, was tormented in his righteous soul by their lawless deeds that he saw and heard)." In this latter text, Lot is held up as a model for Christians. As Lot remained faithful in the midst of lawlessness, so ought they.

SUGGESTIONS FOR GETTING TO THE SITES

To get to Lot's Cave/Dayr 'Ayn 'Abata, follow the Airport Road/Desert Highway south of Amman until you reach the signs for the Dead Sea. Turn right and follow the signs for the Dead Sea. Lot's Cave is located around two hours southwest of Amman, just to the north of the town of As-Safi. Ancient Zoar is located near As-Safi; however, there is nothing to see there of the remains of the ancient site. A visit to the pilgrimage site and As-Safi takes about a half day. There is a rest house and museum associated with Lot's Cave.

The Church of Saints Lot and Procopius is located at Khirbat al-Mukhayyat. It may be visited at the same time as a visit to either Madaba and/or the Memorial of Moses at Mount Nebo, since it is located between those two sites. The visit can be short, unless you have an interest in the other churches at the site. It may be best to visit the Memorial of Moses first, since the ticket to that site also provides admission to Khirbat al-Mukhayyat.

FIG. 11.1   Aerial view of Jabal Haroun (© David L. Kennedy, APAAMe, APA_2005-10-02_DLK-10).

11 THE MEMORIAL OF AARON
JABAL HAROUN (NEAR PETRA)

JOSEPHUS the Jewish historian, as well as early Christian and later Muslim traditions associate Jabal Haroun ("Mountain of the Prophet Aaron") with the death and burial place of Aaron. Later, these traditions are attested in the Crusader period (11th–13th centuries AD) and up to recent times (Peterman and Schick 1996: 477).

Early twentieth-century archaeological explorations on the peak of Jabal Haroun (fig. 11.1) uncovered evidence for the existence of an early Christian church at the place where a Muslim shrine (*weli*) is presently located (Peterman and Schick 1996: 475–77). Following up on this work, Peterman and Schick also examined the remains of a monastic complex on a plateau just below and to the west of the peak (1996: 473–75). More recently, the Finnish Jabal Haroun Project (FJHP) has excavated this complex and has established that the complex consists of a church, chapel, and associated quarters, including a possible hostel. The FJHP found evidence that the church was dedicated to Saint Aaron. All this indicates the pilgrimage character of the site.

AARON IN THE BIBLE – AN OVERVIEW

Aaron is the brother of Moses and Miriam; his association with the former is particularly strong. For example, the expression "Moses and Aaron" appears frequently in the Old Testament/Hebrew Scriptures. However, there are also a few places where the expression "Aaron and Moses" occurs (see, for example, Exodus 6.26; Numbers 3.1).

At the time of the Israelites' sojourn in Egypt and their enslavement there, the LORD appointed Aaron as his spokesperson because of Moses' difficulty in speaking (Exodus 4.10–16). At the beginning of the plague stories, Aaron also played a leading role (Exodus 5–8). Nevertheless, Moses is given the primary position in the departure of the Hebrews from Egypt and in subsequent events.

Aaron is the ancestor of the priestly Aaronites, the priests who claim descent from Levi through him; they are referred to as "the sons of Aaron" (Leviticus 3.8, 21.1; Numbers 10.8). Aaron is the model for later priests. He and his descendants are the ones who perform the most holy rituals, who handle the holiest of sacred objects, and who enter the holiest of places. They oversee all priestly functions and groups and monitor the activities of the priests at both the temple and the tabernacle (see Exodus 28–29; Leviticus 8–9; 1 Chronicles 6.49, 23.13, 24.19). Aaron is given instructions from the LORD through Moses as to how he and his sons are to bless the Israelites, which is to be done in the following fashion: "The LORD bless you and keep you; the LORD make his face shine upon you, and be gracious to you; the LORD lift up his countenance upon you and give you peace!" (Numbers 6.24–26).

But not all the biblical passages portray Aaron in a positive light. For example, Aaron joins his sister Miriam in opposing Moses because of Moses' marriage to a non-Israelite, challenging his authority. The LORD intervenes, sides with Moses, and is angry with Aaron and Miriam (Numbers 12). According to Numbers, there is no doubt that Aaron is second to Moses.

During the period between the departure from Egypt and the entering of the "Promised Land," Aaron once again was among the group who rebelled against the LORD at the waters of Meribah, the "place of quarreling," at Rephidim. The people were unhappy with Moses because of the lack of water and asked him why he made them leave Egypt to die of thirst in the desert. The situation is defused when the LORD commands Moses to strike the rock and the thirst of the people is quenched (Exodus 17.1–7). The incident at Meribah is cited below as the reason why Aaron must die and is not allowed to enter the land that the LORD has given to the Israelites.

Another role Aaron played during the wilderness wandering of the Israelites after their departure from Egypt is in the battle against the Amalekites, a people of southern Palestine and the Sinai peninsula. The Israelites, led by Joshua, were victorious against the Amalekites as long as Moses, who had climbed to the top of a hill with Aaron and Hur, held the staff of God in his hand and kept it raised. As he tired and was no longer able to hold his hands high, the Israelites began to lose the battle. The solution was for Moses to sit on a rock while Aaron and Hur, one on each side, supported his hands. Moses' hands remained steady till sunset and Joshua and his followers defeated the Amalekites (Exodus 17.8–13).

When Moses was up the mountain of Sinai speaking with God and receiving the two tablets of the covenant, he delayed in coming down. The people became restless, since they did not know what had happened to him. They gathered around Aaron and asked him to "make gods for us, who shall go before us." Aaron "took the gold from them, formed it in a mold, and cast an image of a calf." He next built an altar before the image, and the people "offered burnt offerings and brought sacrifices of well being; and the people sat down to eat and drink, and rose up to revel." When Moses came down from the mountain with the two tablets of the covenant in his hands, he heard the sounds of the revelers and found that the Israelites had sinned against God by making for themselves an image of a calf (the "Golden Calf") (Exodus 32). The LORD was angry with Aaron for his leadership in the affair and would have destroyed him except for the intercessory prayer of Moses and the complete destruction of the image (Deuteronomy 9.15–20).

In the New Testament, the Letter to the Hebrews speaks of Jesus being called to the priesthood by God, just like Aaron (5.1–6). However, to distinguish Jesus' priesthood from that of other contemporary priests, the author of Hebrews writes that Jesus is a priest "according to the order of Melchizedek," not to that of Aaron or Levi (Hebrews 7.4–22).

From the above, it is evident that Aaron appears in both a positive and negative light in the Bible. Despite the negative portrayal, he is remembered by Jews, Christians, and Muslims as a prophet and priest.

BIBLICAL TEXTS AND COMMENTARY ON THE DEATH OF AARON

There are three biblical texts that deal with the death of Aaron, but there is no general agreement about the place where it took place. Two of the passages place Aaron's death at Mount Hor (Numbers 20.22–29; Deuteronomy 32.48–51), while the third places it at Moserah (Deuteronomy 10.6). It is only this third passage that provides the explicit information that Aaron was buried where he died.

Numbers 20.22–29

> They set out from Kadesh, and the Israelites, the whole congregation, came to Mount Hor. Then the Lord said to Moses and Aaron at

Mount Hor, on the border of the land of Edom, "Let Aaron be gathered to his people. For he shall not enter the land that I have given to the Israelites, because you rebelled against my command at the waters of Meribah. Take Aaron and his son Eleazar, and bring them up to Mount Hor; strip Aaron of his vestments, and put them on his son Eleazar. But Aaron shall be gathered to his people, and shall die there." Moses did as the LORD had commanded; they went up Mount Hor in the sight of the whole congregation. Moses stripped Aaron of his vestments, and put them on his son Eleazar; and Aaron died there on the top of the mountain. Moses and Eleazar came down from the mountain. When all the congregation saw that Aaron had died, all the house of Israel mourned for Aaron thirty days.

Deuteronomy 32.48–51

On that very day the LORD addressed Moses as follows: "Ascend this mountain of the Abarim, Mount Nebo, which is in the land of Moab, across from Jericho, and view the land of Canaan, which I am giving to the Israelites for a possession. You shall die there on the mountain that you ascend and shall be gathered to your kin, as your brother Aaron died on Mount Hor and was gathered to his kin; because both of you broke faith with me among the Israelites at the waters of Meribath-kadesh in the wilderness of Zin, by failing to maintain my holiness among the Israelites."

Deuteronomy 10.6

The Israelites journeyed from Beeroth-bene-jaakan to Moserah. There Aaron died, and there he was buried. His son Eleazar succeeded him as priest.

According to Numbers and Deuteronomy, the death of Aaron took place at Mount Hor after the Israelites had left the oasis of Kadesh, generally located at either 'Ayn Qadeis or about 8 km to the north–northwest at 'Ayn al-Qudeirat on the southern edge of the Negev Desert (MacDonald 2000: 69). Thus, the mountain in question ought to be located to the east of the oasis. There is no mention of the burial of Aaron, but it is assumed that it was on the mountain, since Moses and Eleazar came down the mountain and no mention is made of the body. Moreover, the reason cited for Aaron's death, the lack of faith in God at Meribah, is the same in both texts.

The biblical authors evidently thought that a mountain peak was an appropriate place for the death of a leader such as Aaron, as it was for Moses. But locating the death of Aaron at Mount Hor is not in accordance with Deuteronomy 10.6, where Aaron dies at Moserah.

Most contemporary biblical commentators and geographers have difficulty in locating Mount Hor and therefore conclude that its positive identification is impossible (MacDonald 2000: 99, note 2).

Since Mount Hor is mentioned immediately after Kadesh, which lay to the west of the territory of the Edomites, the place of Aaron's death ought to be located on the western border of Edom or near the western segment of its territory and, therefore, far from Petra, which is to the east. The biblical writers obviously wanted the death of Aaron to occur outside the land of Canaan, so that the priestly version of the decree that the entire Exodus generation will perish in the "wilderness" (the Sinai Desert) would be fulfilled (Numbers 14.26–35).

The modern Bedouin have a great liking for being buried on mountain tops. There is much evidence for this in Jordan, where already existing watchtowers have become places of burial. Sometimes the body of a distinguished person is brought three or four days out of the steppe that it may be so buried. The Bedouin believe that they retain their union with the tribe if they can look out over the tribal camp from the mountain top.

In Deuteronomy 10.6, Moserah, which means "chastisement," is given as the place of both Aaron's death and burial. However, neither it nor Beeroth-bene-jaakan (the "wells of the Bene-jaakan") can be identified with any certainty (MacDonald 2000: 99, note 2).

Thus, we have two traditions in the biblical texts regarding the place of Aaron's death. No attempt, however, is made to reconcile them.

OTHER ANCIENT TEXTS

Despite the above, Josephus places the death of Aaron on one of the high mountains that encompass Petra:

> Now when this purification, which their leader made upon the mourning for his sister, as it has been now described, was over, he caused the army to remove and to march through the wilderness and through Arabia; and when he came to a place which the Arabians esteem their metropolis, which was formerly called *Arce*, but has now the name of *Petra*, at this place, which was encompassed with high mountains, Aaron went up one of them in the sight of the

whole army, Moses having before told him that he was to die, for
this place was over against them. He put off his pontifical garments,
and delivered them to Eleazar his son, to whom the high priesthood
belonged, because he was the elder brother; and died while the
multitude looked upon him. He died in the same year wherein he
lost his sister, having lived in all a hundred twenty and three years…
(*Antiquities* 4.4.7).

Josephus clearly locates the death of Aaron on one of the high mountains in the vicinity of Petra, a place he describes as a "metropolis" of the
Arabians. But, as indicated previously, neither *Arce* nor *Petra* is cited in
the biblical texts as the place of Aaron's death (and burial).

Both Eusebius, *Onomasticon*, and Jerome, *Book on the Sites and Names
of Places of the Hebrews*, place the death of Aaron at Or, a mountain near
Petra:

> Or (Num 20: 22, 28) A mountain in which Aaron died near the city
> of Petra, in which even until today the rock is shown that Moses
> struck. (176); and **Or**. The mountain where Aaron died, near the city
> of Petra, where even until today the stone is shown which Moses
> struck and gave water to the people (177) (Taylor et al. 2003: 98).

Eusebius and Jerome's location of the death of Aaron at Mount Hor
would appear to fit Jabal Haroun, since this is where later Islamic tradition located both Aaron's death and burial.[1]

EVIDENCE OF EARLY CHRISTIAN PRESENCE
AT PETRA AND JABAL HAROUN

There is no lack of evidence for Christian presence within ancient Petra
itself. Indeed, immediately following his conversion, Paul claims, "but
I went away at once into Arabia" (Galatians 1.17). The Arabia of Paul's
time would have been the Nabataean kingdom, of which Petra was the
capital.

Early 20th-century explorers speak of churches at Petra. Excavations
on the part of the American Center of Oriental Research, Amman, within the city proper in the 1990s and early years of the present century have
resulted in the uncovering of three ecclesiastical structures: the Church

---

1   Eusebius and Jerome also locate the place where Moses struck the rock and gave water to
the people in the same area as the death of Aaron. It is for this reason that the modern town
associated with Petra is called "Wadi Musa."

FIG. 11.2   The Petra Church in the central segment of the city of Petra (photo by Sherry Hardin).

of Saint Mary or "Petra Church" (late fifth–early seventh century; figs. 11.2–3), the Ridge Church (sixth century; probably destroyed in the earthquake of AD 551), and the Blue Chapel (late fifth or early sixth century). Moreover, the Ad-Dayr ("the monastery") monument also indicates Christian presence.

Bishops are attested at Petra beginning in the fourth century. The names of a number of them are known, since some attended church councils in that and subsequent centuries. An inscription in the Urn Tomb within Petra commemorates its conversion into a church in AD 446. A number of references also provide information to the

FIG. 11.3   Chancel screen in the Petra Church (photo by Sherry Hardin).

effect that Petra was a place of banishment for exiled ecclesiastical leaders in the fifth and sixth centuries.

John Moschus (late sixth–early seventh century) recounts the "saying" of Abba John of Petra to him and Sophronios (Moschus 1992: 94, ch. 113) and also mentions Abba Athenogenes, Bishop of Petra (chs. 127–29; Moschus 1992: 103–7). On one or more of his various sojourns, John Moschus could have visited Petra.

The Petra Papyrus Inventory 6, dated to June 15, AD 573 (or earlier), mentions the existence of "the Monastery (Holy House) of our Lord the Saint High-Priest Aaron" outside the city of Petra (Gagos and Frösén 1998: 477; Frösén and Fiema 2004: 7). The best candidate for this "monastery" is the ruins of a Byzantine monastery on Jabal Haroun (see below).

The Life of Saint Stephen the Sabaite mentions that the monks who walked around the Dead Sea during Lent in the mid-eighth century stopped, among other places, at the caves of *Mar Aaronis*, which could be at Jabal Haroun: "He was living with them (…) in the caves of the Arnon, or of Saint Lot, or of Saint Aaron, or beyond the Dead Sea" (*Vita S. Stephani Sabaitae* 17:3). However, a detour to this mountain while walking around the Dead Sea would be a significant one.

Al-Mas'udi, an Arab historian and traveler writing in 955–956, lists Jabal Haroun as a holy mountain of the Christians. He reports that it was in the possession of Melkite Christians (Peterman and Schick 1996: 477).

The monastery on Jabal Haroun was still in existence when the Crusaders arrived in Transjordan. Fulcher of Chartes mentions it during Baldwin's expedition in 1100: "Furthermore we found at the top of the mountain the Monastery of Saint Aaron where Moses and Aaron were wont to speak with God. We rejoiced very much to behold a place so holy and to us unknown" (see Peterman and Schick 1996: 477).

Gilbert the Abbot mentions an oratory there, while Master Thetmarus mentions it during his visit to Petra in 1217: "At length I came to Mount Or, where Aaron died, on whose summit is built a church in which live two Greek Christian monks. The place is called Muscera" (see Peterman and Schick 1996: 477).[2]

Islamic Tradition on Jabal Haroun

Jabal Haroun, sometimes referred to in modern Arabic as *Jabal Nebi Haroun* ("Mountain of the Prophet Aaron"), is today the location of a

---

[2] The place name is possibly a reference to Moserah of Deuteronomy 10.6.

Muslim shrine (*weli*) (fig. 11.4; UTM coordinates: 0731420 E/3356530 N; elev. 1340 m). The construction of the shrine is recorded by an Arabic inscription above its entrance. There are different versions as to what the inscription reads. According to E. H. Palmer, it states: "the building was restored by esh-Shim'ani, the son of Mohammed Calaon, sultan of Egypt by his father's orders, in the year 739 of the Hirjah" (AH 739 = AD 1338–1339). Others, however, read that it was built AH 728 (AD 1327–1328) or ca. AH 900 (AD 1495). The Muslim shrine was built reusing materials from the monastery. Within it, there is another Arabic inscription that records the construction of the tomb to an-Nasir Muhammad ibn Qalaun (for all the above see Peterman and Schick 1996: 477–78).

Evidence from Medieval Jewish Literature

FIG. 11.4 The Muslim shrine atop Jabal Haroun. Detail from aerial view (© David L. Kennedy, APAAMe, APA_2005-10-02_DLK-10).

Medieval Jewish pilgrims also record Jabal Haroun. In a list of Jewish tombs outside the Holy Land, Rabbi Jacob (1238–1244) notes: "It is three days journey on the road thence (from Sodom and Gomorrah) to Mount Hor where Aaron is buried." Moreover, an anonymous author in 1537 included it in a list of places where Jewish patriarchs are buried outside the Holy Land. Rabbi Yehezkel came to the site in 1851 and in his diary he refers to earlier visits by Jewish pilgrims in 1624 and 1732. However, none of these writers mention any Christian presence there (see Peterman and Schick 1996).

The Bilingual Sign at the Bottom of the Stairs leading to the Muslim Shrine

A modern, bilingual sign – in Arabic and in English – near the bottom of the stairs leading up to the Muslim shrine reads:

The Shrine of Prophet Aaron:
Prophet Aaron is the brother of Moses, peace be upon him. Aaron
died in the Sinai (Deut. 10:6) but his tomb was later moved to Mount
Hor, south of Petra. Sultan al-Nasir Muhammad son of Qalawun restored the shrine in AD 1320. The shrine is surmounted by a white
dome and a crypt is located under the prayer hall. Aaron is venerated by the local people of Wadi Musa and the Bdul Bedouins and
is commemorated by an annual festival in autumn.

THE ARCHAEOLOGY OF THE MUSLIM SHRINE
AND THE MONASTERY OF SAINT AARON

The peak of Jabal Haroun is ca. 1340 m above sea level. From it, facing
westward, one is able to look down on Wadi 'Arabah and across it to the
eastern Negev desert. Looking to the northeast, one looks over the site
of Petra.

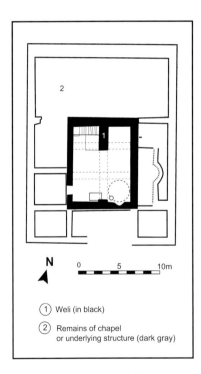

FIG. 11.5 Ground plan of the Muslim
shrine (*weli*) and remains of the underlying structure at the peak of Jabal
Haroun (adapted from Wiegand 1920).

History of Exploration

As mentioned previously, the peak is occupied today by the 14th-century Muslim
shrine. Within the shrine is a tomb believed
to contain the remains of Aaron. However,
early 20th-century visitors to the area reported the remains of a centrally planned church
at the peak of the mountain, built over by
the Muslim shrine. They also report Jewish
graffiti, marble fragments, mosaic cubes,
and a multi-colored marble floor beneath
the carpet that now covers the floor of the
Muslim shrine. Also on the peak, Peterman
and Schick (1996) reported five pieces of
marble colonnettes, which could have once
been part of a chancel screen. More recently,
the Finnish Jabal Haroun Project (FJHP) discovered fragments of marble floor tiles and
limestone tesserae also on the summit of the
Muslim shrine. Project team members also
found a cache of carved and inscribed marble
fragments on the bedrock ledge southeast of
and below the Muslim shrine and two large

pieces of a round, well-made, polished black granite vessel on a lower ledge to the east of the Muslim shrine. Thus, it is probable that a Christian structure existed at the peak before the Muslim shrine was built there (fig. 11.5). The shrine may, indeed, be a refurbished Byzantine church which was originally built in the time of Justinian I (reigned AD 527–565).

Peterman and Schick (1996) provided the first detailed description of an extensive ruined architectural complex located at ca. 1270 m elevation on a wide plateau of the mountain, ca. 70 m below and 150 m to the west of the peak with the Muslim shrine. At that time, they suggested that it represented the ruins of a Byzantine monastery (UTM coordinates: 0731209 E/3356542 N; elev. 1268 m), most likely dedicated to Saint Aaron.

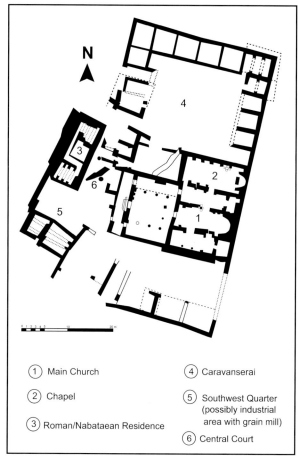

N

1. Main Church
2. Chapel
3. Roman/Nabataean Residence
4. Caravanserai
5. Southwest Quarter (possibly industrial area with grain mill)
6. Central Court

FIG. 11.6 Plan of the Monastery of Saint Aaron at Jabal Haroun (adapted from Frösén and Fiema 2004).

Investigations on the part of the FJHP, with an archaeological reconnaissance season in 1997 and excavations beginning in 1998, have uncovered the monastic complex that Peterman and Schick described in the 1990s. The complex included a large church and a chapel, along with some auxiliary structures and rooms (fig. 11.6). An uncovered mosaic floor dates to the sixth century. The excavators conclude "that the complex, in addition to its monastic function, had most probably also served as a pilgrimage center dedicated to the veneration of Saint Aaron, between the late 5th and the 8th centuries AD, possibly continuing up to the Crusader times (12th century AD)" (Frösén and Fiema 2004: 6).

FIG. 11.7 The main church of the monastic complex on Jabal Haroun, facing east (photo by Sherry Hardin).

Monastic Complex

According to the FJHP, the monastic complex measures ca. 62 (N–S) × 48 (E–W) m. Its various structures are located along the perimeter or inside this area. Back walls of all external rooms served as an enclosure of the entire complex, which may be divided into four main components and is situated around three courts. The components are: the church and chapel, which occupy the central location; the western and northern areas; the southwestern quarter; the central court.

Church and Chapel

Of all the structures comprising the complex, the church and chapel are the most significant. The church, which was most probably built in the late fifth century AD, was originally a large, rectangular basilica, internally measuring ca. 22.6 × 13.6 m (fig. 11.7). It was divided by two east–west rows of columns – with seven columns in each row – into the nave and two side aisles. The columns supported large horizontal beams, which in turn supported the roof construction. The sanctuary or altar area, which consisted of the apse and the rectangular low platform (*bema*), was located at the eastern end of the structure. The apse had a two-tiered, curving installation built against it. The liturgy of the church would have been

FIG. 11.8 Baptistry and chancel screen of the main church (photo by Sherry Hardin).

performed in this area and, thus, the altar was located here. Rectangular sacristy rooms were located on both sides of the apse. The church was decorated with marble furnishing; it had a marble floor and the *bema* had marble enclosures (chancel screens; fig. 11.8). The church's three doors were located in its western wall (Frösén and Fiema 2004: 9–10).

The chapel was built at the same time as the church and shared a wall with it. Its eastern end featured an apse flanked on both sides by high cupboards or cabinets. It is probable that marble once covered the floor of the chapel. At the western end of the chapel are the remains of an octagonal pit chiseled out of the bedrock. This was the area where a small baptismal font, cruciform in shape, was located. Close by were found the fragmented remnants of plaster. One of the fragments contained a Greek inscription that read *Prodromos* (ΠΡΟΔΡΟΜΟC), "the Forerunner," a reference to John the Baptist. Would pilgrims have been baptized here?

An earthquake is probably responsible for the destruction of the entire complex sometime in the sixth century. The church was restored but divided by a wall into eastern and western parts. The former continued to function as a church, but only two of the original columns were retained. Inside the apse, a throne for the bishop was installed in the middle of the two-tiered, curving installation. The western part of the original church was turned into an open court with two porches and probably served as

FIG. 11.9 Main columned courtyard of the monastic complex, facing east, toward the church (photo by Sherry Hardin).

a gathering place for the monks and pilgrims before and after liturgical ceremonies (fig. 11.9). A formal porch, with a colorful mosaic floor, was erected to the west of this open court. It was an enclosed space with a portico of four columns in the front.

After the destruction, some changes also occurred in the chapel. However, the baptismal font continued to fulfill its original function.

Sometime in the seventh century, another destruction occurred at the site. Again, major changes were made to the church. In the chapel, the baptismal font was abandoned and filled in. In its place, a new but also cruciform font was erected in the northern side of the chapel's rectangular low platform, on which was also placed the masonry base of a large altar or pedestal. An inscription, reading *[A]aron*, was found on a marble fragment in front of the pedestal.

Further changes to the church and chapel occurred in the eighth century. These may have been initiated by another destruction and/or to reinforce the structure against future earthquakes. The church still functioned in this century, but, as Byzantine iconoclasm targeted sacred images, stone tesserae forming mosaic faces of humans and animals were removed and replaced with large plain ones.

FIG. 11.10 Southwest corner of the caravanserai, facing west (photo by Sherry Hardin).

The Western and Northern Areas

The so-called western wing of the monastic complex is located to the west of the church. It is a monumental structure consisting of separate rooms. It appears that the entire western structure preceded the Byzantine monastery at the site, as it was built in the Nabataean–Roman period (first century BC–third century AD). Its function is unknown but it could have been a large residence. Once the monastery was built, this structure seems to have been incorporated into it, possibly as living quarters or a meeting place. A sloping wall, located directly west of the early monumental structure, could have served defensive purposes and/or as a reinforcement against potential earthquakes. It may date to the Crusader–Ayyubid period (12th–13th centuries AD). Relative to this later structure, the excavators think that even after the church and monastery were no longer in use, pilgrimages to the tomb of Saint Aaron would have continued. In their opinion, the reinforced western building would have provided safety and protection for visitors (Frösén and Fiema 2004: 13).

A large court, surrounded on three sides by 14 rooms of substantial size, is located to the north of the chapel. The excavators posit that this part of the monastery complex is reminiscent of a *caravanserai* – a typical Near Eastern hostel for travelers or pilgrims (fig. 11.10). One of the

FIG. 11.11   Main columned courtyard of the monastic complex, facing southeast (photo by Sherry Hardin).

excavated rooms is primarily dated to the fifth-sixth centuries and has multi-phased occupation. It is possible that the courtyard was used by visitors/pilgrims to prepare food and/or house their pack animals (Frösén and Fiema 2004: 13).

Southwestern Quarter

The southwestern quarter, located to the south of the church, consists of another court that is bordered by a series of rooms on its southern side. One of the rooms excavated in this area was spanned by two arches and probably occupied during the Byzantine and Islamic periods. The room could have served an industrial function, for example, as a grain mill.

Central Court

The central court with a cistern appears to have been the main communication hub of the entire complex (fig. 11.11). Through it, one could proceed from the southern to the northern court. The area around the cistern was paved with large flagstones. Three channels carried water from the area of the church into the cistern. There is evidence for very late temporary or casual occupation here (Frösén and Fiema 2004: 14–15).

CONCLUSIONS

The complex on the plateau below and to the west of the peak of Jabal Haroun was a monastery, built next to a memorial church to Aaron at the peak. This church is possibly dated to the late fifth century of the early Christian era and most probably coexisted with the monastery complex with its own church and chapel.

The type of monastery could have been similar to Late Roman agricultural estates, which were self-sufficient complexes. Thus, by means of its gardens and orchards, it would have served some of the needs of the pilgrims visiting the holy place associated with the prophet Aaron's death and burial. The thought of agricultural activity in such a presently barren region is not fanciful, since local informants have told the excavators that dams and associated cultivation fields were in use around Jabal Haroun as late as the early 20th century. However, as to this date there is very little archaeological support for such a conclusion (Lavento, et al. 2006).

SUGGESTIONS FOR GETTING TO THE SITE

The site of the Muslim shrine at the peak of Jabal Haroun and the monastery on a plateau to the west of the peak are not easily accessed. Although there are roads, general vehicular traffic is prohibited from the area. One dirt road, used by licensed archaeologists, leads to it; other roads in the area lead to Bedouin encampments in the region to the southwest of Petra.

Those who wish to visit Jabal Haroun can do so by foot, donkey, and/or camel. If you go by foot, doing so with a guide is strongly advised. Of course, if you do so by donkey or camel, the owner of the animal will accompany you. Guide prices are negotiable!

It is a distance of around 15 km from the ticket office at the entrance to Petra to the site. The walking is at times difficult and steep. Be sure to take plenty of water and some food. Allow a day for a leisurely visit. Thus, begin early.

BIBLIOGRAPHY

Ali, A.

2001 *Al-Qur'an: A Contemporary Translation*. Princeton, NJ: Princeton University.

Alliata, E.

1990 Nuovo settore del monastero al Monte Nebo-Siyagha. Pp. 427–66 in *Christian Archaeology in the Holy Land. New Discoveries: Essays in Honour of Virgillo*, eds. G. C. Bottini, D. Di Segni, and E. Alliata. Jerusalem: Franciscan Printing.

1999 The Legends of the Madaba Map. Pp. 47–101 in *The Madaba Map Centenary 1897–1997: Travelling Through the Byzantine Umayyad Period* (Proceedings of the International Conference held in Amman, 7–9 April 1997), eds. M. Piccirillo and E. Alliata. Studium Biblicum Franciscanum – Collectio Maior 40. Jerusalem: Franciscan Printing.

Alliata, E., and Bianchi, S.

1998 The Architectural Phasing of the Memorial of Moses. Pp. 151–91 in *Mount Nebo: New Archaeological Excavations 1967–1997*, eds. M. Piccirillo and E. Alliata. Studium Biblicum Franciscanum – Collectio Major 27. Jerusalem: Studium Biblicum Franciscanum.

Alt, A.

1935 Aus der 'Araba. II: Römische Kastelle und Strassen. *Zeitschrift des deutschen Palästina-Vereins* 58: 1–78 (see especially pp. 64–72 "Griechische christliche Inschriften aus *Fēnān*").

Applebaum, S., and Segal, A.

1993 Gerasa. Pp. 470–79 in *The New Encyclopedia of Archaeological Excavations in the Holy Land*, 2, ed. E. Stern. Jerusalem: The Israel Exploration Society & Carta.

Arculfus

1895 *The Pilgrimage of Arculfus in the Holy Land (About the Year A.D. 670)*. Translated and annotated by J. R. MacPherson. The Library of the Palestine Pilgrims' Text Society, Vol. 3. New York: AMS.

Avi-Yonah, M.
1954   *The Madaba Mosaic Map: With Introduction and Commentary.*
        Jerusalem: The Israel Exploration Society.

Benjamin ben Jonah of Tudela
1840–41 *The Itinerary of Rabbi Tudela.* Translated and edited by A. Asher.
        2 vols. London: Asher.

Bikai, P. M.
1996   Petra Church Project, Petra Papyri. *Annual of the Department of
        Antiquities of Jordan* 40: 487–89.

Bowsher, J. M. C.
1986   The Church Inscriptions. Pp. 319–22 in *Jerash Archaeological
        Project 1981–1983,* ed. F. Zayadine. Amman: The Department of
        Antiquities of Jordan.

Braemer, F., and Seigne, J.
1987   L'histoire de Jerash du Bronze moyen aux Omayyades. *Dossiers
        Histoire et Archéologie* 6: 50–55.

Browning, I.
1982   *Jerash and the Decapolis.* London: Chatto and Windus.

Bujard, J.; Piccirillo, M.; and Poiatti-Haldimann, M.
1992   Les Églises Géminées d'Umm er-Rasas: Fouilles de la mission
        archéologique suisse (Fondation Max van Berchem). *Annual of
        the Department of Antiquities of Jordan* 36: 291–306.

Burchardus de Mont Sion
1896   *A Description of the Holy Land (A.D. 1280).* Translated by A.
        Stewart with geographical notes by C. R. Conder. London: The
        Library of the Palestine Pilgrims' Text Society, Vol. 12.

Clamer, C.
1999   The Hot Springs of Kallirrhoe and Baarou. Pp. 221–25 in *The
        Madaba Map Centenary 1897–1997: Travelling Through the
        Byzantine Umayyad Period* (Proceedings of the International
        Conference held in Amman, 7–9 April 1997), eds. M. Piccirillo
        and E. Alliata. Studium Biblicum Franciscanum – Collectio
        Maior 40. Jerusalem: Franciscan Printing.

Clark, V. A.
1986   The Church of Bishop Isaiah at Jerash. Pp. 303–18 and 323–41
        in *Jerash Archaeological Project 1981–1983*, ed. F. Zayadine.
        Amman: The Department of Antiquities of Jordan.

Cohen, R.
1993   Kadesh-Barnea. Pp. 841–47 in *The New Encyclopedia of
        Archaeological Excavations in the Holy Land*, 3, ed. E. Stern.
        Jerusalem: The Israel Exploration Society & Carta.

Colgrave, B.
2003   Willibald of Eichstätt, St. P. 761 in *New Catholic Encyclopedia*.
        Second Edition. Vol. 14. Washington, DC: Catholic University
        of America.

Corbo, V.
1967   Nuovi scavi archeologici nella cappella del battistero della ba-
        silica del Nebo (Siyagha). *Liber Annuus* 17: 241–58.
1970   Scavi archeologici sotto I mosaici della basilica del Monte Nebo
        (Siyagha). *Liber Annuus* 26: 281-318

Crowfoot, J. W.
1931   *Churches at Jerash. A Preliminary Report on the Joint Yale-
        British School Expeditions to Jerash 1928–1930*. British School of
        Archaeology in Jerusalem, Supplementary Papers 3. London:
        British School of Archaeology in Jerusalem.
1941   *Early Churches in Palestine*. The Schweich Lectures of the British
        Academy 1937, Reprinted 1980. London: British Academy.

Al-Daire, M.
2001   Umm Qays 1998: The Fourth Century AD Memorial Basilica
        of Gadara. Pp. 553–60 in *Studies in the History and Archaeology
        of Jordan VII*. Amman: Department of Antiquities.

Devos, P.
1967   La date du voyage d'Égérie. *Analecta Bollandiana* 85: 165–97.

Dietz, M.
2005   *Wandering Monks, Virgins, and Pilgrims: Ascetic Travel in
        the Mediterranean World A.D. 300–800*. University Park, PA:
        Pennsylvania State University.

Di Segni, L.
1992   The Date of the Church of the Virgin in Madaba. *Liber Annuus*
        42: 251–57.
2006   The Use of Chronological Systems in Sixth–Eighth Century
        Palestine. *ARAM* 18.1: 113–26.

Donner, H.
1982   Mitteilungen zur Topographie des Ostjordanlandes anhand der
        Mosaikkarte von Madeba. *Zeitschrift des Deutschen Palästina-
        Vereins* 98: 174–90.
1984   Transjordan and Egypt on the Mosaic Map of Madaba. *Annual
        of the Department of Antiquities of Jordan* 28: 249–57
1992   *The Mosaic Map of Madaba: An Introductory Guide.* Kampen:
        Kok Pharos.

Donner, H., and Cüppers, H.
1977   *Die Mosaikkarte von Madeba.* Teil I: *Tafelband.* Abhandlungen
        des Deutschen Palästinavereins. Wiesbaden: Harrassowitz.

Elsner, J., and Rutherford, I.
2005   *Pilgrimage in Graeco-Roman and Early Christian Antiquity:
        Seeing the Gods.* Oxford: Oxford University.

Eusebius
1999   *Life of Constantine* (*Vita Constantini*). Ed. Heikel; translated by
        A. Cameron and S. G. Hall. Oxford: Clarendon.

Fiema, Z. T.
2001   Byzantine Petra. A Reassessment. Pp. 111–34 in *Urban Centers
        and Rural Contexts in Late Antiquity*, eds. T. S. Burns and J. W.
        Eadie. East Lansing, MI: Michigan State University.

Fiema, Z. T., and Frösén, J.
2008   *Petra – The Mountain of Aaron: The Finnish Archaeological
        Project in Jordan.* Volume 1: *The Church and the Chapel.*
        Helsinki: Societas Scientiarum Fennica.

Fiema, Z. T., Kanellopoulos, C., Waliszewski, T., and Schick, R.
2001   *The Petra Church.* Amman: American Center of Oriental
        Research.

2003   The Byzantine Monastic/Pilgrimage Centre of St. Aaron
        near Petra, Jordan. Pp. 343–57 in *One Land – Many Cultures:*
        Archaeological Studies in Honour of Stanislao Loffreda OFM, eds.
        G. C. Bottini; L. Di Segni; and L. D. Chrupcala. Studium
        Biblicum Franciscanum – Collectio Major 41. Jerusalem:
        Franciscan Printing.

Frank, F.
1934   Aus der ʿAraba. I. Reiseberichte. *Zeitschrift des deutschen*
        Palästina-Vereins 57: 191–280 (see especially pp. 221–24 and Plan
        19, 20 A and B, 21; Tafel 32 A and B; trip made in 1932).

Freedman, D. N. (ed.)
1992   *The Anchor Bible Dictionary*. Vols. 1–6. New York: Doubleday.

Frescobaldi, L.; Gucci, G.; and Sigoli, S.
1948   *Visit to the Holy Places of Egypt, Sinai, Palestine and Syria in 1384.*
        Translated from the Italian by T. Bellorini and E. Hoade, with
        a preface and notes by B. Bagatti. Publications of the Studium
        Biblicum Franciscanum 6. Jerusalem: Franciscan Printing.

Frösén, J., et al.
2001   The 2000 Finnish Harun Project: Preliminary Report. *Annual*
        of the Department of Antiquities of Jordan 45: 359–76.
        The 1998-2000 Finnish Harun Project: Specialized Reports.
        Annual of the Department of Antiquities of Jordan 45: 377–92.
2002   *The Petra Papyri I*. Amman: American Center of Oriental
        Research.

Frösén, J., and Fiema, Z. T.
2004   *Excavating the Monastery of St. Aaron: The Finnish Archaeological*
        Project in Jordan. Vantaa: Finnish Institute in the Middle East.

Gagos, T., and J. Frösén
1998   Petra Papyri. *Annual of the Department of Antiquities of Jordan*
        42: 473–81.

Gawlikowski, M., and Musa, A.
1986   The Church of Bishop Marianos. Pp. 137–62 in *Jerash*
        Archaeological Project 1981–1983, ed. F. Zayadine. Amman: The
        Department of Antiquities of Jordan.

Geyer, P., ed.

1898   *Itinera Hierosolymitana Saeculi IIII–VIII: Recensuit et com-
        mentario critico Instruxit.* Corpus Scriptorum Ecclesiasticorum
        Latinorum 39. Prague: Tempsky.

Grabois, A.

1982   Christian pilgrims in the Thirteenth Century and the Late
        Kingdom of Jerusalem: Burchard of Mount Sion. Pp. 285–96
        in *Outremer: Studies in the History of the Crusading Kingdom
        of Jerusalem,* eds. B. Z. Kedar; H. E. Mayer; and R. C. Smail.
        Jerusalem: Ben-Zvi.

Harpur, J.

2002   *Sacred Tracks: 2000 Years of Christian Pilgrimage.* Berkeley, CA:
        University of California.

Hirschfeld, Y.

1992   *The Judean Desert Monasteries in the Byzantine Period.* New
        Haven, CT: Yale University.

1995   Spirituality in the Desert: Judean Wilderness Monasteries.
        Biblical Archaeology Review 21.5: 28–37, 70.

1997   Hammath-Gader. Pp. 468–70 in *Oxford Encyclopedia of
        Archaeology in the Near East,* vol. 2, ed. E. M. Meyers. New
        York: Oxford University.

Hobbs, T. R.

1985   *2 Kings.* Word Biblical Commentary 13. Waco, TX: Wood Books.

Horn, C.

2005   A Chapter in the Pre-History of the Christological
        Controversies in Arabic: Readings from the Works of John
        Rufus. *Parole de l'Orient* 30: 133–56.

2006   *Asceticism and Christological Controversy in Fifth-Century
        Palestine: The Career of Peter the Iberian.* Oxford: Oxford
        University.

Hunt, E. D.

1982   *Holy Land Pilgrimage in the Late Roman Empire A.D. 312–460.*
        Oxford: Clarendon.

2000   The Itinerary of Egeria: Reliving the Bible in Fourth-Century
        Palestine. Pp. 34–54 in *The Holy Land, Holy Lands, and*

Christian History, ed. R. N. Swanson. (Papers read at the 1998 Summer Meeting and the 1999 Winter Meeting of the Ecclesiastical History Society.) Studies in Church History 26. Woodridge: Boydell and Brewer.

Hoffman, A., and Kerner, S. (eds.)
2002   *Gadara – Gerasa und die Dekapolis*. Mainz: von Zabern.

Holmgren, R., and Kaliff, A.
1997   The 1995–1996 Excavation of Dayr al-Qattar al-Byzanti: A Preliminary Report. *Annual of the Department of Antiquities of Jordan* 41: 321–40.
2005   The Hermit Life on Al-Lisan Peninsula – Results of the Swedish Dead Sea Expedition: A Preliminary Report. *Annual of the Department of Antiquities of Jordan* 49: 167–76.

Jäggi, C.; Meier, H.-R; and Brenk, B.
1997   New Data for the Chronology of the Early Christian Cathedral of Gerasa: The Third Interim Report on the Jarash Cathedral Project. *Annual of the Department of Antiquities of Jordan* 41: 311–20.
1998   Temple, Kiln and Church – Fourth Interim Report on the Jarash Cathedral Project (Autumn 1997). *Annual of the Department of Antiquities of Jordan* 42: 425–32.

Josephus
1987   *The Works of Josephus*. Translated by W. Whiston. Peabody, MA: Hendrickson.

Khouri, R. G.
1986   *Jerash. A Frontier City of the Roman East*. New York: Longman.
1988   *Jerash: A Brief Guide to the Antiquities*. Amman: Al Kutba.
1990   *Madaba, Mount Nebo, Umm er-Rasas: A Brief Guide to the Antiquities*. Amman: Al-Kutba.
1999   Tell Mar Elias, Jordan. *The Jordan Times*, November 11.

Kopp, C.
1963   *The Holy Places of the Gospels*. Montreal: Palm.

Kraeling, C. H. (ed.)

1938   *Gerasa. City of the Decapolis. An account embodying the re-
        cord of a joint excavation conducted by Yale University and the
        British School of Archaeology in Jerusalem (1928–1930), and Yale
        University and the American Schools of Oriental Research (1930–
        1931)*. New Haven, CT: American Schools of Oriental Research.

Lavento, M.; Hertell, E.; Kouki, P.; Mukkala, A.; Silvonen, S.; Ynnilä,
H.; Haggren, H.; Junnilainen, H.; and Erving, A.

2006   *The Finnish Jabal Haroun Project Survey: Preliminary Results
        from Six Seasons of Archaeological Fieldwork in Jordan*. Vantaaa:
        Finnish Institute in the Middle East.

Loffreda, S.

1981   Preliminary Report of the Second Season of Excavations at
        Qal'at El-Mishnaqa-Machaerus. *Annual of the Department of
        Antiquities of Jordan* 35: 85–94.

MacDonald, B.

1980   The Hermitage of John the Abbot at Hamman 'Afra, Southern
        Jordan. *Liber Annuus* 30: 351–64.

2000   *"East of the Jordan:" Biblical Sites and Territories of the Hebrew
        Scriptures*. Boston, MA: American Schools of Oriental Research.

MacDonald, B., and Politis, K.D.

1988   Deir 'Ain 'Abata: A Byzantine, Church/Monastery Complex in
        Ghor es Safi. *Liber Annuus* 38: 289–97.

MacDonald, B.; 'Amr, K.; Broeder, N. H.; Skinner, H. C. W.; Meyer, C.;
Neeley, M. P.; Reese, D. S.; and Whitcomb, D. S.

1992   *The Southern Ghors and Northeast 'Arabah Archaeological
        Survey 1985–1986, Southern Jordan*. Sheffield Archaeological
        Monographs 5. Sheffield: Collis.

Magen, Y.

1995   Martyrius: Lavish Living for Monks. *Biblical Archaeology
        Review* 21.5: 38–49.

1993   *The Monastery of Martyrius at Ma'ale Adummim: A Guide*.
        Jerusalem: Israel Antiquities Authority.

Magen, Y., and Hizmi, H.
1985   The Monastery of St. Martyrius at Ma'ale Adummim.
          Qadmoniot 18.3–4: 62–92.

Mango, C.
1995   The Pilgrim's Motivation. Pp. 1–9 in *Akten des XII.*
          Internationalen Kongresses für Christliche Archäologie (Bonn
          22.–28. September 1991, Teil 1). Jahrbuch für Antike und
          Christentum Ergänzungsband 20, 1. Münster: Aschendorff.

Maraval, P.
1995   Les Itinéraires de Pèlerinage en Orient (entre le 4e et le 7e s.).
          Pp. 291–300 in *Akten des XII. Internationalen Kongresses für*
          Christliche Archäologie (Bonn 22.–28. September 1991, Teil 1).
          Jahrbuch für Antike und Christentum Ergänzungsband 20, 1.
          Münster: Aschendorff.

Mason, S. (ed.)
2001   *Flavius Josephus: Translation and Commentary,* Vol. 9: *Life of*
          Josephus. Leiden: Brill.

Meehan, D. (ed.)
1958   *Adamnan's De locis Santis.* Dublin: Dublin Institute for
          Advanced Study.

Meimaris, Y. E.
1992   *Chronological Systems in Roman-Byzantine Palestine and Arabia:*
          The Evidence of the Dated Greek Inscriptions. Athens: The
          National Hellenic Research Foundation, Research Centre for
          Greek and Roman Antiquity.

Meimaris, Y. E., and Kritikakou-Nikolaropoulou, K. I.
2005   *Inscriptions from Palaestina Tertia.* Vol. Ia. *The Greek Inscriptions*
          from Ghor es-Safi (Byzantine Zoora). Athens: Eptalofos.

Michel, A.
2001   *Les Églises d'Époque Byzantine et Umayyade de la Jordanie Ve*
          –VIIIe Siècle: Typologie architecturale et aménagements liturgiques.
          Turnhout: Brepols.

Mkhjian, R.
2005   Preliminary Report Rhetorius Monastery Bethany Beyond the
        Jordan. *Annual of the Department of Antiquities of Jordan* 49:
        403–10.
2007   Bethany Beyond the Jordan where Jesus was Baptized. *Annual
        of the Department of Antiquities of Jordan* 51: 239–41.

Mkhjian, R., and Kanellopoulos, C.
2003   John the Baptist Church Area: Architectural Evidence. *Annual
        of the Department of Antiquities of Jordan* 47: 9–18.

Montgomery, J. A., and Gehman, H. S.
1951   *A Critical and Exegetical Commentary on the Books of Kings*
        (ICC). Edinburgh: Clark.

Morinis, E.A.
1992   Introduction: The Territory of the Anthropology of Pilgrimage.
        Pp. 1–28 in *Sacred Journeys: The Anthropology of Pilgrimage*, ed.
        E. A. Morinis. Westport, CT: Greenwood.

Moschus, J.
1992   *The Spiritual Meadow (Pratum Spirituale)*. Introduction, trans-
        lation and notes by J. Wortley. Cisterian Studies Series 139.
        Kalamazoo, MI: Cistercian.

Pappalardo, C.
2006   Ceramica e piccoli oggetti dallo scavo della chiesa del
        Reliquiario ad Umm al-Rasas. *Liber Annuus* 56: 389–98.

Patrich, J.
1995   Church, State and the Transformation of Palestine – The
        Byzantine Period (324–640 CE). Pp. 470–87 in *Archaeology
        of Society in the Holy Land*, ed. T. E. Levy. Washington, DC:
        Leicester University.

Peterman, G., and Schick, R.
1996   The Monastery of Saint Aaron. *Annual of the Department of
        Antiquities of Jordan* 40: 473–80.

Piccirillo, M.

1976   Campagna archeologica nella basilica di Mosè sul Monte Nebo-Siyagha (1 luglio–7 settembre 1976). *Liber Annuus* 26: 281–318.

1979   First Excavation Campaign at Qal'at El-Mishnaqa-Meqawer (Madaba) (September 8–October 28, 1978). *Annual of the Department of Antiquities of Jordan* 33: 177–83.

1988   The Mosaics of Um er-Rasas in Jordan. *Biblical Archaeologist* 51.4: 208–13, 227–31.

1989   *Chiese e Mosaici di Madaba*. Studium Biblicum Franciscanum – Collectio Maior 34. Jerusalem: Franciscan Printing.

1992   *The Mosaics of Jordan*. American Center of Oriental Research Publication 1. Amman: American Center of Oriental Research.

1993a   La Chiesa dei Sunna' a Madaba. *Liber Annuus* 43: 277–313.

1993b   Umm er-Rasas. Pp. 1490–93 in *The New Encyclopedia of Archaeological Excavations in the Holy Land*, ed. E. Stern. Jerusalem: The Israel Exploration Society & Carta.

1995   Le antichità cristiane del villaggio di Mekawer. *Liber Annuus* 45: 293–318.

1997a   La chiesa di San Paolo a Umm al-Rasas – Kastron Mefaa. *Liber Annuus* 47: 375–94.

1997b   Machaerus. Pp. 391–93 in *The Oxford Encyclopedia of Archaeology in the Near East*, 3, ed. E. M. Meyers. New York: Oxford University.

1998a   Pilgrims' Texts. Pp. 71–83 in *Mount Nebo: New Archaeological Excavations 1967–1997*, eds. M. Piccirillo and E. Alliata. Studium Biblicum Franciscanum – Collectio Major 27. Jerusalem: Franciscan Printing.

1998b   The Monastic Presence. Pp. 193–219 in *Mount Nebo: New Archaeological Excavations 1967–1997*, eds. M. Piccirillo and E. Alliata. Studium Biblicum Franciscanum – Collectio Major 27. Jerusalem: Franciscan Printing.

1999a   Madaba: One Hundred Years from the Discovery. Pp. 15–24 in *The Madaba Map Centenary 1897–1997: Travelling Through the Byzantine Umayyad Period* (Proceedings of the International Conference held in Amman, 7–9 April 1997), eds. M. Piccirillo and E. Alliata. Studium Biblicum Franciscanum – Collectio Maior 40. Jerusalem: Franciscan Printing.

1999b   Ainon Sapsaphas and Bethabara. Pp. 218–21 in *The Madaba Map Centenary 1897–1997: Travelling Through the Byzantine Umayyad Period* (Proceedings of the International Conference held in Amman, 7–9 April 1997), eds. M. Piccirillo and E.

Alliata. Studium Biblicum Franciscanum – Collectio Maior 40. Jerusalem: Franciscan Printing.

2002   The Ecclesistical Complex of Saint Paul at Umm ar-Rasas – Kastron Mefaa. *Annual of the Department of Antiquities of Jordan* 46: 535–59.

2006a   The Sanctuaries of the Baptism on the East Bank of the Jordan River. Pp. 433–43 in *Jesus and Archaeology*, ed. J. H. Charlesworth. Grand Rapids, MI: Eerdmans.

2006b   La Chiesa del Reliquiario a Umm al-Rasas. *Liber Annuus* 56: 375–88.

Piccirillo, M., and Alliata, E.

1994   *Umm al-Rasas – Mayfa'ah I: Gli scavi del complesso di Santo Stefano*. Studium Biblicum Franciscanum – Collectio Maior 28. Jerusalem: Franciscan Printing.

1998   *Mount Nebo: New Archaeological Excavations 1967–1997*. Studium Biblicum Franciscanum – Collectio Major 27. Jerusalem: Franciscan Printing.

Politis, K. D.

1992   Excavating Lot's Sanctuary in Jordan: Evidence of a Forgotten Biblical Episode. *Minerva: The International Review of Ancient Art and Archaeology* 3.4: 6–9.

1995   Excavations and Restorations at Dayr 'Ayn 'Abata 1994. *Annual of the Department of Antiquities of Jordan* 39: 477–91.

2001   Early Byzantine Monasticism in Southern Jordan. Pp. 585–89 in *Studies in the History and Archaeology of Jordan VII*. Amman: Department of Antiquities.

2004   Where Lot's Daughters Seduced Their Father. *Biblical Archaeology Review* 30.1: 20–30, 64.

Riesner, R.

1992   Bethany Beyond the Jordan. Pp. 703–5 in *The Anchor Bible Dictionary* I, ed. D. N. Freedman. New York: Doubleday.

Roll, I.

1999   The Roads in Roman-Byzantine Palaestina and Arabia. Pp. 109–20 in *The Madaba Map Centenary 1897–1997: Travelling Through the Byzantine Umayyad Period* (Proceedings of the International Conference held in Amman, 7–9 April 1997), eds. M. Piccirillo and E. Alliata. Studium Biblicum Franciscanum – Collectio Maior 40. Jerusalem: Franciscan Printing.

Saller, J. S.
1941   *The Memorial of Moses on Mount Nebo*. Part I. *The Text*. Part
        II. *The Plates*. Part III. *The Pottery*. Publications of the Studium
        Biblicum Franciscanum 1. Jerusalem: Franciscan Printing.

Saller, J. S., and Bagatti, B.
1949   *The Town of Nebo (Khirbet el-Mekhayyat), with a Brief Survey of
        Other Ancient Christian Monuments in Transjordan*. Publications
        of the Studium Biblicum Franciscanum 7. Jerusalem:
        Franciscan Printing.

Schick, R.
1988   Christian Life in Palestine during the Early Islamic Period.
        Biblical Archaeologist 51.4: 218–21, 239–40.
1995   *The Christian Communities of Palestine from Byzantine to Islamic
        Rule: A Historical and Archaeological Study*. Studies in Late
        Antiquity and Early Islam 2. Princeton, NJ: Darwin.
1997   Umm er-Rasas. Pp. 279–81 in *The Oxford Encyclopedia of
        Archaeology in the Near East*, vol. 5, ed. E. M. Meyers. New
        York: Oxford University.
2001a   Christianity in Southern Jordan in the Byzantine and Early
        Islamic Periods. Pp.581–84 in *Studies in the History and
        Archaeology of Jordan VII*. Amman: Department of Antiquities.
2001b   The Ecclesiastical History of Petra. Pp. 1–5 in Z. T. Fiema, C.
        Kanellopoulos, T. Waliszewski, and R. Schick, *The Petra Church*.
        Amman, Jordan: American Center of Oriental Research.

Seigne, J.
1992   Jérash romaine et Byzantine. Pp. 331–41 in *Développement ur-
        bain d'une ville provinciale orientale*, ed. G. Bisheh. Studies in
        the History and Archaeology of Jordan 4. Amman: Department
        of Antiquities.

Shahid, I.
1995   The Islamic Pilgrimage. Pp. 340–47 in *Akten des XII.
        Internationalen Kongresses für Christliche Archäologie (Bonn
        22.–28. September 1991, Teil 1)*. Jahrbuch für Antike und
        Christentum Ergänzungsband 20, 1. Münster: Aschendorff.
1998   The Madaba Mosaic Map Revisited: Some New Observations
        on its Purpose and Meaning. Pp. 147–54 in *The Madaba
        Map Centenary 1897–1997: Travelling Through the Byzantine*

Umayyad Period (Proceedings of the International Conference held in Amman, 7–9 April 1997), eds. M. Piccirillo and E. Alliata. Studium Biblicum Franciscanum – Collectio Maior 40. Jerusalem: Franciscan Printing.

Stemberger, G.
2000   *Jews and Christians in the Holy Land: Palestine in the Fourth Century.* Translated by R. Tuschling. Edinburgh: Clark.

Swanson, R. N. (ed.)
2000   *The Holy Land, Holy Lands, and Christian History.* (Papers read at the 1998 Summer Meeting and the 1999 Winter Meeting of the Ecclesiastical History Society.) Studies in Church History 26. Woodridge: Boydell and Brewer.

Taylor, J. E.
1993   *Christians and the Holy Places: The Myth of Jewish-Christian Origins.* Oxford: Clarendon.

Taylor, J. E.; Freeman-Grenville, G. S. P.; and Chapman III, R. L.
2003   *Palestine in the Fourth Century A.D.: The Onomasticon by Eusebius of Caesarea* (with Jerome's Latin translation and expansion in parallel from the edition of E. Klostermann). Translated by G. S. P. Freeman-Grenville, indexed by R. L. Chapman III, and edited and introduced by J. E. Taylor. Jerusalem: Carta.

Tsafrir, Y.
1983   *The Excavations of Kursi – Gergesa.* 'Atiqot 16. Jerusalem: Department of Antiquities and Museums/Ministry of Education and Culture.
1995   Jewish Pilgrimage in the Roman and Byzantine Periods. Pp. 369–76 in *Akten des XII. Internationalen Kongresses für Christliche Archäologie (Bonn 22.–28. September 1991, Teil 1).* Jahrbuch für Antike und Christentum Ergänzungsband 20, 1. Münster: Aschendorff.

Waheeb, M.
1998   Wadi al-Kharrar Archaeological Project (Al-Maghtas). *Annual of the Department of Antiquities of Jordan* 42: 635–38.

2001a   Wadi al-Kharra Archaeological Project (Al-Maghtas). Pp. 591–600 in *Studies in the History and Archaeology of Jordan VII*. Amman: Department of Antiquities.

2001b   Recent Discoveries East of the Jordan River: Wadi al-Kharrar Archaeological Project. *Annual of the Department of Antiquities of Jordan* 45: 419–25.

Walker, P. W.

1990   *Holy City, Holy Places? Christian Attitudes to Jerusalem and the Holy Land in the Fourth Century*. Oxford: Clarendon.

Weber, T., and Khouri, R.

1989   *Umm Qais – Gadara of the Decapolis: A Brief Guide to the Antiquities*. Amman: Al Kutba.

1995   Gadara in Byzantinischer Zeit. Pp. 1273–81 in *Akten des XII. Internationalen Kongresses für Christliche Archäologie (Bonn 22.–28. September 1991, Teil 2)*. Jahrbuch für Antike und Christentum Ergänzungsband 20, 1. Münster: Aschendorff.

1998   Gadara 1998. The Excavation of the Five-Aisled Basilica at Umm Qays: A Preliminary Report. *Annual of the Department of Antiquities of Jordan* 42: 443–56.

Wiegand, Th. (ed.)

1920   *Sinai*. Wissenschaftliche Veröffentlichungen des Deutsch-Türkischen Denkmalschutz-Kommandos 1. Berlin: de Gruyter.

Wilken, R.

1992   *The Land Called Holy: Palestine in Christian History and Thought*. New Haven, CT: Yale University.

Wilkinson, J.

1976   Christian Pilgrims in Jerusalem during the Byzantine Period. *Palestine Exploration Quarterly* 108: 75–101.

1995   Visit to Jewish Tombs by Early Christians. Pp. 452–65 in *Akten des XII. Internationalen Kongresses für Christliche Archäologie (Bonn 22.–28. September 1991, Teil 1)*. Jahrbuch für Antike und Christentum Ergänzungsband 20, 1. Münster: Aschendorff.

1999   *Egeria's Travels*. Third edition. Warminster: Aris & Phillips.

2002   *Jerusalem Pilgrims before the Crusades*. Second edition. Warminster: Aris & Phillips.

Wilson, C. W. (ed.)
1895   *The Pilgrimage of the Russian Abbot Daniel in the Holy Land, 1106–1107 A.D.* Palestine Pilgrims' Text Society 4. London: Palestine Exploration Fund.

Wood, S. (ed.)
1996   *The Holy Sites of Jordan.* Amman: Turab.

Zayadine, F. (ed.)
1986   *Jerash Archaeological Project, I. 1981–1983.* Amman: Department of Antiquities of Jordan.

Ziegler, A. W.
2003   Milan, Edict (Agreement) of. P. 625 in *New Catholic Encyclopedia.* Vol. 9, second edition. Washington, DC: Catholic University of America.

ARCHAEOLOGICAL PERIODS & DATES

Early Bronze Period	ca. 3300–1950 BC
Middle Bronze Period	ca. 1950–1550 BC
Late Bronze Period	ca. 1550–1200 BC
Iron I Period	1200–1000 BC
Iron II Period	1000–539 BC
Persian Period	539–332 BC
Hellenistic Period	332–63 BC
Nabataean	ca. 300 BC–AD 106
Roman Period	63 BC–AD 324
Early Roman	63 BC– AD 135
Late Roman	AD 135–324
Byzantine Period	AD 324–640
Early Byzantine	AD 324–491
Late Byzantine	AD 491–640
Early Islamic Period	AD 640–1099
Umayyad	AD 661–750
Abbasid	AD 750–878
Fatimid	AD 878–1099
Middle Islamic Period	AD 1099–1516
Crusader Period	AD 1099–1187
Ayyubid/Mamluk	AD 1174–1516
Late Islamic Period	AD 1516–1918
Modern Period	AD 1918–Present

INDICES

INDEX OF SUBJECTS

T Theodosius 30, 91–93, 95, 106,   V Valerius 29
    130
                                        W Willibald 34–35, 96, 106

INDEX OF PLACE NAMES (INCLUDING ARCHAEOLOGICAL SITES)

INDEX OF BIBLICAL PASSAGES

Old Testament/Hebrew Scriptures